49.50

D0463149

Flora Domestica

A History of British Flower Arranging
1500–1930

MARY ROSE BLACKER

SPECIAL PHOTOGRAPHY BY
Andreas von Einsiedel

THE NATIONAL TRUST

Harry N. Abrams, Inc., Publishers

First published in Great Britain in 2000 by
National Trust Enterprises Ltd,
36 Queen Anne's Gate, London SW1H 9AS

http://www.ukindex.co.uk/national trust/bookshelf

Text © Mary Rose Blacker 2000
Step-by-step instructions © The National Trust 2000

The quotation from *John Bull's Island* is reproduced by permission of
The Society of Authors, on behalf of the Bernard Shaw Estate.

Distributed in 2000 by Harry N. Abrams, Incorporated, New York

British Library Cataloguing in Publication Data
A catalogue record for this book is available from the British Library.

Library of Congress Catalog Card Number: 99–67638

ISBN 0 7078 0380 2
ISBN 0-8109-6703-0 (Abrams)

Picture research by Mary Rose Blacker, Philippa Reynolds and
Margaret Willes

Edited by Margaret Willes

Designed by the Newton Engert Partnership

Production management by Bob Towell

Phototypset in Sabon by SPAN Graphics Limited,
Crawley, West Sussex

Printed and Bound in China
Phoenix Offset

HALF TITLE: A late eighteenth-century style arrangement – Rosa Mundi
rose, honeysuckle, geum, nigella and lavender – in a Wedgwood vase
(see pages 88 and 89).

FRONTISPIECE: 'Jeanie' Hughes, painted by G. F. Watts in 1858. She is
shown watering lilies of the valley in an ornate pot. On the floor are cut
flowers which presumably will be arranged in the trumpet vase on the table.
Watts is using the language of flowers to provide a moral allegory, for
his sitter was a philanthropist who became the first female inspector of
workhouses. Thus the lilies of the valley represent the 'return of happiness',
and by watering them, she is providing purity and temperance.

To Ted Fawcett and John Hardy

Contents

1	Tuberose flower.	9	Camomile double.	17	Long blowing Honeysuckle.	25	Musk Scabious.
2	Single Nasturtium.	10	Semper Augustus Auricula.	18	Spiked Aster.	26	Double white Musk rose.
3	Yellow peren.t Poppy.	11	Indian Tobacco.	19	Belladona Lilly.	27	Box leav'd Myrtle.
4	Purple Polyanthos.	12	Arbutus double.	20	Ever green Honeysuckle.	28	Michaelmas Daisie.
5	Saffron flower.	13	Best flowering Geranium.	21	Leonurus, or Archangel tree.	29	Yellow Passion flower.
6	Strip'd double Colchicum.	14	Guernsey Lilly.	22	Black Cranes bill.	30	Holly hock always double.
7	Single blew Periwinkle.	15	Autumn Carnation.	23	Scarlet Cranes bill.	31	Virgina Shrub Acre.
8	Trumpet flower.	16	Agnus Castus.	24	Marigold tree.		

OCTOBER

Design'd by P.r Casteels.

From the Collection of Rob.t Furber Gardiner at Kensington 1730.

Engrav'd by H. Fletcher.

Introduction

'Dear Miss Nora, don't pluck the little flower. If it was a pretty baby you wouldn't want to pull its head off and stick it in a vawse of water to look at'. So 'Father' Keegan admonishes a young girl for plucking nervously at some heather in George Bernard Shaw's play *John Bull's Other Island*. Shaw was no flower arranger, but in this, as in other matters, he was in the minority. Over the centuries men and women have decorated their houses with plants and flowers, and looking at 'vawses' of flowers has been a particular delight.

In this book I have traced the use of flowers and plants in houses from the sixteenth century, when we begin to get some idea of which varieties were used and how they were arranged. I have concentrated on country houses, especially those belonging to the National Trust and therefore possible to visit. I have also introduced Het Loo Palace in The Netherlands and Colonial Williamsburg in the United States, where historic flower arranging has been studied and can now be seen. I have used sources and images from Europe and America for my research.

At the end of the book I have given dates of the arrival of many plants into Great Britain and their places of origin, so that anyone wishing to make an accurate recreation of an arrangement can see when particular varieties were available. I have, of course, included in the text descriptions of vases and containers used over the centuries. Not many of us are blessed with seventeenth-century pyramid vases in Delftware, but modern reproductions of these and other period vases can now be bought.

As well as contemporary pictures, the illustrations include specially commissioned photographs of recreations of historic flower and plant arrangements. These range from an Elizabethan wedding bouquet and a well-filled Regency plant stand through to a lavish dining-table decoration that would have enlivened a grand Edwardian party. Nearly all the flowers used are of the period, but on occasion, when an 'old' variety could not be found, we have substituted a modern variety as indicated. We have avoided using modern materials such as oasis, except on a very few occasions.

From the seventeenth to the mid-nineteenth centuries, many vases had pierced tops – both fixed and loose – and some had interior metal fittings. From the 1860s damp sand was widely used, enabling flowers to be placed in the exact positions wanted. Moss covered the sand but, as sphagnum moss is becoming rare, please use it sparingly and, when possible, use the moss from your lawn. From the Edwardian period, all kinds of flower holders were introduced, including glass 'roses', strips of folded lead and pin holders. Wire netting stretched across the top of a vase with a pin holder in the base can make a good substitute for 'old' holders.

'October' from Robert Furber's *The Flower Garden Display'd* ... first published in 1732 (see pages 42 and 43).

This book would have been written in partnership with Gervase Jackson-Stops, the National Trust's Architectural Adviser, had he not sadly died five years ago. We laid the plans together, and I hope he would have been pleased with the result. It has been especially complex to put together as it draws on so many subjects, including the development of architecture and interior design, ceramics, garden history, social history and the history of flower arrangement. I therefore have a very large number of people to thank for their valuable help and contributions.

The idea for the book originally came from Ted Fawcett and was set into action by Liz Drury. Without the continual encouragement and help I have received from them, together with John Hardy and Charlotte Gere, it could never have been written. Vital roles were played by Cathy Gere, who helped to organise the text and fill in gaps, and by Corinna Rock who helped to ensure that the book was finished. My husband David's enthusiasm for jaunts to National Trust properties all over the country and his wise criticism have been a constant support.

I am indebted to many others for generously helping and sharing their knowledge: Robert Treadway, who from New York supplied most of the American material and was always ready to discuss any problems; Cathy Grosfils and Libbey Oliver of Colonial Williamsburg; Wies Erkelens and Willem Zielerman of Het Loo Palace; Martin Einchcomb of Hampton Court Palace, who taught me a great deal about flower arranging of the William and Mary period; Tony Lord, who painstakingly checked all the dates of the plant introductions; Lady Ashbrook; Anneka Bambery of the Museum and Art Gallery in Derby; Thomasina Beck; David Bostwick; Tony Boulding; Peter Brown of Fairfax House in York; Jim Buckland and Sarah Wain of West Dean in Sussex; Oliver Davies; Lyn Ferguson; Philippa Glanville; Peter Goodchild; Rosamund Griffin; Anthony Heald; Catherine Lachlan; Amanda Lange; Lady Legard who lent plants from Scampston Hall in Yorkshire; Todd Longstaff-Gowan; Jonathan Marsden; Roger Meek; Gerard Noel; Tim Rock; and Arthur Shufflebotham.

I am grateful for the gracious permission of Her Majesty the Queen to publish material from the Royal Archives at Windsor Castle, and to Jill Kelsey for her help in finding it. Also to the Trustees of the Wedgwood Museum at Barlaston, Stoke-on-Trent, Staffordshire, for allowing me to publish material from their archives, and to Gaye Blake Roberts for her help in locating it. Also to Dr Brent Elliot and Jennifer Vine at the Lindley Library of the Royal Horticultural Society, to the staff of the London Library, the Linnaean Society, the British Art Library at the Victoria & Albert Museum, and the British Library who patiently helped me to find books on their hi-tech computers which baffle me still.

Many people within the National Trust gave freely of their time and knowledge. I am particularly grateful to Jim Marshall for his advice on horticultural matters in general and Malmaison carnations in particular, and to Anthony du Boulay who identified many of the ceramic vases and patiently answered many questions. And to many others, who include Andrew Barber, John Chesshyre, Christopher Corry-Thomas, Martin Drury, Jonathan Elphick, Oliver Garnett, Julian Gibbs, Ceri Johnson, Tim Knox, Alastair Laing, Helen Lloyd, John McVerry, Maggie McKean, Anthea Palmer, James Rothwell, Christopher Rowell, Andrew Sawyer, David Stone, Anne Stoker and Sam Youd.

One of the seventeenth-century style flower arrangements from an exhibition mounted at Hampton Court Palace in May 1999. A cistern of Nevers faience and two reproduction pyramids are shown in the hearth of the Queen's Audience Chamber. The cistern arrangement is based on paintings by the artist Jan van Huysum (1682–1749), but rounded in overall effect. The first flowers put in were a rose, iris and kniphofia, off centre at the top, and the red peonies. Oasis was used in this cistern and other large vases in the exhibition.

I am truly grateful to Andreas von Einsiedel and to his assistant Philip Harris for the excellent photographs they have taken, which are such an enhancement to the book. And to Sonia Beresford Hobbs who created the arrangements taken in the studio, on the Sudbury Hall staircase, and on the dining table at Polesden Lacey. I am delighted that we are able to use photographs of the superb arrangements done by Martin Einchcomb, Christine Jermyn, Pat Lague and members of the National Association of Flower Arrangement Societies (Surrey Area) for an exhibition of flowers of the William and Mary period which took place in the Queen's Apartments at Hampton Court Palace in May of last year, organised by Terry Gough and Tony Boulding. And my great thanks to those who arranged the flowers at National Trust houses, and with whom it was such a pleasure to work: Dai Evans and Doris Codling at Lyme Park; Linda Cusdin, Jean Grieve, Leslie Orton and Sally Rogers at Osterley Park; Sallyann Hardwick, Delia Webster, Madelaine Abey-Koch and Paul Dearn at Polesden Lacey.

Lastly my huge thanks to Margaret Willes for the enormous amount of work and skill she has put into editing and publishing this book, and to her assistants, Sophie Blair and Philippa Reynolds.

Mary Rose Blacker
August 1999

CHAPTER ONE

Decking the House

1500–1677

'The most beautiful flowers should crown the vase like a beautiful head of hair crowns a beautiful body.' So wrote G.B. Ferrari in *De Florum Cultura*, published in Italy in 1633. The cultivation of flowers and their use in houses to decorate and scent rooms has been part of our style of living for centuries, indeed millennia. But the story of flower arranging in Europe really begins with the Renaissance, when a revival of interest in the natural world is reflected in more realistic portrayals in illuminated manuscripts and details in religious paintings. From the early fifteenth century simple bunches of identifiable flowers appear in paintings of the Holy Family and of the saints.

Craftsmen and artists fleeing the wars of religion bedevilling Europe often found their way to Britain in the sixteenth century, and spread the message of the Renaissance. One such was the German artist, Hans Holbein the Younger, whose first visit took place from 1526 to 1529. His portrait of Sir Thomas More and his family features vases of flowers decorating the room. Another was Jacques le Moyne, who escaped from France some time after 1580. He probably joined the Sidney household as tutor, for his book *Le Clef des Champs*, published in 1586, is dedicated to Lady Mary Sidney. His exquisite flower and fruit paintings are now in the Victoria & Albert Museum in London.

Books played an important part in the spread of knowledge about flowers. Monk physicians had compiled herbals or catalogues of plants in the Middle Ages describing in detail their medicinal uses. Later, florilegia (paintings or drawings of collections of flowers) proclaimed their decorative value and were commissioned by rich patrons to illustrate the plants in their gardens. An early seventeenth-century florilegium in the library at Blickling Hall in Norfolk is very unusual. It was compiled by Fabio Colonna, one of the leading natural scientists of his time. Not only does it have paintings of various flowers, but also the impression of plants produced by pressing inked specimens.

This dissemination of knowledge of flowers and horticulture was, of course, considerably accelerated by the invention of printing in the mid-fifteenth century. At first printed books were imported into Britain from France and Italy, but more sophisticated herbals and books on gardening began to be produced in England in the sixteenth century.

One of the first books to give advice on the cultivation of flowers was Thomas Tusser's *A Hundred Pointes of Good Husbandrie*, published in 1557 with many later editions. A man of many parts, the author was in turn musician, schoolmaster, courtier and farmer. The book is of especial interest in that it would appear to provide the first mention of flowers used to decorate the house, with its list of 'hearbs, branches, and flowers for windows and pots'. His suggestions are set out in Table 1.

LEFT: *Sir Thomas More and his family*. The original group portrait by Hans Holbein the Younger, painted in the 1520s, is lost, but a copy was made by Rowland Lockey later in the sixteenth century. In the background the artist has depicted three flower arrangements: details of two of these are shown on page 23.

BELOW: A page of poppies from Columna's *Icones*. Fabio Colonna, a distinguished natural scientist of the late sixteenth and early seventeenth centuries, collected plant specimens, inked them and pressed them on to paper.

TABLE 1: Thomas Tusser, *A Hundred Pointes of Good Husbandrie*, 1557.

Baies sow or set in plants in January

Batchlors buttons [double buttercup]

Bottles, blew, red and tawnie [cornflowers]

Campions

Columbines

Cowslips

Daffadowndillies

Eglantine or Sweet Brier

Fetherfew

Flower de luce [iris]

Flower gentle white and red [amaranthus]

Gilleflowers red, white and carnation set in the spring and at the harvest in pots, pails, or tubbes, or sow summer in beds

Hollihockes white, red and carnation

Lavender of all sorts

Larks foot [larkspur]

Lilium con vallium [lilies of the valley]

Lilies red and white, sow or set in March and September

Marigold double

Nigella Romana

Paoncies or hartease

Pinkes of all sorts

Queenes gilleflowers

Rosmarie

Roses of all sorts

Snap dragons

Sops-in-wine [pinks that are white or pink with red edgings and markings]

Sweet Williams

Star of Bethlehem

Stocke gilliflowers of all sorts

Velvet flowers or French Marigolds

Violets yellow or white

Wall gilleflowers of all sorts [wallflowers]

Most of Tusser's recommendations appear in a herb garden created in the 1960s at Hardwick Hall in Derbyshire. They are represented too in the exquisite embroideries with which Elizabeth Talbot, Countess of Shrewsbury furnished her splendid new house in the 1590s. Bess of Hardwick, as she is familiarly known, was a skilled needlewoman in her own right, but also employed professional embroiderers to provide the rich collection of needlework that survives along with tapestries and other textiles at Hardwick.

Among these is a collection of 'slips' of single flowers worked with silk in tent stitch or *petit point* and then appliquéed onto chair and stool covers and bed and canopy hangings. The technique may have been introduced to her by Mary, Queen of Scots, another skilled and enthusiastic needlewoman. In 1569 Queen Elizabeth appointed the Earl of Shrewsbury as Mary's custodian, so she lived with Bess for many years of her confinement. An inventory of her effects taken in 1586, the year before her execution, lists '52 different flowers in *petit point* drawn from life'.

Bess always hoped that Queen Elizabeth would visit Hardwick Hall. In anticipation of this event, the plaster frieze in the High Great Chamber is an allegory in celebration of the Virgin Queen. Diana, the virgin huntress, is enthroned in the centre of the frieze. Every flower set among the trees in the hunting scene has been chosen for its association with virginity: lilies, the flower of purity; the foxglove known as 'virgins' fingers'; pinks, which the herbalist Gerard calls 'this virgin-like pink'; and the purple iris. These flowers would also have filled pots around the house had the Queen paid that eagerly awaited visit.

ABOVE: Part of the plaster frieze on the upper walls of the High Great Chamber at Hardwick. This detail shows Diana the huntress in the forest, amid a menagerie of animals and a profusion of flowers. Many of the animals may be exotic, but the flowers are native English, chosen for their emblematic association with virginity.

LEFT: Detail of an Elizabethan cushion at Hardwick Hall. The crimson velvet background is decorated with strapwork cut from cloth of silver and with needlework slips of flowers. Gardeners still refer to plant cuttings as slips, but here the term refers to flowers in tent stitch. A variety of flowers can be seen including roses (probably eglantine which were associated with Bess of Hardwick), the pot marigold and honeysuckle.

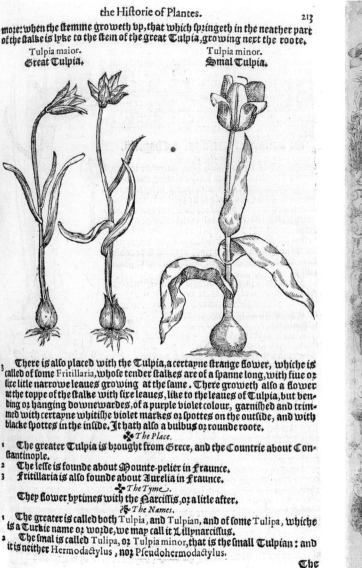

moꝛe: when the ſtemme groweth vp, that which ſpꝛingeth in the neather part of the ſtalke is lyke to the ſtem of the great Tulpia, growing nert the roote.

Tulpia maior.
Great Tulpia.

Tulpia minor.
Smal Tulpia.

³ There is alſo placed with the Tulpia, a certayne ſtrange flower, whiche is called of ſome Fritillaria, whoſe tender ſtalkes are of a ſpanne long, with fiue oꝛ ſire litle narrowe leaues growing at the ſame. There groweth alſo a flower at the toppe of the ſtalke with ſire leaues, like to the leaues of Tulpia, but bending oꝛ hanging downewardes, of a purple violet colour, garniſhed and trimmed with certayne whitiſhe violet markes oꝛ ſpottes on the outſide, and with blacke ſpottes in the inſide. It hath alſo a bulbus oꝛ rounde roote.

❧ The Place.

¹ The greater Tulpia is bꝛought from Grece, and the Countrie about Conſtantinople.
² The leſſe is founde about Mounte-pelier in Fraunce.
³ Fritillaria is alſo founde about Aurelia in Fraunce.

❧ The Tyme.

They flower bytimes with the Narciſſis, oꝛ a litle after.

❧ The Names.

¹ The greater is called both Tulpia, and Tulpian, and of ſome Tulipa, whiche is a Turkie name oꝛ woꝛde, we may call it Lillynarciſſus.
² The ſmal is called Tulipa, oꝛ Tulpia minor, that is the ſmall Tulpian: and it is neither Hermodactylus, noꝛ Pſeudohermodactylus.

The

THE
HERBALL
OR GENERALL
Hiſtorie of
Plantes.
Gathered by Iohn Gerarde
of London Maſter in
CHIRVRGERIE.

Imprinted at London by
Iohn Norton.
1597

ABOVE: A page from Henry Lyte's *Niewe Herball*, 1578, with woodcut illustrations of tulips.

RIGHT: On the frontispiece of his *Herball*, 1597 edition, John Gerard illustrates some of the produce from his garden. Flowers in various pots and baskets surrounding the title include *Carlina acaulis* (the alpine thistle) and *Hermodactylus tuberosus* (widow iris).

It is possible that some of Bess's embroidered slips were copied from the woodcuts of flowers in herbals. In 1578 Henry Lyte, of Lytes Cary Manor in Somerset, translated Dodoen's *Cruedeboek* and published it as his *Niewe Herball or Historie of Plantes*. Twenty years later, the barber surgeon John Gerard published his famous *Herball* with woodcuts of all the flowers he purported to grow in his garden.

Gerard was employed by William Cecil, Lord Burghley, as his gardener at Theobalds in Hertfordshire and at Cecil House in London, and dedicated his herbal to him. It was chiefly concerned with the medicinal qualities of the plants, but his wife added some snippets 'mainly for women', and between them they produced a book that became a bestseller. One assumes that Mrs Gerard was responsible for the references to the flowers suitable for 'decking up' a house: 'Pinks ... esteemed for their use in garlands and nosegays'; 'Columbine ... blue or red or purple or white ... used especially to deck garlands and houses'; 'Meadowsweet ... the leaves and flowers ... far excel all other herbs for to decke up houses ... for the smell thereof makes the heart merrie and joyful and delighteth the senses.'

Gerard lived in Holborn, then a village surrounded by meadows and woods. He tells us that in Gray's Inn Lane he gathered mallow, shepherd's purse, sweet woodruff, bugle, and in the meadows nearby red-flowered clary, white saxifrage, the 'sad-coloured' rocket, yarrow, lesser hawkweed and trefoil, which were presumably put in pots and vases to decorate his house.

His garden contained not only native English plants, but also those that had been introduced to Western Europe via Constantinople. The Turks were notable gardeners, and it was from them that we have acquired some of our best known flowers: the tulip, hyacinth, ranunculus, pinks, narcissi and lilies, as well as the crown imperial and sweet sultan. Some were brought home by the Crusaders. A variety of narcissus known as the 'Findern flower' was brought back from the Holy Land by a crusading ancestor of Jane Findern, who married Richard Harpur in the 1540s. Findern flowers are still to be seen in the Derbyshire village of Findern and at Calke Abbey, purchased in the seventeenth century by Jane and Richard Harpur's descendants.

Gerard referred to these introductions as 'strangers', often noting in his herbal 'these be strangers in England, yet I have them in my garden', sometimes adding triumphantly 'where they flourish as in their natural place of growing'. William Lawson, whose book *The Countrie Housewife's Garden* was published in 1617, was also proud to grow 'strange flowers ... for the making of nosegaies and garlands ... whose colours being glorious and different ... are both wondrous, pleasant and delectable to behold'. A nosegay was either a bunch of flowers carried in the hand to ward off unpleasant smells, also known as a tussie-mussie, or a bunch of flowers in a vase to decorate and scent the house.

As they arrived in England, these flowers were treasured like jewels. Indeed John Parkinson, author of *Paradisus Terrestris* in 1629, who had a garden at Long Acre next to Covent Garden, and received many foreign plants, wrote: 'I do wish all Gentlemen and Gentlewomen, whom it may concern for their own good, to be as careful whom they trust with the planting and replanting of these fine flowers, as they would be with so many Jewels'. He was very aware of the decorative value of plants, and amongst those he singled out as being especially suitable to 'deck up a house' were 'Daffodils ... Many are so exceeding sweet that a very few are sufficient to perfume a whole chamber'; 'Wallflowers ... the sweetness of the flowers causeth them to be generally used in nosegays, and to deck up houses'; 'The Flagg [iris] ... it well doth serve to deck up both a Garden and a House with natures beauties'; and 'Thrift ... in the summertime it will send forth many short stalks of pleasant flowers, to decke up a house among other sweet herbs.'

Parkinson writes of 'the pride of delight', the tulip, introduced into England in 1577 and passionately admired, but never to the fever pitch experienced in Holland. The striped tulip was especially desired. This was caused by a 'break' in some blooms, resulting from a virus transmitted by aphids – a mundane cause of the phenomenon called 'tulipomania' in

'Smell' from the Five Senses by the Flemish arist Frans Floris and engraved by Cornelis Cort in 1561. Flora is shown creating an arrangement of flowers in a basket container made in the fashionable baluster shape, while carnations growing in a terracotta pot stand on the ledge behind. Flora's bouquet includes two slender tulips, recently introduced to the Low Countries from Turkey.

Holland, with bulbs fetching astronomic prices, which reached its height in 1637. One specimen of the 'Viceroy' tulip was sold for 2,500 florins which, as a pamphlet complaining of the evils of tulipomania pointed out, could have bought 'two loads of wheat, four loads of rye, four fat oxen, eight fat pigs, twelve fat sheep, two hogsheads of wine, four barrels of beer, two barrels of butter, 1,000 pounds of cheese, a bed, a suit of clothes and a silver beaker.'

One of Parkinson's illustrious friends was John Tradescant. He and his son, also John, were gardeners successively to Charles I and Charles II. John Tradescant the Elder travelled extensively in Europe and the Mediterranean region, bringing back many plants that included *Gladiolus communis* subsp. *byzantinus* with its wine red flowers; white and orange Martagon lilies, so called because their petals resembled a turban worn by the Turkish sultan known as a martagon; *Gentiana asclepiadea* with its azure blue trumpets; scarlet beans that were valued for their decorative flowers; and the invaluable laurustinus (*Viburnum tinus*) which flowered prolifically in the winter, and was decorative all the year round, with shining evergreen leaves that were happy to be clipped into different shapes.

From Virginia, where the family had business interests, he and his son acquired plants that included *Amaranthus hypochondriacus* (prince's feather); *Rudbeckia laciniata* (coneflower); *Tradescantia virginiana* (the blue-flowered variety was known as spiderwort because it was believed to cure the bite of a spider, and the white known as Moses in the Bulrushes); and *Aster tradescantii*.

The Tradescants lived in Lambeth on the south bank of the Thames. The church in

which they worshipped now houses the Museum of Garden History, founded in 1977, where a replica of a seventeenth-century knot garden contains only their introductions or plants of the period.

In medieval times, flower cultivation was chiefly confined to gardens of monasteries or large manorial demesnes, where they were grown amongst vegetables in simple beds, principally for medicinal purposes, but also for church decoration and for making garlands. Towards the end of the fifteenth century a more orderly way was adopted, with rectangular flower-beds enclosed by low fences made of railings or trelliswork. These in turn gave way to flower-beds in the shape of knots, edged with box or yew, or herbs such as cotton lavender, rosemary or thrift. At Hampton Court Palace in the 1530s Henry VIII's privy gardens included both rectangular beds edged with railings painted green and white in the Tudor colours and a knot garden. The fashion for knots spread rapidly, inspired by patterns and plans – some simple, some elaborate – in gardening books.

A detail from Jan Breughel the Elder and Adriaen Stalbent's early seventeenth-century painting of *The Archduke Albert and Isabella in a Collector's Cabinet*. Many of the flowers, like the objects in the cabinet, come from foreign lands – the sunflower was introduced from America, the crown imperial from India and Iran, and these valued flowers, with a hollyhock, madonna lilies and guelder roses, form the 'crowning' flowers in the vase. A flower-piece is hung amongst the paintings on the wall.

Elizabethan Bouquet

This arrangement is based on a bouquet of herbs, flags and flowers from Joris Hoefnagel's *Wedding Feast at Bermondsey*, now hanging in Hatfield House in Hertfordshire. Because the detail is so tiny, it is difficult to make out the flowers, but they were probably clove pinks. Sweet williams have been substituted, which have a similar colour combination, and were used by the Elizabethans.

The rosemary was held in the flower arranger's hand, and single stems of sweet williams were added to the bouquet. Once the arrangement looked effective, the whole bunch was then placed in the china vase. A few small sprigs of rosemary were added to give a full effect. Wire-edged ribbon was attached to the topmost stem of sweet william.

Garden Scene after Abraham Govaerts. This early seventeenth-century picture originally contained figures of Vertumnus and the garden nymph Pomona, but these have been painted out to make it more marketable. Instead, the plants and gardening tools take centre stage. Covered arbours are shown on the left and at the far end of a gravelled walk that progresses between borders with railed edges adjoining high hedges. An abundance of vegetables include globe artichokes, fruit is represented by orange trees, and flowers include tulips, narcissi and hollyhocks.

The great advantage of this style of horticulture was that the flowers and herbs mixed in the knots looked pretty and colourful in summer, but were still decorative in winter with their evergreen edgings and sprinkling of evergreen herbs.

After the Restoration of Charles II in 1660, the fashion was for gardens in the French style, as created by André le Nôtre at Vaux le Vicomte and then at Versailles. Gardens were extended by formal walks of sweeps of grass, the knots were replaced by parterres that were more likely to be filled with grass and gravel, and flowers were grown in a compartment nearby. On 22 July 1666 Samuel Pepys wrote in his diary that 'flowers are best seen in a little plat by themselves: besides their borders spoil [the walks of] any other garden.' He was walking up and down at Whitehall Palace with the architect Hugh May 'discussing the present fashion of gardens, to make them plain ... with a little mixture of statues or pots, which may be handsome, and so filled with another pot of such and such, a flower or a green, as the season of the year will bear.'

And so it was indoors, with pots of 'such and such' placed inside handsome urns, lining the walls, flanking the furniture or the fireplace, or set out in rows in the gallery.

The fashion for exotic fruit trees had begun in England a century earlier when Sir Francis Carew imported some for his estate at Beddington, near Croydon. Sir William Cecil, not to be outdone, wrote to Sir Thomas Windebank in Paris on 25 March 1562: 'Mr Caroo meaneth to send home certen orege [orange] pomgranat lymon and myrt [myrtle] trees. I have already an orrege tree, and if ye price be not too much, I pray you procure for me a lymon, a pomgranat and a myrt tree, and help that they may be sent home to London with Mr Caroo's trees, and before hand send me in wryting a perfect declaration how they ought to be used, kept and ordered.'

The great attraction of the orange tree was not so much the fruit, which only occasionally ripened to perfection, but the deliciously sweet scent of the flowers and the glossy green leaves. When Henrietta Maria came to England as the bride of Charles I in 1625, she brought over orange trees which she kept at Oatlands Palace in Surrey and at the Manor House at Wimbledon. An inventory made at Wimbledon after Charles I's execution in 1649 describes 'one large garden house ... fitted for the keeping of oringe trees' which contained 'Forty two oringe trees bearing fair and large oringes standing in square boxes.'

Elizabeth Murray, Countess of Dysart, indulged in a flurry of building at Ham House in Surrey soon after marrying John Maitland, Duke of Lauderdale in 1672. Their additions would seem to have included the orangery, although it may have been built earlier. An inventory of 1683, taken after her husband's death, lists his goods and chattels, trees and plants. In the orangery there were 42 boxes, as at Henrietta Maria's Wimbledon Manor, but here in addition to the large orange trees, there were lemons, myrtles, oleanders and pomegranates.

During the sixteenth and seventeenth centuries, the main living rooms of a house were known as chambers, the more informal rooms as parlours. Size varied, and so did nomenclature, from great chambers, withdrawing chambers, antechambers and inner chambers to great parlours, little parlours and winter parlours sited near the kitchen for warmth. Any of these rooms, when in use, might have flowers in them, placed on a table, on the shelved buffet alongside the display of family treasures, on a window sill or chimneypiece, or on the floor.

Our principal form of reference for how flowers were displayed in houses are oil paintings of the period. Exquisite still-life paintings of flowers in vases, known as flower-pieces, appeared at the beginning of the seventeenth century. These found a ready market, perhaps because bulbs were so expensive that it often proved cheaper to have a painting of them rather than the actual flowers. It might also have been thought preferable to enjoy paintings of these precious, wonderful flowers all the year round, rather than for the short time of their blooming. They surely had an influence on how flowers were arranged, but they do not usually represent an actual domestic arrangement for they often portrayed flowers of different seasons in one vase.

If flower-pieces can be misleading about the composition of flower arrangements, other paintings provide more accurate information. Hans Holbein the Younger's portrait of Sir Thomas More and his family painted in the 1520s provides a case in point. The original is lost, but a late sixteenth-century copy by Rowland Lockey hangs at Nostell Priory in Yorkshire. It shows a room decorated with flowers, no doubt from More's renowned Chelsea garden, described in 1556 by Ellis Heywood, a friend of the family, as a 'place of marvellous beauty full of lovely flowers and blossoming fruit trees with a beautiful view of the

A *Flower-piece* by Jan Brueghel (1568-1625). As with many flower-pieces, this probably took years to complete and includes flowers of different flowering periods and with stems of exaggerated length. It does show how the large and small flowers were arranged together in an upright manner.

Brueghel has shown here an earthenware pot, but vessels of glass and even gold were often depicted. The 'crowning' flowers are various tulips and irises, accompanied by *Leucojum aestivum* (summer snowflake) which has small flowers but is 3 ft (1m) tall. The smaller flowers include double daisies and kingcups, forget-me-nots and scilla.

Details from the More family portrait (page 10) showing vases and flowers. LEFT: Double white narcissus, a double aquilegia, an iris, borage, stock gilliflower and peony are displayed in a white maiolica ewer on the buffet. RIGHT: A medieval ewer on the windowsill holds an iris, a peony, aquilegia, violas and buttercups.

Thames'. Here he received the foremost men of the age, including the Dutch humanist Erasmus and Henry VIII, who spent whole days there. One of Sir Thomas's favourite plants was rosemary, of which he wrote, 'I let it run all over my garden walls, not only because my bees love it, but because it is the herb sacred to remembrance and to friendship.'

When examining the More family portrait in detail, it is important to bear in mind that this version was painted at the end of the sixteenth century, and therefore shows some flowers familiar to Holbein and some that were probably introduced later in the century. The peony, *Paeonia tenuifolia* for instance, is not recorded in cultivation until 1594.

On the left-hand side of the painting are two vases of flowers standing on the top shelf of the buffet, alongside a gold plate, a pewter mug, a guitar, a lute and several books. The vase on the left contains white lilies, pink roses and pink and red carnations. The long-stemmed carnations are proudly displayed in a prominent position: perhaps they were a new variety, recently introduced into England by religious refugees from Europe. The vase on the right is a white maiolica ewer (tin-glazed earthenware), probably early sixteenth-century Italian. The flowers – narcissus, aquilegia, iris, borage, stock gilliflower and a peony – are tightly

Two paintings from the series of flower-pieces set in the frieze of the Cartoon Gallery at Knole. These two had been taken down and were rediscovered recently. LEFT: Summer snowflake and Madonna lilies in a two handled vase. RIGHT: A lemon tree in an Italian maiolica vase.

The origin of these paintings is not known, though it has been suggested that they might be Spanish.

packed into it with some greenery. A third vase, a late medieval metal alloy ewer, stands on the window sill and contains an iris, a peony, aquilegia, violas and buttercups.

A portrait of George Gisze, a German merchant working in London, was painted by Holbein in 1532. Carnations in a glass vase stand beside him on a table. The vase is in the shape of a decanter, with a very long neck. This portrait is now in the Staatliche Museum in Berlin. In a portrait of the Nuremberg goldsmith Wenzel Jamnitzer painted by Nicholas Neufchatel, *c*.1562, a silver gilt vase of similar shape filled with silver flowers and ferns appears in a niche. This portrait is now in the Musée d'Art et d'Histoire in Geneva.

At this time, and throughout the seventeenth and eighteenth centuries, a vase for flowers was usually referred to as a 'pot' or 'flower pot'. To add to the confusion, the term was used for containers for both growing and cut flowers. Peter Thornton tries to get to grips with the matter in his book, *Seventeenth Century Interior Decoration in England, France and Holland*: 'In the seventeenth century a "flower pot" could be a large urn with two handles, or it could be a vase. In French a distinction was sometimes made between a "*pot à bouquets*" or a "*vase à fleurs*" on the one hand, and a "*pot à fleurs*", which was usually an altogether more substantial vessel, but the distinction is often blurred.'

As has been noted in the More family portrait, in the sixteenth century domestic jugs with handles, or wine ewers, were used as vases. So too were household glass bowls, decanters and tumblers, particularly the Dutch 'Roemer', a beaker with decorative knobs round the base. Vessels made of plain earthenware, or of Italian maiolica were also used. In the Rothschild Collection at Waddesdon Manor in Buckinghamshire there is a very rare

vessel made in Valencia in Spain in the later fifteenth century. It is an *alfabeguer* or basil pot. Such vessels of basil were used to remove unpleasant smells and to keep the air fresh, but it is clear from paintings that pots like this could also be filled with flowers.

Substantial maiolica pots are to be seen in several of the fascinating flower paintings in the Cartoon Gallery at Knole Park in Kent. These were set high up as a frieze when the room was remodelled for Thomas Sackville, 1st Earl of Dorset between 1605 and 1608. Twelve are still in place; nine additional panels have recently been discovered. They show various arrangements, some with simple mixtures such as white lilies and red roses, or lilies and summer snowflakes. Others show single flower types, unusual for the period.

Bowls and ovoid vases made in Delftware (the Dutch equivalent of Italian maiolica) were also used for flower arrangements. In a painting in the Golfi Collection in Rome by Franz Francken II of *The Study of a Collector c.*1600, amongst the clutter of the room is a blue-and-white bowl with a tall upright arrangement of flowers. A long-stemmed tulip rises above tall columbines, beneath them are carnations, while the lower part of the arrangement consists of short-stemmed roses. A blue-and-white Delft bowl appears in a painting by Alexander Marshall *c.*1650, now in the Mellon Collection at Yale. This time the arrangement consists of just a stem of roses and buds, a carnation and auriculas.

The baluster vase became popular in the seventeenth century. Probably the first vases to

The Cartoon Gallery at Knole, originally known as the Matted Gallery because of the type of covering on the floor. The ornate decoration of the gallery dates from the early years of the seventeenth century when Thomas Sackville, 1st Earl of Dorset, undertook a major refurbishment of the house. On the left of the photograph, above the statue in a niche, can be seen two of the series of paintings of flowers and plants in vases and pots, reflecting the idea that the gallery should combine with the garden. This concept is also reflected in the decoration of the ceiling, where the King's Plasterer, Richard Dungan, modelled botanical emblems from a herbal in the spaces between the ribs.

Illustration from G.B. Ferrari's *De Florum Cultura*, published in Italy in 1633, showing a vase of the fashionable baluster shape, with a removable lid through which the flower stems might be inserted. Ferrari suggested that the flowers could be refreshed by removing the lid with the flowers still in place, and changing the water, preferably every three days.

have tops pierced with holes were urns of this form illustrated in G.B. Ferrari's *De Florum Cultura*. They have intertwined serpents as handles, and the tops are removable. Apparently they could be used for both small and large arrangements, for in one illustration only a few holes are filled, with tulips, narcissi and carnations. In the other, all the holes are filled with a whole mixture of flowers, including daffodils, poppy anemones, lilies, hyacinths, cyclamen and fritillaries. Eight of these magnificent flower-filled vases appear in the scagliola decoration of the *Reiche Kapelle*, added by Maximilian I of Bavaria to the Palace of the Residenz in Munich in 1607.

Ferrari also illustrates a vase of this shape that is almost entirely covered with holes for flowers, and has a complicated interior arrangement that supplies water to all of them. This surely must have influenced Daniel Marot's designs for Queen Mary's pyramid vases (see page 56). Ferrari gives three fundamental principles for arranging flowers in these vases. First, only flowers that carry a single flower on a stem are suitable, such as anemones and roses, so that they can be placed close to the vase, thus keeping its shape distinct. Next, the flowers must be of different colour and arranged neatly. Lastly, the most beautiful flowers should crown the vase like a beautiful head of hair crowns a beautiful body, as stated at the beginning of this chapter. Paintings of the period show that this last instruction was often followed with 'most beautiful flowers', such as crown imperials, lilies, iris, sunflowers or tulips standing well clear of the rest.

Round baskets of flowers appear frequently in pictures. Usually the flowers are in a low, crowded arrangement, but with each bloom clearly visible. Often it is clear that the flowers have no water to sustain them and were changed every day, as the base too is filled with flowers that show through the sides of the woven basket. An engraving of *c*.1640 by Abraham Bosse shows a large basket of flowers on top of a cloth-covered cupboard flanked by a pair of tall pots. A painting of 1647 by Hieronymus Janssens portrays a party in a Dutch house, where a large basket occupies the entire space on top of a tall black cabinet.

Carved wooden baskets of flowers crown the newel posts of the principal staircases at Ham House and at Sudbury Hall in Derbyshire. Both were built in the 1670s as magnificent preludes to the splendours to be found in the state rooms on the first floor. At Ham the Roman concept was recalled that 'when arms and armour are laid aside, then agriculture flourishes'. Thus the vases of fruit and flowers surmount a balustrade composed of martial trophies. The baskets at Sudbury, by the great woodcarver Edward Pearce, are removable; perhaps branches of candelabrum were placed in the holes to light the way up the stairs. Gervase Jackson-Stops has additionally suggested that they might have been replaced with baskets of fresh flowers on special occasions. An echo of this way of decorating a staircase can be seen at Lyme Park in Cheshire when, at the beginning of the twentieth century, watercolours and photographs show spreading palms and waving ferns balanced on the newel posts of the great staircase (see page 211).

Amongst the vases shown in the Cartoon Gallery flower paintings at Knole is a golden one, with a tall stem and elaborate wrought decoration. A rather surprising reference to silver flower pots comes in the description of a dinner given to Oliver Cromwell at the Grocer's Hall in London in 1649. The Protector was presented with decorative silver, including flower pots, fruit baskets and a warming pan, which, as Philippa Glanville

A door panel in *pietra dura*, probably Italian, set in an ebony cabinet made in Flanders in the mid-seventeenth century, and kept in the private apartments at Hinton Ampner in Hampshire. The blue flower on the left is probably *Lignum vitae*, a Jamaican flower not introduced into England until 1694, but well known to Italian craftsmen. Moving to the right, the flowers are a rosebud, tulip, poppy anemone, snakeshead fritillary, either a primrose or a pomegranate bud, and a carnation.

writes, 'belie our suspicion of puritanical simplicity in his household plate and suggest that he expressed his wishes as to the content of the gift'.

Silver flower pots reach their apogee, less surprisingly, at the court of Louis XIV. His mistress, Madame de Montespan, liked to have silver baskets filled with flowers on the floor. The scent of blossom must have filled the rooms at Versailles, where orange trees were displayed in abundance in silver pots specially designed for them by Charles le Brun. In a late seventeenth-century tapestry of a setting for a masquerade, large orange trees in silver pots are raised on pedestals high above the heads of revellers. In an engraving of the *Gallerie des Glaces* at Versailles they are placed on either side of every pier and side-table in the gallery. In 1698 these vases, along with mirrors, candelabra and firedogs, were melted down to pay for the wars against William III and his allies.

Sudbury Flower Baskets

In 1676 George Vernon commissioned the woodcarver Edward Pearce to decorate his great staircase at Sudbury Hall in Derbyshire. Originally it was to have been decorated with pineapples, but these were abandonned in favour of baskets of flowers and fruit, which could be removed at night and replaced by candelabra or lanterns. The theory has been advanced that baskets of real flowers might have been used for parties and special occasions.

In the recreation, neither the basket nor the manner of arranging are typical of the seventeenth century, though the sunflowers and marigolds echo those in Pearce's carving. The other flowers used are peonies, bearded iris, asphodel, sweet williams, lilies and cornflowers, which were all used for interior decoration in the seventeenth century. The marigold is a modern variety.

Wire netting was pushed down into a plastic container and secured with mossing wire. Do not use string as it can act as a siphon. The container was placed within the basket, with a little moss arranged around the edge to keep it steady, and filled with water. The flowers were then placed within the wire netting, starting with the largest, the sunflower, and moving down to the smallest.

In 1560 a Dutchman, Levinus Leminus, visited England, and after he returned to Holland wrote of how he was pleased to find flowers in the chambers, parlours and bedchambers of English houses. 'Their nosegays finely intermingled with sundry sorts of fragraunt flowers with comfortable smell cheered me up and entirely delighted all my senses.' And he went on to write of the greenery that decorated rooms, favourably comparing the English way of doing it with that of the Dutch. 'Altho' we do trimme up our parlours with green boughs, fresh herbs or vine leaves, no nation does it more decently, more trimmely, nor more sightly than they do in England.'

In 1608 Sir Hugh Platt published his *Floraes Paradise*, a book on gardening containing a section headed 'A Garden within doors'. Platt, the son of a wealthy brewer, also wrote books on cookery and diet, and created ingenious systems such as a grate to burn coal, the fuel of the future. Enthusing about the practice of having a 'Fair gallery, great Chamber or other lodging' opening onto the sun and decorated with growing plants, he instructs the reader: 'First, you may have fair sweet Marjerom, Basil, Carnation, or Rosemary-pots, etc., To stand loosely upon fair shelves.... In every window you may make square frames either of Lead or of Boards, well pitched within: fill them with some rich earth, and plant such Flowers or Hearbs therein as you like best; if Hearbs, you may keep them in the shape of green borders, or other form'. For the 'shady places' of the room, he suggests trying to grow 'sweet Bryars, Bays, Germander, etc', but urges his readers frequently to open the windows as they 'delight and prosper best in the opon Air'.

He also describes the habit of having plants climbing up inside windows, over the walls and even over the ceiling. If rosemary is planted in the frames or boxes on the window sills it should be encouraged to run 'up the Transomes and movels of your windows'. Vines, or apricot or other plum trees, should be planted without the walls 'which being let in at some quarrels may run about the sides of your windows and all over the sealing of your Rooms'. This remarkable idea is shown in a group portrait of the English and Spanish pleni-potentiaries at a conference at Somerset House in 1604. Behind the massed ranks of the distinguished gentlemen, greenery curls its way round the windows.

Another unusual idea is to hang 'in the Roof, and about the sides of the Room, small Pompions or Cowcumbers, pricked full of Barley, first making holes for the Barley (quaere what other seeds or flowers will grow in them) and these will be overgrown with green spires, so as the Pompion or Cowcumber will not appear.' This idea, Platt says, comes from Italy where these 'fancies are hung up in their Rooms to keep the Flies from their Pictures'.

He suggests that to keep the indoor plants healthy 'the pots you may let down at your pleasure in apt frames with a pulley from your Chamber window into your Garden, or you may place them upon shelves made without the Room, there to receive the warm Sun, or temperate Rain at your pleasure, now and then you see cause'.

Another method devised by Platt of making sure the plants had enough water was as follows: 'From platforms of lead over your windows, rain may descend by small pipes and so be conveyed to the roots of your hearbs or flowers that grow in your windows. These pipes would have holes in the sides, for so much of them as is within the earth, and also holes in the bottom, to let out the water when you please in great showers.' It is not surprising to learn that Hugh Platt was knighted for his prowess in mechanical inventions.

The Somerset House Conference, 1604 by an unknown English artist. Greenery decorates the window behind the conference table, in the style recommended by Sir Hugh Platt in *Floraes Paradise*. Thomas Sackville, 1st Earl of Dorset from Knole, is sitting at the top, on the right side of the table.

He tells us how it is possible to have roses or carnations growing in winter by keeping them 'in a Room that may some way be kept warm, either with a dry fire, or with the steam of hot water conveyed by a pipe fastened to the cover of a pot, that is kept seething over some idle fire, now and then exposing them in a warm day, from twelve to two, in the Sun, or to the rain if it happen to rain, or if it rain not in convenient times, set your pots having holes in the bottom in pans of rainwater, and so moisten the roots'. He adds 'I have known Master Jacob of the Glass-house to have Carnations all the Winter by the benefit of a Room that was near his Glass-house fire.'

He describes how to make pyramids or other shapes out of rosemary, thyme or hyssop crowned with a flower:

Cause large Carnation pots to be made, viz. double in bigness to the usual pots; let them have ranks of sloping holes, of the bigness of one's finger, each rank one inch [2.5 centimetres] distant from another. Set in the midst of the pot a Carnation or a Lilly, and in every of the holes, a plant of Thyme or Hysop, keep the Thyme or Hysop as it groweth, even with clipping. . . . Also you may make piramides, losinges, circles, pentagons, or any form of beast or fowl, in wood or burnt clay, full of slope holes (as before). . . . these being planted with hearbs will very speedily grow green, according to the form they are planted in: And in this manner may you in two years space make a high piramid of Thyme, or Rosemary.

These wonderful shapes of greenery could then be added to 'the Garden within Doors to grace it in winter' or be set upon 'fair pillars in your Garden, to make a beautiful shew'.

In 1653, after Sir Hugh Platt had died, a new edition of his book was published, renamed *The Garden of Eden*. To this was added a second part in 1660, giving instruction on how to grow the exotic 'Olive, Pomgranate, Orange and Lemon Trees and such like.' And how to force these trees to grow 'in pots or wooden vessels', suggesting 'Let every Outlandish Plant be set in such soil as cometh nearest in kind to that soil wherein it did naturally grow beyond the seas, or if you can, bring over sufficient of the same earth wherein it grew.' In order to ensure the survival of these trees the editor does not think it 'an unseemly sight to have some dozen or twenty of those Dwarf-trees ranked in good order upon high shelves in our Winter Parlors, where we may also make a second use of our chargeable fires.'

In the sixteenth and seventeenth centuries dinner was the main meal of the day, starting at 11am, but getting later as the decades passed. For the household it might be served in the great hall, as in the Middle Ages, but for the family and honoured guests it was taken in the great chamber or the parlour. There is no evidence of flowers being used to decorate the table, but then there would have been scant room with the quantities of dishes of meat, fish, pies and puddings that were served as the first two courses, in the style of a modern Chinese meal. But the room itself was often decorated with flowers. At Cowdray Park in Sussex at the end of the sixteenth century, Viscount Montagu ordered that the rooms where he dined should be kept 'sweet with perfumes, flowers, herbs and boughs in their season.' For a feast at Knole on 3 July 1636, Edward Sackville, 4th Earl of Dorset ordered his servants to have 'fresh bowls in every corner and flowers tied upon them, and sweetbriar, stock, gilly flowers, pinks, wall-flowers and any other sweet flowers in glasses and pots in every window and chimney.'

After these two courses came a third, the 'banquet', later known as the dessert, for which guests withdrew to the withdrawing room, or to a banqueting house built especially for the purpose, often reached by a walk across the garden. A temporary house was made in Greenwich Park when Queen Elizabeth entertained the French Ambassador in 1560. It was made of fir poles 'and decked with birch branches and all manner of flowers both of the field and of the garden, as roses, julyflowers, lavender, marygolds, and all manner of strewing herbs and rushes.' At Montacute in Somerset, Edward Phelips built little decorated pavilions for banquets in his garden. At Hardwick Hall in Derbyshire, Bess not only had banqueting houses in her garden, but also one on the roof of her magnificent mansion. Guests, having dined in the High Great Chamber, would cross the leads of the roof to reach their banquet, taking in, of course, the grandeur of the rugged landscape below.

At the banquet the table would be covered with fresh and preserved fruits, sugar paste centrepieces and decorative biscuits. Flowers would be used to garnish the pyramids of fruit, as recorded by the diarists of the time. On 18 July 1670, by which time the banquet was becoming known as the dessert, John Evelyn wrote in his diary after dining at Goring House: 'at Dinner my Lord Viscount Stafford rose from the Table in some Disorder, because there were roses stuck about the fruite, when the Discert came in and was set on the Table; such an Antipathie it seems he had to Roses.'

Seventeenth-Century Table Decoration

This decoration is based on an illustration for an al fresco party from *Il Trinciante* published in Italy in 1593. It uses lengths of yew, marigolds (a modern variety) and apples.

Lengths of galvanised wire, ⅛ inch (3 millimetres) thick, were measured, cut to length and covered with stem wind (Guttacoll™).

Yew sprigs were placed along the wire and bound on with mossing wire. It is important to work down the wire, ensuring the yew is even and that there are no gaps.

Using a staple gun, the yew strips were then fixed to the table cloth, with the cross-overs alternating. To keep the distances correct, the cross-overs were lightly wired.

Each marigold flower was wired (see page 107 for method). The apples were also wired by placing the wire right through the fruit three quarters of the way down the apple. Ensuring the wires are the same length, bend them down to the bottom of the apples, and twist twice round. Cut the ends of the wires to leave a length of 2-3 inches (5-8 centimetres). The wired flowers and fruit were then stabbed into the yew strips.

34

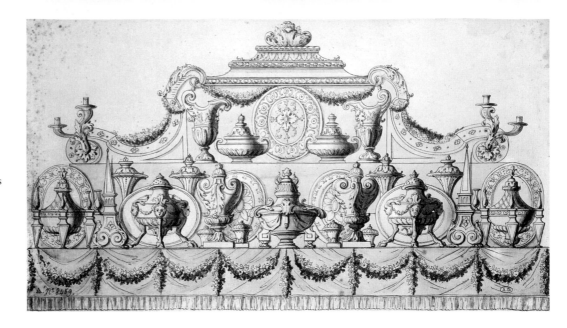

Proposal for dressing a *buffet* by Jean Bérain, *c*.1670, with garlands draping the display of plate and fixed along the front of the board cloth. Bérain was designer to the *Menus Plaisirs*, an organisation that provided equipment and decoration for the numerous elaborate festivities at the French Court.

Lord Stafford's allergy was well known; on 12 July 1666 Samuel Pepys noted in his diary, 'By and by, the Dessert coming with roses upon it, the Duchess [either of Albemarle or York] bid him try touching his skin with one to see if it would make it rise and pimple.' From a chance remark in Pepys' diary for 13 September 1665 it is known that a large pot of flowers might stand on a side-table. 'Sir W. Hicke's – it is a good seat but ill furnished and miserably looked after – not so much as a latch to his dining room door which saved him nothing, for the wind blowing into the room for want thereof, flung down a great Bowpott that stood upon the side table, and that fell upon some Venice-glasses, and did him a crown's worth of hurt'.

Bowpot, bough pot or bogh pot is a term often used in the seventeenth and eighteenth centuries to describe a large pot or vase for flowers and 'boughs'. This was usually put in the fireplace, although on this occasion it was placed on a side-table – with disastrous results. Towards the end of the eighteenth century the term seems to have also been used to describe all vases, both large and small, that have tops pierced with holes for flowers (see pages 80 and 82).

Flowers were used in profusion to decorate the buffet or sideboard, where the plate was displayed both for indoor or outdoor feasts. Garlands were draped over and around the silver dishes and cups, over the pyramids of fruit too, and were hung in swags round the edges of the buffet and along the top, or wherever there was a suitable place for them. Smaller side-tables also might be decorated with swags, or even a lattice-work of garlands.

Fireplaces, with their large openings, must have looked cavernous and unwelcoming without a fire. A picture of a Dutch interior by Nicolas de Gyslaer, *c*.1621, shows a vase of flowers standing between the firedogs on the hearth in front of the fireplace. With very little furniture in the room, the flowers in their tall vase stand out as a dominant feature. The flowers are in a loose, round arrangement.

Sir Hugh Platt suggested that during the summer months the chimney 'may be trimmed with a fine bank of moss and planted with columbine' or even 'filled with a fine bank of moss … or with orpin … and at either end and in the middest place one of your Flower or

A Dutch interior by Nicolas de Gyslaer, 1621, showing flowers in a metal vase in the fireplace, probably the earliest record of a fireplace decorated in this way. Here, as in most arrangements of this period, the flowers are placed carefully in their container so that each bloom can be clearly seen and appreciated.

Rosemary Potts'. In the 1675 edition of *The Queen-like Closet or Rich Cabinet*, Hannah Wolley made similar suggestions:

> To dress a chimney very fine for the summertime, as I have done many, and they have been liked very well. First take a pack thread and fasten it to the inner part of the chimney, so high as you can see no higher as you walk up and down the house.... Then get a good store of old green moss from trees and melt an equal proportion of Beeswax and Rosin together and while it is hot, dip in the wrong ends of the moss in it, and press it down hard with your hand ... then several other kinds of moss ... then any kind of fine snail shells, in which the snails are dead, and little toad stools that look like velvet, or any other thing that is old and pretty, and place it here or there as your fancy serves ... then for the hearth orpen sprigs (it will grow as it lies), according to season what flowers you can, and a few sprigs of sweetbriar. The flowers you must renew each week, the moss will last all summer till it will be time to make a fire. The orpen will last near two months. A chimney doth grace a room exceedingly.

CHAPTER TWO

Parterres to Flower Pots

1677-1740

'If possible to have flowers in all seasons in order to make two or three bouquets for the service of Her Highness every week.' These instructions, signed on 5 November 1678 by Prince William of Orange, were given to Charles du Buisson, the gardener at Honselaarsdijk, a palace not far from The Hague. A later note requested that 'her rooms should be abundantly furnished each day with all kinds of flowers'.

William of Orange had brought his bride, Mary Stuart, daughter of James, Duke of York, and niece of the English King, Charles II, to Honselaarsdijk a year earlier, following their wedding in London. A record of the bouquets ordered by the Prince, bound in ribbon, was made in a flower painting, one of a series specially commissioned.

When William and Mary built their palace at Het Loo near Apeldoorn, an apartment in the basement was made for the Princess, consisting of 'a chamber, a kitchen cellar and a grotto'. Inventories and recent excavations show that many flower vases were kept in these rooms, which can be thought of as forerunners of the 'flower room' (see pages 154 and 204). From the apartment a door opened out into Mary's private garden and a staircase led directly up to her private apartments. With this easy access, it is most likely that she would have arranged the flowers herself, and no doubt picked some of them too. Both William and Mary enjoyed domestic pleasures above court life.

In 1689 the couple jointly ascended the English throne as William III and Mary II, and the embellishment of Mary's rooms with flowers continued in all their palaces – Whitehall, Kensington and Hampton Court. From April 1689, George London had to supply flowers for the royal apartments at Whitehall from his nursery at Brompton Park in West London. At Hampton Court the flowers, flowering shrubs and other exotics in pots were brought into the palace by the gardener from various areas of the garden, including the Flower Quarter on the west side of the Privy Garden that has recently been restored. Flowers had now taken on a new importance, enjoyed in quantities indoors.

Mary II figures so largely in this chapter because her influence at the time was great. As Stephen Switzer, the famous gardener, nurseryman and author wrote, 'the Nobility and Gentry of Great Britain were all this while very busy in Imitation of the Royal Examples of the King and Queen'. Not only did she love flowers, but was equally interested in ceramics, and thus responsible for the development of a great variety of vases. Her position as Queen allowed her to give full rein to these interests, for she had both plentiful resources at her disposal and William's architect and designer, Daniel Marot, to advise her. Marot had fled to Holland in 1685 following Louis XIV's Revocation of the Edict of Nantes, which drove many French Protestants or Huguenots into exile. He worked for William and Mary

Portrait of Princess Mary painted by Adriaen de Hennin in 1677, the year of her marriage to William of Orange. She points to an orange tree, loved since ancient times for its decorative fruit, sweet-scented flowers and glossy leaves. In the seventeenth century, orange trees were placed in decorative pots and tubs, and served to decorate both the house and the garden.

first at Het Loo and later at Hampton Court, where, as Gervase Jackson-Stops has written, 'he designed everything from coaches to clocks, state beds to snuff boxes, parterres to flower pots'.

Parterres to flower pots indeed. There was a similarity between the arrangement of flowers displayed in vases and the manner of growing them in late seventeenth-century gardens. Whether these were attached to a palace or a modest town house, they were now laid out with formality and overall symmetry. Knot gardens, so popular with the Elizabethans, had been replaced by parterres, some of most intricate design, of grass or different coloured gravel surrounded by low box hedges. The simple compartments containing a jumble of flowers gave way to 'plates bandes' – long narrow beds, also edged with box, and often surrounding the parterres. In these 'plates bandes' the flowers were grown singly with space between them so that the plant could be seen from all angles. Large and small stood side by side, and there was no attempt at a colour scheme. Although they were part of, and set in, a formal decorative scheme, they were grown for themselves as individuals. This sparse method of planting flowers may have been due to the fact that the botanical aspect of a plant was much studied and admired, its growth and development noted day by day.

John Evelyn of the celebrated diary, and author of books on many subjects, advocated growing flowers specifically for cutting for the house. In *Directions for the Gardener at Sayes Court* (his home near Deptford to the east of London) written in 1687 he declared:

> In this quarter of the Nurserie, you should raise in their distinct beds, all sorts of flowers, which spring, and are increased from seedes, bulb or other rootes ... that they may be ready to ... be gathered for Bough-pots and adorning the house ... Anemones,

An engraving for a *trompe l'oeil* painting of a pedestal-supported vase, published *c.*1700 by Daniel Marot, 'architect' to William III, and intended as decoration for an over-door or over-mantel. The flowers in the urn include a large tuberose, roses, tulips and opium poppies, while the garland in which the putti frolic is made up of poppy anemones, tulips, roses and smaller flowers.

Auriculas, Carnations, Crocus, Crown Imperials, Iris, Jacynths [hyacinths], Junquills, Martagon, Narcissus, Peonie, Poulanthos, Ranunculus, Stock-gilly flower [*Matthiola* species], Tulips.

He directs that the 'choicer shrubs' grown in the nursery should include 'Althea frutex, Honeysuckle, Jasmine, Roses the severall sorts, Sweete-briar and Syringa', and on the hotbed he suggests growing 'Marvell of Peru, Nasturtium Indicum, Limons, Myrtles, Oranges and Tuberose'. A hotbed at this period consisted of a deep brick-lined pit filled with dung, sometimes topped up with tan bark. Usually covered with glass and looking like the present-day cold-frame, it was intended for 'starting off' and 'bringing on' flowers and plants. Serious, large-scale forcing, however, did not take place until later in the eighteenth century.

Further advice to the Sayes Court gardener was 'to give his Mistris notice when … any Flowers or plants under his care are fit to be spent, cutt and to be gathered … and to receive her directions.' Among the 'Toles and Instruments necessary for a Gardiner' he includes '2 flower googes, Flower baskets of severall sizes, Tubs, Cases and Boxes, Flower Pots and Finer thread to bind up Nose-gays with.'

Evelyn translated the work of Monsieur de la Quintinie, supervisor of Louis XIV's enormous kitchen gardens at Versailles. Published in France in 1690, it was translated as *The Compleat Gard'ner or Directions and Right Ordering of Fruit Gardens and Kitchen Gardens* and came out in England three years later. Mixed up amongst the produce of fruit and vegetables that he advises growing for each month of the year are lists of flowers plainly to be used for decoration indoors. Three extracts are given in Table 2.

TABLE 2: M. de la Quintinie, *The Compleat Gard'ner or Directions and Right Ordering of Fruit Gardens and Kitchen Gardens*, translated by John Evelyn, 1693.

January We have now naturally but few Flowers, except those of Laurus Thymus (Laurustine) & Snowdrops, but by the help of Hot Beds we may have some single Anemones, Narcissus's of Constantinople, Crocus's etc. And we have now Laurel Rose-leaves to garnish the dishes we serve up to Table.

June We have abundance of flowers, as well to garnish Dishes, to set out Flower-Pots, viz Double Poppies of all colours, white, pale, violet, flesh-coloured, or Carnation, flame coloured, purple, violet coloured and panached or striped, yellow and violet pansies, Larks Heels [larkspurs], Julians [stocks], … Roses of all sorts, viz double, panached or striped, double Eglantine or Dog Roses, Roses of Gueldres [*Viburnum opulus*], white lilies, yellow lilies, Matricaria's or Feather-fews, Calves-snowts [antirrhinum], Golden Rod, Gladiolus's, Veronica's or Fluellins, Spanish Carnations, Verbascum or Mullein Flowers, Valerians, Lady-Gloves [foxgloves], Tuberoses, Anemonies …

September As to flowers, we have now great store of Tuberoses, Asters or Oculus Christis, of Flower gentles, Velvet Flowers or Amaranthus, of Indian Gilliflowers or French Marigolds, of Indian Roses, Marvels of Peru, … Laurel or Bay Roses, both White and Carnation, Ultramarine Roses, Ordinary Stock, Gilliflower both of white and violet sorts, etc, Ciclamens, and some Orange-Flowers, with single Anemones.

The Sunken Parterre at Hanbury Hall, restored in 1993 to the designs provided for Thomas Vernon *c*.1700 by the gardener George London. The flowers that now make up the parterre are marigolds, Brompton stocks, alpine strawberries, pinks and pasque flowers, while the border, 'ranked' in the traditional seventeenth-century manner, runs around the edge, with a repeating pattern of rose campion, nettle-leaved campanula, peony, pinks and dictanmus.

March, July and November from Robert Furber's *The Flower Garden Display'd. . . .* It was first published in 1732 to illustrate the flowers available from his nursery in Kensington Gore, and to show the months in which they would bloom.

This month-by-month approach was also adopted by Robert Furber, who founded a nursery at Kensington Gore soon after 1700. In 1732 he published as his catalogue '*The Flower Garden Display'd, Four Hundred Representations of the most Beautiful Flowers regularly dispos'd in the respective Months of their Blossom . . . and Coloured to the Life.*' Each month is depicted by an urn or vase filled with flowers in bloom, including branches of red- and white-flowering larch, maple, bay, myrtle and laurustinus, and tender exotics such as orange, lemon and olive. He gives instructions as to how the plants should be grown, including directions as to where they would best flourish – in 'Stoves, Green-Houses, Hot Beds, Glass-cases, Open Borders or against Walls'.

For each month he recommends thirty to forty blooms. Each flower is numbered, its name is given in a list below, and the same number is assigned wherever that name appears in the descriptive text. Furber suggests that the pictures will be useful 'Not only for the curious in Gardening . . . but also for the Ladies as Patterns for Working and Painting in Watercolours.'

The qualities most sought after in flowers at this time were threefold: first, stripes, speckles or spots of dark colour on paler petals. This applied particularly to carnations,

1 Ficoides or fig Marigold.
2 White Periwinkle.
3 Earliest flowering Laurustinus.
4 Blew Periwinkle.
5 Tree Candy tuft.
6 Embroider'd Cranes bill.
7 Yellow spik'd Eternal.
8 Strip'd single Anemone.
9 Borage.
10 Thyme leav'd Myrtle.

11 French Marigold.
12 Colchicum Alpina major.
13 Ilex leav'd Jasmine.
14 Great purple Cranes bill.
15 Arbutus or Strawberry tree.
16 Double Nasturtium.
17 Broad leav'd red Valerian.
18 Myrto Cistus.
19 Virginian Aster.
20 Campanula Canariensis.

21 Pheasants Eye.
22 Perennial dwarf Sun flower.
23 Double Feather few.
24 Carolina Star flower.
25 Scarlet Althæa.
26 Spanish white Jasmine.
27 Lavender with divided Leaves.
28 Golden Rod.
29 American Viburnum.

30 Yellow Dwarf Aloe.
31 Single blew Anemone.
32 Purple Ficoides.
33 Groundsell tree.
34 Pellitory with Daisy flowers.
35 Scarlet single Anemone.
36 White Egyptian holly hock.
37 Taper Bush.
38 Dwarf Colutea.

NOVEMBER

Design'd by P.r Casteels.

From the Collection of Rob.t Furber Gardiner at Kensington 1730.

Engrav'd by H. Fletcher.

pinks and tulips; secondly, double flowers, such as anemones (the poppy anemone seen so often in flower paintings), narcissus, rockets, violets, polyanthus, etc; thirdly, flowers with strong scents.

New flowers that arrived in England during this period were proudly displayed in vases indoors. These included the sweet pea (*Lathyrus odoratus*), a Sicilian wild flower with maroon-coloured wings and a blue or purple standard, introduced into England in 1700. In 1722 the nurseryman Thomas Fairchild of Hoxton in East London wrote: 'the scent is somewhat like Honey and a little tending to the Orange-flower Smell'.

Gerard had described the nasturtium *Tropaeolum minus* which had yellow flowers. Now *Tropaeolum majus* was introduced from Peru in 1686 and known as Indian cress because of the resemblance between the hot peppery taste of the leaves and the flavour of watercress. This, rather than *minus*, is the variety we grow today. The passion flower (*Passiflora caerulea*) came to England from South Brazil in 1699 and was first mentioned growing in the Duchess of Beaufort's garden at Badminton in Gloucestershire. It is a hardy variety, differing from the earlier type of passion flower grown by Parkinson and described by him as 'a pretty thing of semi-herbaceous habit' which needed to be grown indoors to bring its flower to perfection.

The Paris daisy (*Argyranthemum frutescens*) was introduced from the Canaries in 1699. It is sometimes known as the marguerite because Marguerite de Valois, Queen of Henri IV, grew it in her garden at Issy near Paris in 1600. The name, however, correctly belongs to the wild ox-eye daisy.

From America in 1684 came prince's feather (*Amaranthus hypochondriacus*). It is similar to love-lies-bleeding, but has upright rather than drooping flowers. The collaboration between two Quakers, the English horticulturist Peter Collinson and the American John Bartram, brought many new plants from North America to Britain. One was *Lilium superbum* with its brown-spotted, crimson petals. It flowered in Peter Collinson's London garden in 1738, delighting him and inspiring his collection of American plants (see page 79).

The Chinese aster (*Callistephus chinensis*) was a native of China where, wrote John Hill in *Eden, or Compleat Body of Gardening* (1757), 'in that gay Country [it is] as frequent about the Hedges as Mallows or Thistles are with us'. Seeds were sent to Paris in 1728 and thence to Philip Miller of the Chelsea Physic Garden in 1731. They were particularly appreciated for their double forms in purple, white and red, and there were some striped varieties too.

Not only were new flower introductions coming into Europe at this period, but also shrubs known as exotics and greens. Exotic meant that they 'came from abroad', or as John Evelyn described them 'plants such as are sent from beyond the seas'. Greens meant evergreens. In winter tender varieties were kept either in orangeries, also known as greenhouses (houses for greens), or in hothouses, also known as stoves or glass cases. In summer months they were carried out into the gardens. M. de la Quintinie recommended May as the correct month for this. Some were displayed indoors all year round to decorate and scent rooms. In 1694 Celia Fiennes, visiting New College, Oxford, where her grandfather had been a Fellow, wrote in her diary, 'They [the Fellows] take much delight in greens of all

A *Flower-piece* in the style of Jan van Huysum (1682-1749). His paintings, although exaggerated and contrived, show the fashion for free flowing and spacious arrangements in contrast to the earlier, simple and upright ones with their 'crowning' flowers. Resting on the ledge are nasturtiums (*Tropaeolum majus*) and a gentian. In the vase going up and round from the left are the pale pink *Rosa × centifolia*, *Rosa × alba* 'Alba Maxima', carnations, cyclamen, auriculas, *Saxifraga umbrosa*, a double red geum, an opium poppy, a tall branch of *Prunus avium* 'Plena', tulips, *Narcissus aureus*, marigold, double hyacinth, and stock.

The interior of an orangery from Jan Commelin's *Nederlantze Hesperides*, 1676. Two of the stoves for heating the orangery in the winter months can be seen on the left. The gardeners are shown moving the orange trees with poles through the handles of the pots, in the style of sedan chairs.

sorts Myrtle Oringe and Lemons and Lorrestine growing in potts of earth and so moved about from place to place and into the aire sometymes.'

In 1675 William, then Prince of Orange, had requested the Dutch East India Company to bring him back plants with their cargoes from the Far East and Cape of Good Hope, and this they did each year. These exotics were kept first in the enormous orangery at his palace of Honselaarsdijk and later at Hampton Court where three glass cases were built in the Pond Yard to house them.

In 1689, the year after William and Mary arrived in England, Stephen Switzer wrote 'that active Princess lost no time but either measuring, directing or ordering her Buildings, but in Gardens Especially Exotics, she was particularly skilled'. In 1701 the glass cases at Hampton Court were replaced by a larger building known as the Lower Orangery, and *Magna Britannia* reported that 'the Gardens are improved to a wonderful degree ... the Green-houses ... have stoves under them, so artificially contrived that all foreign Plants are here preserved in gradual Heats, suitable to the Climes of their respective Countries, where they naturally grow, and from whence they are brought.'

The remains of the Queen's exotics survived there until 1921 when the building was altered to display Mantegna's cartoons from the great art collection of Mary's grandfather, Charles I. Now again a collection of the exotics grown by William and Mary is being built up in the glasshouse nursery in the seventeenth-century melon ground. They are put out on the terraces overlooking the Privy Garden in the summer, and include oleanders, olives, yuccas, agaves and aloes. In the winter they are replaced by greens such as bay, laurustinus, holly, Portugal laurel and Spanish broom.

In the middle of the King's Apartments, William and Mary incorporated another orangery with large glass doors and windows for their orange, lemon and bay trees. This was finished and in use by 1700. Twenty-four years later, Daniel Defoe on his travels noticed 'The Orange Trees and Fine Dutch Bays' still there. Attempts to revive this custom by overwintering the citrus collection in this orangery have not proved successful, so the citrus trees are kept alongside other exotics in the glasshouse nursery and are staged out on the orangery terrace from mid-May.

While William was collecting his exotics via the East India Company, Henry Compton, Bishop of London, took advantage of his missionary network to bring plants from all corners of the earth. He kept them in his stoves at Fulham Palace, where he had over 1,000 species. Compton may well have inspired Queen Mary's love of flowers, for he had been religious instructor to her and her sister Anne, confirming both princesses in 1676. When Mary was married to Prince William a year later, he performed the wedding ceremony.

By the 1680s, Henry Compton's exotics had multiplied, and some were sold off by his gardener, George London, through the Brompton Park Nursery that he had founded in 1681. Enthusiastic gardeners rushed to buy them, including the Duchess of Beaufort, who built up a large collection at Badminton. At the same time the Physic Gardens at Oxford, founded in 1621, and Chelsea, founded by the Society of Apothecaries in 1673, were collecting exotics and, as they multiplied, distributing them to nurseries and collectors.

George London had also worked at Hampton Court for the King and at Petworth in Sussex, where Charles Seymour, 6th Duke of Somerset had a rectangular walled orange garden laid out next to the chapel with an orangery standing at the north end. Within the garden trees were set in painted tubs in formal patterns in the parterre, marked out by 'Border boards'. The Duke took a particular interest in his orange trees, asking his gardener, Miller, in July 1703, 'if the orange trees are in blossom and how much' as he liked to decorate the house with the flowers. In late August he instructed Miller to take the trees back into the orangery for overwintering, replacing them with bays and laurustinus.

For those not in easy reach of nurseries, the exotics and greens had to be transported by ship. When, in 1694, the Duke of Hamilton bought from Brompton Park ten baskets of growing trees for Hamilton Palace, his home to the south of Edinburgh, he gave five shillings extra to the seamen for carrying them carefully into the ship, watering them and taking care of them during the voyage. He gave orders that 'his flowers in the pots must be kept from the sea water'. Sir William Carew, laying out his gardens at Antony in Cornwall in 1710, commissioned the Lambeth nurseryman Humphrey Bowen to ship greens, fruit trees and shrubs from London to Plymouth on the *Loving Brothers*. The shrubs were divided into baskets, 242 in all, labelled to indicate for which part of the garden they were destined.

With the increasing popularity of exotics and greens, the orangery became an indispensable feature of a country estate. Some were incorporated into the house, as at Dyrham Park

in Gloucestershire, where William Blaythwayt, Secretary at War to William III, had one built onto the east front in 1701. Others were separate garden buildings, as at Felbrigg Hall in Norfolk, where in 1705 Ashe and Katherine Windham wrote of purchasing 'sashes, shutters, doors, pavement for the orenge house'. In the 1720s a charming small orangery was built at Dunham Massey in Cheshire. Here now, as in the eighteenth century, myrtle trees with their scented leaves are overwintered in tubs for placing outside in summer. At Hanbury Hall in Worcestershire the orangery, built in 1745, also still overwinters exotics representing species introduced to England before 1700, including *Citrus aurantium*, the Seville orange, which has the largest and best scented flowers (and can be grown from a pip), *Citrus limon* 'Quatre Saisons' which produces large blossoms and heavy crops of pointed lemons, pomegranates, oleanders and olives.

Indoors, as in the garden, rooms were arranged formally, with furniture set against the walls. For dining or for social functions, the furniture would be brought into the centre of the room. From a flower-arranging point of view, this meant that there were few surfaces on which to place vases. One place was on the side-table against an inner wall, another the pier-table that stood against the pier between the windows, and in daytime the tall candle-stands that by custom flanked it. A Gobelins tapestry of a reception held for the Spanish Ambassador at Versailles shows four candlestands bearing bowls of cut flowers. A portrait at Antony House of Lady Anne Coventry, who married Sir William Carew in 1713, shows

ABOVE: The orangery at Hanbury Hall, a free-standing brick building with baskets of fruit and flowers in the pediment, dates from *c.*1745. Orange and lemon trees in pots are ranged on the terrace in front.

LEFT: The orangery at Dyrham Park was built in 1700 by William Blaythwayt. Unusually for this period, he attached it to the east front of his house – in this photograph, the orangery can be seen on the left. A hot air system of flues ensured that his exotics survived the winter and it provided a pleasant place for entertainment, with furnishings that in 1710 included eighty-eight prints, nine chairs, two tables and two carpets.

RIGHT: Flowers deck a golden *torchère* in the Queen's Gallery at Hampton Court. They include larkspur, monkshood, moluccella (the everlasting, known also as bells of Ireland and shell flower), statice, stocks and a little ivy.

FAR RIGHT: Portrait of Lady Anne Coventry who married Sir William Carew in 1713 and provided the money to make the substantial alterations in the house and garden at Antony. In this portrait by Michael Dahl, the basket is typical of the period, waisted with thin upright slats. An open tulip crowns the arrangement.

RIGHT & FAR RIGHT: The walls of the Grand Staircase at Powis Castle, painted by Gerard Lanscroon c.1705. Above the doorcases, an assistant, possibly Montingo, has painted vases of flowers within the broken pediments, and it is believed that vases of real flowers may have been placed here on special occasions.

a basket of flowers placed on a pedestal which might otherwise be used to support a sculptured bust.

From pictures of interiors, wall and overdoor paintings, it seems certain that vases of flowers were sometimes placed on projecting cornices, and likely that they would also have been sited above doors, especially in the gaps provided by broken pediments. Gervase Jackson-Stops wrote of a *trompe-l'oeil* picture of a vase of flowers painted over a door at Montagu House in London by Jean Baptiste Monnoyer in 1692, 'it creates the illusion that a footman might only recently have climbed a ladder to create this profuse arrangement of lilies, peonies, carnations and auriculas.' Perhaps this illusion was based on reality? If there was a shortage of places to put flowers, there was no shortage of footmen in larger households to run up and down ladders.

Vases always contained a mixture of different flowers and colours, though there was seldom a central point or any symmetry to the arrangement. Flowers on either side never matched each other and colours that today would be considered clashing were often put beside each other. Wild flowers and grasses from the fields were often included, and in England virtually no greenery was used except for that growing on the same stalk as the flower. Some flowers were purposely placed facing backwards and sideways, and there nearly always seems to have been at least one or two red flowers in the arrangements. Flowers were never chosen to match the colour scheme of a room, although a flower painted in a picture or on the wall or ceiling might be echoed. They were not crowded in the vase – the aim was to make each bloom clearly visible.

This style of flower arranging has been recreated at Het Loo, where the palace and gardens have been restored to their former magnificence. Flowers of the right period are grown in the nursery garden for cutting, and a special part of the park is left unmown to provide the wild flowers of the field, such as daisies, poppies and sorrels, that Princess Mary liked to mix with the garden flowers in her vases.

Just as William had taken advantage of the Dutch East India Company's trade with the Far East to bring him exotic plants, so Mary acquired blue-and-white oriental porcelain. The shapes, colours and decoration of these pieces were copied by factories in the town of Delft in tin-glazed earthenware, known as Delftware or Delft. At Het Loo many of Mary's original vases made especially for flowers still exist: flower pyramids, flower pots and bowls, together with large Kangxi porcelain vases from China, which may have been used for flowers. Modern copies of a late seventeenth-century earthenware urn have been made. Silk flowers are used for the pyramid vases, while fresh flowers fill the large vases and bowls of porcelain and Delftware. These flowers are picked by one of the gardeners and arranged by him in a basement room rather than Queen Mary's 'garden-room-cum-grotto', which is now open to the public. He arranges the flowers in plastic containers covered in velvet so that there is no danger of the priceless vases being damaged when the flowers are carefully lowered into them.

Likewise at Hampton Court during the summer season, flowers are displayed in King William's apartments. A proportion of them are grown in the nursery garden and supplemented by bought ones. They are arranged in a room off the Fountain Court, not in the King's Delftware vases, but in more modern examples of a similar style. Inspiration for

Flowers of Princess Mary's time, grown in the cutting garden at Het Loo Palace and arranged by Willem Zieleman in one of the Princess's smaller Delft urns.

1 *Helianthus annuus* (sunflower) 2 *Papaver somniferum* (red opium poppy) 3 *Physostegia virginiana* (dragon's head or obedient flower) 4 *Centaurea cyanus* (cornflower) 5 *Consolida ajacis* (larkspur) 6 *Zinnia elegans* 7 *Tanacetum parthenium* (feverfew) 8 *Tagetes erecta* (African marigold) 9 *Calendula officinalis* (pot marigold) 10 *Papaver somniferum* (white opium poppy) 11 *Antirrhinum majus* (snapdragon) 12 *Convolvulus tricolor* (dwarf convolvulus) 13 *Hedera helix* (common ivy) 14 *Liriodendron tulipiferum* (Virginian tulip tree).

Princess Mary's 'garden-room-cum-grotto' at Het Loo with Delft tiles of blue, white and manganese, most of which are decorated with vases of flowers. The room contains some of her collection of Delftware pots and vases, including, on the left, an extraordinary flower pagoda. In the middle is a two-handled urn with eight spouts along the upper rim, and on the right a bowl in the form of a flower basket.

the arrangements is provided by paintings on the ceiling of the Banqueting House, in the borders of garlands surrounding wall paintings by Antonio Verrio in the Queen's Drawing Room, and by the Dutch flower paintings displayed in the King's apartments.

At Ham House, where the Duke and Duchess of Lauderdale had a fine collection of blue-and-white ware, both oriental and Delft, volunteers arrange flowers from the kitchen garden in the rooms along the southern *enfilade*. They use as their source of reference the engravings of Daniel Marot, which show so clearly the importance he attached to flowers as part of interior decoration.

Marot probably designed several of the exquisite Delftware flower vases owned by William and Mary and their courtiers. Examples can be seen at Dyrham, Lytes Cary, Uppark in Sussex and Chatsworth in Derbyshire, as well as at Hampton Court. The highest quality

A late seventeenth-century embroidered chair cover from Doddington Hall depicts a Delft vase filled with flowers that include peonies, carnations, tobacco plants, a hyacinth and a rose. Similar flowers fill a fan-shaped vase on the seat. This chair indicates that not only tulips, but many different flowers were displayed in the spouts of pyramid and fan-shaped vases, and that more than one flower could occupy a single spout.

was made at the Greek A Factory in Delft under the proprietorship of Samuel van Eenhoorn from 1674-1686, and Adrian Kocks, 1686-1701. Their monograms help to date pieces. Delftware containers for flowers were also made in England at factories in Bristol, Lambeth and Southwark, and continued to be popular until the arrival of creamware and fine English porcelain in the mid-eighteenth century.

The magnificent Delft pyramid vases derive their shape from obelisks, or pyramids as they were called in the seventeenth century, hence their name. Some took the shape of Chinese pagodas: examples of these can be seen at Het Loo Palace and Castle Howard in Yorkshire. Each tier – and some had as many as ten – was made to contain water for cut flowers placed in the spouts that protruded from the corners. Misleadingly they are often now called tulip vases, but all sorts of flowers were displayed in them, as can be seen in an

LEFT: Delftware in the Diogenes Room at Dyrham Park. The flower pyramids that flank the table were made c.1690 by Adrian Kocks at the Greek A Factory in Delft. Each of the seven tiers can be removed and filled with water for cut flowers. On the table are a pair of baluster urns bearing the insignia of William and Mary, which are thought to have been presented to William Blaythwayt by the King and Queen for services rendered. Also on the table are a condiment set and a sweetmeat tray.

BELOW: Delft vase made c.1690 at the Greek A factory by Adrian Kocks. It reflects the style advocated by Ferrari in *De Florum Cultura*, 1633 (see page 26), but this vase has spouts to provide support for flowers. It stands in the Red Drawing Room at Uppark.

A reproduction Delftware fan-shaped vase, also known as a quintal horn. The earliest known vase of this type was excavated in the garden beside Princess Mary's garden room at Het Loo. A white martagon lily, apothecary's rose, astrantia, Jacob's ladder, sweet sultan, borage, Rosa Mundi roses and nasturtiums are displayed in this vase.

embroidered chair covering at Croft Castle in Herefordshire and another at Doddington Hall in Lincolnshire, where the spouts of pyramid vases are filled with lilies, peonies, roses, carnations and other flowers.

A fine pair of pyramid vases, 51 inches (130 centimetres) high, and decorated with bust portraits of William III, can be seen at Dyrham Park. Made *c.*1690 at the Greek A Factory in Delft, and marked AK (for Adrian Kocks), they are recorded in the inventories taken in 1703 and 1710. The Delft factories produced a whole series of vases with spouts in different shapes and sizes. One, now at Uppark, reflects the vase illustrated in Ferrari's *De Florum Cultura* of 1633 (see page 26), but it has spouts instead of holes, making it easier to support heavy flowers. Also at Uppark is a fan-shaped vase with five spouts. The earliest known example of this type was excavated in the garden beside Princess Mary's 'garden-room-cum-grotto' at Het Loo. It is now possible to buy modern reproductions of these vases known as quintal horns.

ABOVE: A Delft flower pot decorated with the arms of William and Mary that stands in the Tapestry Room at Erddig. In the seventeenth century, exotic plants were so precious that magnificent pots such as this were made in which to display them. Even a small orange tree would not seem out of place.

RIGHT: A flower brick in Delftware, made either in England or Holland c.1700, from Sudbury Hall.

A very exotic example of a Delft vase with spouts survives at Drayton Park in Northamptonshire. Shaped like a circular tureen, it has a flattish lid with protruding fish heads with open mouths. It may be one of the flower pots described in an inventory of 1710 as set on black pedestals in the long gallery. The Drayton inventory records 'two little blue and gold rollwagons': these cylindrical-bodied containers, as well as the jars and beakers that often formed part of a garniture decorating a cornice or mantelpiece, were sometimes used for flowers. Also appropriate for mantelpiece garnitures were containers that we now call 'flower bricks'. They were made at the Bristol factory by 1735 and, judging by the number that have survived, they must have been very popular. A suggestion that they were originally intended to hold an inkpot and quills has now been scotched by Michael Archer in his book, *Delftware*, supported by the pictorial evidence provided by an early eighteenth-century chimneyboard in the Victoria & Albert Museum (see page 59).

At Erddig in North Wales there is a blue-and-white flower pot, 26 inches (67 centimetres) high from the Greek A Factory in Delft, and dating from c.1690, decorated with the royal arms of William and Mary. This gigantic vase has a hole in the bottom, showing it was intended for a growing plant, such as an orange or myrtle tree. According to family tradition, it was given by Queen Anne to Dorothy Wanley, 'rocker' to her son, Prince William. Dorothy's granddaughter married into the Yorke family of Erddig, taking the pot with her.

A chimneyboard, *c.*1700, decorated with a blue and white pot of flowers that include tulips, passion flowers, roses and lilies. Around the main arrangement are a series of pots of flowers on Delftware tiles, including flower bricks (third up on both sides).

Robert Furber appears to be the first person to write of growing bulbs in glasses containing water only. He describes how he 'bought some Dozens of Flint Tumbler Glasses of the Germans who cut them prettily and sell them Cheap; whole pints to Halves and Quarters; wide at the top and tapering to the bottom.' In these he placed spring bulbs – narcissus, several sorts of hyacinths, tulips, daffodils and jonquils – and 'took particular care that no water shou'd be fill'd up to wet any more than just the Bottoms of the Bulbous Roots, for that would certainly rot them and have destroyed all my hopes'.

The early eighteenth-century chimneyboard in the Victoria & Albert Museum illustrated above, represents a fireplace inside which is a Delftware urn holding a sunflower, rose, tulip, several carnations and the newly arrived hardy blue climbing passion flower (see page 45), with more flower-filled containers, including flower bricks, in the tile surround.

Chimneyboards were produced in a variety of designs to decorate fireplaces when fires were not needed. But flowers were frequently used instead, especially in the summer months when they were plentiful. Virtually any fireplace in the house might have been decorated in this way with cut or growing flowers. At Dyrham the early eighteenth-century inventories recorded that no less than nine rooms were equipped with a 'Delft flower pott in ye Chimney' (some have survived and can still be seen there). Richard Bradley in his *Gentleman & Gardeners Kalender* of 1718 recommended *Campanula pyramidalis* as suitable for 'growing in chimneys'. This is a wonderful herbaceous plant which can grow to 5 feet (1.5 metres) in height and remains covered with a pyramid of white or blue flowers and buds for over four weeks. It is, moreover, undaunted if dug out of the ground and transplanted into a pot when flowering, appearing to thrive as well indoors as in the garden.

During the 1720s gardening books gave plentiful advice to ladies on how to decorate their chimneys. Thomas Fairchild, with his nursery at Hoxton in East London, was able to recommend plants for cultivating both in and out of doors in *The City Gardener*, published in 1722. He noted that 'The chimneys which are generally dressed in Summer with fading Bough Pots might be as well adorn'd at once with Living Plants, as I have observed at her Grace's the late excellent Duchess of Beaufort.' He suggested that 'Box or Privet trained up in a Fan Fashion' inside the fireplace would look well with pots of white lilies, which would 'last beautiful a long time, and perfume the House almost as well as a Tuberose'. Another suggestion was 'to have a Pyramid of Shelves set in the chimney and cover'd with Pots of blossoming Orange-Trees, with Fruit upon them, intermixt with Mirtles, Aloes, etc for Variety-sake', which he thought would be 'extremely beautiful for the summer'. He emphasised that the pots used 'to add to the greater Beauty, might be of Delph Ware, or well painted, to stand in Dishes, which are now in Use, for that when we water the Plants, the water will not run upon the floor'. Practical as always, he recommends that 'the Orange Trees may be brought to such places, when they are in Flower, and remain 'til August, and then be sent back to the garden to be taken Care of for the Winter at the usual price'.

In 1728 Batty Langley, designer and author of numerous practical guides for builders, carpenters and decorators, in *New Principles of Gardening* laid down 'exact Rules for Adorning the Chimneys of Halls, Chambers, etc'. From January to May, he preferred to have pots of mixed growing flowers. From June to September, he suggested plants grown singly. His recommendations are set out in Table 3.

A room set aside solely for eating was a rarity at this period. The inventory of 1677 taken at Ham House refers to 'The Marble Dining Room', but this was in reality a parlour on the ground floor. When people talked of dining rooms – and they often did – they were referring to the various rooms in which meals took place, and which included the hall and saloon for grand occasions, smaller chambers or parlours for family meals and even on occasion, the orangery. After visiting Kensington Palace in 1722, Defoe wrote in his journal, 'the late Queen delighted very much in the place, and often was pleased to make the greenhouse, which is very beautiful, her summer supper house'. The greenhouse to which he refers is the large and splendid orangery designed by Nicholas Hawksmoor and Sir John Vanbrugh and built for Queen Anne in 1704.

TABLE 3: Batty Langley, *New Principles of Gardening*, 1728.

For *January* 'a very large root [bulb] or two of Snow-Drops of the double kind, which environ with a circle of the several sorts of crocus'.

For *February*, polyanthus with blue and white anemones, hyacinths and violets, 'planted in like manner' he thinks will be 'very entertaining'.

For *March* a stock-july-flower with hyacinths and violets about it 'will make a very beautiful Appearance, and their sweet Odors be very agreeable'.

For *April* 'the most beautiful flowers are Hyacinths, Stock-July-Flowers, Wall-Flowers, Tulips, Ranunculus, Anemonies, Jonquils, Narcissus and Auriculas'. He advises planting the taller flowers in the middle, surrounded by smaller ones.

For *May* 'the White Lilies and Crown Imperials are in their beauty, which being planted as aforesaid, and environ'd with a Circle of Double-White Narcissus are very beautiful'.

In *June* and *July* 'our best Ornaments are the several kinds of Pinks, Carnations, Amaranthus, Tricolor and Coxcombe, Lychnis, Campanulas, Tuberose, Larkspurs, Sweet-Williams, and Sweet Basil; all which are best to be planted singly, being tied to a handsome flower-stick placed in the centre of each Pot'.

In *August* and *September* there are 'the Amaranthus's, Pinks, July-Flowers, Campanulas, Marvel of Peru, Female Balsam, Capsicum indicum and Larkspurs. To which may be added White and Red Calvills and other beautiful sorts of Apples; as also round-headed plants of the large Sweet-Briar, White Jessamine and Honey-Suckles, for the several Months of their Blooming'. Of the jasmine and honeysuckles he says: 'It has been the practice of Breeding this plant up in headed plants, yet I cannot commend it, feeling that it naturally hates to be confined, or stumped with Sheers.' Batty Langley seems to have been the first person to yearn for the more natural look, which became all the rage in the 1740s.

In the months of *October*, *November*, *December* and *January* (although he had earlier suggested flowers for January) he rightly thinks that 'a good fire is the best Ornament for Chimneys; excepting such where little Use is made of the Rooms, whose best Furniture is small Hedge Laurus-Tinus Plants, planted in large Flower Pots'.

His last word on the subject is that 'the diligent Gardiner … must always observe to remove such as are fading and introduce fresh ones in their stead … so as to be free from a Mixture of disagreeable fading Objects'.

The *Gentleman's Magazine* reported on 17 August 1732: 'At a dinner and dancing given by Sir Robert Walpole, Her Majesty, His Royal Highness the Prince, His Highness the Duke and the three eldest Princesses were elegantly entertained by Sir Robert in the greenhouse of his mansion. For the occasion the walls of the greenhouse had been hung with the finest pictures in Europe.' If kings and queens were pleased to dine in 'greenhouses', without doubt their subjects were doing the same all over the country.

Wherever eaten, the main meal of dinner was usually taken at 2pm, though the hour moved later as the century went on. Small tables would be brought into the room and covered with tablecloths, and chairs taken from their usual positions round the walls and

François Massialot's suggestion for decorating a dining table with a large vase of flowers in the middle, and single flowers adorning pyramids of fruit (see table 4 for a list of the recommended flowers). From a chapter headed '*Des Garnitures et Enjolivement des Services*' in his book published in 1698.

set round the tables. There would have been no flowers on the table during the two main courses as the many dishes of food left no room for decoration. It was only when all these dishes were cleared away and the last course of fruit and sweetmeats brought in that there was room for flowers. This course, known in medieval and Tudor times as the banquet and now called the dessert, using the French word derived from *desservir*, to clear the table, formed the climax of the meal.

It is from a French chef, François Massialot, that we realise to what extent flowers were used to decorate the dessert. Massialot was a *cuisinier royal* in 1698 when the court of Louis XIV was setting the standard for dining throughout Europe. French cookery reigned

---

TABLE 4: François Massialot, '*Des Garnitures et Enjolivement des Services*', translation of 1698 edition.

For January he recommends 'Anemones of all colours, winter Cyclamen, winter Hyacinths, Narcissi from the Levant, Primroses; failing these Orange or Oleander leaves, Everlasting flowers or realistic artificial flowers.'

For March he gives 'Bulbous Irises, all kinds of Anemones, spring Cyclamen, all sorts of Hepaticas, Narcissi, Fritillaries, Buttercups, spring Crocuses, Hyacinths, Jonquils, early Tulips, Primroses of every colour and early Auriculas.'

For July he includes 'Campanula, Scabious, Love-in-a-mist, Catchfly [*Lychnis* species], Lilies of all kinds …, Comfrey, double Marigolds, Everlasting flowers, Indian Knapweed [*Gonocaulon glebrum* from East Indies], Jerusalem cross [*Lychnis chalcedonica*], Fraxinella [*Dictamnus albus*], Convolvulus, Chamomile, St Bruno lilies, Scillas, Asters, Orchids, Eryngiums, …, Amaranths, Balsam, Statice, Hellebores, Ox-eye [*Anthemis* species], Valerian, Parnassia [Grass of Parnassus].'

For September he recommends 'Tricolour Amaranth, Marvel of Peru, Narcissus from Portugal, French Marigolds, Passion flower.'

supreme, and books written by French chefs were translated into English. Massialot's book, *Nouvelles Instructions pour les Confitures, les Liqueurs et les Fruits*, published in France in 1692, was translated into English in 1702 as *The Court and Country Cook*. In a chapter entitled '*Des Garnitures et Enjolivement des Services*' he gives lists of those flowers he considers suitable for each month. A selection of these are set out in Table 4.

An illustration in Massialot's book shows a table covered with a tablecloth sweeping down to the ground. In the middle is a grandiose vase in the baroque style filled with flowers standing on a board which it shares with objects that appear to be sugar sifters and cream jugs. It is surrounded by very tall pyramids of fruit and sweetmeats in baskets (probably plain wicker or gilt) or on dishes (probably of blue-and-white Delftware or of the Chinese and Japanese porcelain which was popular for this course). Some of the pyramids have single flowers beside them. And all around this scene of *enjolivement* are smaller plates filled with biscuits and other sweetmeats.

As earlier, the buffet or sideboard on which was displayed the family's plate would sometimes have been garlanded with flowers. A description of a wedding in 1680 at Versailles might have inspired those keen to follow French fashion:

A table fifty feet [20 metres] long and six and a half feet [2.5 metres] wide bearing nineteen open-work baskets of silver or gilded copper filled with anemones, hyacinths, Spanish jessamine and orange blossoms. A garland of flowers also natural bound one basket to the next. Sixteen candles illuminated each basket, adding to the brilliance of the baskets themselves, and the ribbons which ornamented them, the whole offering a truly ravishing spectacle to the eye.

Other descriptions of flowers decorating the dessert at Versailles refer to 'a table ornamented with twenty-four silver pots filled with flowers'; 'little potted shrubs decorated the table for dessert, hung with preserved fruit and ribbon garlands' (these were probably smartly clipped in the manner of garden topiary work); 'at a gala – a vase of silver filigree held an orange tree covered with flowers and fruit'. All around the base were 'eight baskets and eight smaller vases, all sixteen filled with flowers'. *Le Mercure* in February 1700 reported an unusual decoration at Versailles, where 'all the tables were covered with turf as green as if in the month of May; all were encircled with garlands charged with leaves, flowers and fruit'. Georgiana Smith in her book *Table Decoration* suggests that these were on the new round tables made fashionable at this time by Louis XIV, who hit upon them as a clever way to defy protocol and place his mistress, Madame de Maintenon, opposite him rather than at the far end of a long narrow table.

These decorations, of course, were for the grandest occasions. At the other end of the scale, Richard Bradley's *Family Dictionary* of 1725 gives a description of a more simple arrangement: 'the whole desert is to be set out with Flowers, Greens and other Ornaments, according to the Season. ... You should cover the board with marbled or painted Paper, and set it out always with Leaves and Flowers, or other Ornaments according to the Season, most especially in the void Spaces at Intervals caused by the indenting on the Top of the Board.' The 'board' had cut-in, rounded or hollowed corners, and these were the voids that needed particular attention. It was probably made of wood or wicker, the precursor of the

surtout de table of porcelain, and the mirror plateau, used to display decoration during the dessert later in the eighteenth century.

When no fresh flowers were available to decorate the dining table, silver ones might have been used. At Burghley the 1688 inventory refers to 'thirty-seven bunches of silver flowers in use as table decorations'. Or as M. Massialot advised for the mid-winter months, one could be reduced to using 'cut paper and artificial flowers'.

There is a close relationship between long galleries and gardens. Almost invariably their windows provided the best viewpoint over the garden, and in bad weather they were used for the exercise that otherwise might have been taken outdoors. They were rooms where not only tapestries and pictures, but flowers too, could be displayed and admired to advantage. In her gallery at Honselaarsdijk, Princess Mary had six pyramids for cut flowers and eleven flower pots for growing trees, all of blue-and-white Delftware and works of art in themselves. The flower pots could have contained orange and lemon trees, myrtles, bays, aloes or any other exotics.

When Celia Fiennes made her last journey through England in 1703, she visited Hampton Court Palace. In the Queen's Gallery she saw 'two marble tables in two piers with two

ABOVE: A display at the top of the Queen's Staircase at Hampton Court. The arrangement is asymmetrical and free flowing, with emphasis on space between flowers and variety of colour. The largest flowers, peonies and roses, were put in first, followed by a mixture that included wild clematis and larkspur, always ensuring the placing was irregular. Some were turned sideways and others backwards.

LEFT: A multi-tiered buffet painted by A.F. Desportes *c.*1700. It had probably been set up for a banquet *en plein air* at Versailles. Garlands festoon the shell-framed mask of Pan, and tumble over the plates and dishes.

A state bedchamber designed by Daniel Marot in the 1690s. The open fireplace is decorated with an orange or myrtle tree in an urn, standing between two large pots. Marot was probably the first designer to include flowers in a design for a room, showing how important they had become.

great open jarrs on each side each table, two such at the end the same for to put potts of orange and mirtle trees in'. This was the fashion that had started at Louis XIV's court at Versailles (see page 27).

In the long gallery at Ham House, the Duchess of Lauderdale's 'seaven boxes carv'd and gilt for tuby roses', recorded in the 1679 inventory, would have been filled with growing tuberoses spreading their scent throughout the gallery. Six of these boxes are still at Ham. Tuberoses arrived in England from Mexico in 1620 and were of immense importance for decorating and scenting rooms throughout the seventeenth and eighteenth centuries. Henry van Oosten, a gardener in Leyden in Holland, wrote a book that was translated into English and published as *The Dutch Gardener* in 1711. He wrote of the tuberose 'this plant bears white Flowers like little Lillies and Leaves like those of Leaks. The Stalk shoots up to Four Foot [1.5 metres] high, somewhat more or less. The flower smells very well. We plant them in Pots, and place them in our Chambers, and one Pot is sufficient to fill a whole Room with its strong and pleasant Smell. We plant them in March in good Earth.' So highly valued were these flowers that they are frequently referred to in letters and diaries, which tell of them being stolen, and of the despair when they died of frost.

Bedroom apartments were often used for entertaining close friends and even for dining. As in other rooms, flowers were used to decorate the bedroom fireplace. Daniel Marot designed a state bedchamber which shows an orange or a myrtle tree in a pot inside the fireplace. At Dyrham, one of William Blaythwayt's Delft flower pyramids (see pages 56 and 57) is recorded in the inventories of 1703 and 1710 as standing 'in ye chimney' of the 'Best bedchamber above stairs'.

An idea for 'Raising Flowers without any Trouble, to blow in full Perfection in the Depth of Winter, in a Bed-Chamber, Closet, or Dining Room' came from the nurseryman Robert Furber in a new chapter that he added to the 1734 edition of his book, *The Flower Garden Display'd*, first published in 1732.

He describes how he procured basins 'about 18 inches [48 centimetres] diameter and 1 foot [30 centimetres] deep' of imitation blue-and-white Delftware, filled them with a 'very good Garden Mould' then planted 'in the midst a strong root of Crown Imperial ... round the Crown Imperial I placed some Tulips, and round them a ring of double white and blew Hyacinths' followed by rings of white and yellow polyanthus narcissus, large double daffodils, different coloured crocus and finally snowdrops. Then on two opposing edges he planted 'two roots of hepatica and some roots of Fritillaries'. He placed the pots 'inside my chamber window' about Michaelmas, 29 September, and they flowered in succession from twelve days before Christmas until the middle of March, by which time 'the Crown Imperial was two and a half feet [6 metres] high with flowerbuds at the top'. He found that anemones did better planted in a basin on their own.

Having discovered, apparently for the first time, that bulbs, or 'roots' as he called them, could be made to flower early indoors in basins, he then did the same with 'Annuals that had been raised upon Hot-beds':

> I likewise set double Africa, Marvel of Peru, Capsicum, Cockscomb, Amaranthus, Orange Mint, and other variegated Herbs which all thrived exceeding well, within the Chamber, the Capsicums changing to their fine Red, and continuing with me til the approach of Winter when I substituted my Spring Flowers.... many of these Beauteous Creatures appeared in all their lustre in the midst of the cold Winter when they perfum'd my Chamber with most odoriferous fragrance.

Furber, as we have seen, was the first person to write of growing bulbs in glasses containing water only. One advantage, he explains, is the 'neater and cleaner way and more acceptable to the curious of the Fair Sex who must be pleased to see a Garden growing, and exposing all the Beauties of its Spring Flowers with the most delicious perfumes thereof, in their Chambers or Parlours.' In that age of botanical study it must indeed have seemed miraculous to be able to see clearly the roots of the bulbs through the glass as they grew in the water. Furthermore, he claims that in the winter months when 'Rooms must have constant fires in them every day' his flowers grown in water 'did not fail in the smoke'. And of course, the growing flowers lasted in bloom much longer than cut flowers 'which usually decay in four or five days'.

CHAPTER THREE

Natural and Haphazard

1740–1800

In 1726 Batty Langley suggested that flowers in the house should be arranged in a 'free loose manner, so as not to represent a stiff bundle of flowers void of freedom, in which the beauty of everything consists'. His was one of several voices that heralded the sweeping changes in fashion that were soon to take place – the 'taste for nature' and for 'glorious irregularity' eventually known as the Rococo style, which was all the rage in England by the 1740s.

The new fashion dictated that ceilings, walls, furniture and porcelain must be decorated with scenes or objects of nature that included shells, rockwork, exotic birds and, above all, flowers. However, the most dramatic change brought about by the new fashion was that which overtook the formal gardens with their orderly arrangements of borders, parterres and straight avenues. Many of these gardens, so painstakingly created, were swept away. Where there had been a straight line, a curved or wavy one now took its place, and serpentine or crinkle-crankle-shaped flower-beds and borders replaced the rectangular flower-beds and straight avenues. The parterres and sometimes the surrounding garden walls disappeared altogether. Lord Burlington's friend, William Kent, who began life as an artist but became an architect, furniture designer and gardener, was a pioneer of this transformation. It was carried to even greater lengths by the architect and landscape gardener Lancelot, known as Capability, Brown, who from the 1750s dismissed the flower-beds from around the house altogether.

At Calke Abbey in Derbyshire, for instance, the beautiful formal gardens, laid out between 1710 and 1715 by George London and Henry Wise, were grassed over in 1772 by William Emes, an eminent landscape gardener and rival of Brown. At the same time the present vast walled garden for flowers and vegetables was built some 150 yards (140 metres) from the house, well screened by trees and evergreen shrubs so that the 'natural' landscape could be enjoyed from the house without distraction.

Blooms were not only grown for cutting alongside vegetables in hidden walled gardens, but were also picked from serpentine-shaped flower-beds or, later, gathered from the flower edgings of 'walks'. On 10 October 1737 the prolific letter writer Mrs Delany (then Mrs Pendarves), whose extraordinary 'floral mosaics' formed by cutting parts of a flower out of coloured paper and fitting them together are now in the British Museum, wrote to her sister from Northend, 'I walked from one flower-plot to another, till I composed a nosegay of anemonies, carnations, roses, honeysuckles, sweet williams, jessamine, sweet briar and myrtle till I turned down the lime walk full of pleasing reflections'.

Although by 1760 there were seldom flowers near the house, there were plenty to be

The Tapestry Room at Osterley was designed in the 1770s by Robert Adam for Robert Child. Horace Walpole, who did not give his approbation lightly, described it as 'the most superb and beautiful that can be imagined'. It is a flowered bower, with Gobelins tapestries woven after medallion paintings of the Elements by François Boucher. Earth is represented by Pomona, the goddess of gardens and orchards. Garlands hang from and interweave all around the cornice in swags and festoons. Even the carpet has baskets of flowers corresponding to the flower vases in the tapestries.

gathered in the walks. In that year Robert Adam created for Lord Scarsdale a Long Walk at his new house, Kedleston Hall in Derbyshire. The walk, encircling the park, was about three miles in length, and at 100-yard (90-metre) intervals along the greater part of it were what Adam called 'diversions' – enchanting outdoor rooms furnished with sweet-smelling flowers to provide resting places and viewpoints. The flowers ordered *en masse* by Scarsdale included 1,000 sweet briar, 100 jasmines, 1,050 syringas (philadelphus), 1,200 lilac, 350 honeysuckle, 100 sweet williams, 300 mixed tulips as well as various roses and carnations. At Woburn Farm in Surrey, a circuitous sandy walk had a continuous flower border on the inner side, consisting mainly of hollyhock, lily, golden rod and crown imperial, with an edging of pinks at the front and mixed shrubs, including roses, syringa, sweet briar and lilac, behind.

Many retired gardeners passed their time writing 'Gardening Calendars' to help ladies direct their gardens. Detailed instructions were provided for each month of the year for growing both flowers and vegetables. While flowers for use indoors were grown in the walled kitchen garden, as they are now at Calke Abbey, tender varieties were wintered in a greenhouse or orangery to protect them from frosts.

Anthony Powell, who proudly proclaimed himself 'Gardener to his late Majesty King George II', published in 1769 *The Royal Gardener or Complete Calendar of Gardening*. For each month the produce for the house is detailed in a catalogue. Four months are set out in Table 5.

Many hardy garden flowers and shrubs were forced amongst the pineapples and other tender plants in hothouses, so that from March onwards they would be ready for cutting or growing in pots, to decorate the house.

John Abercrombie, the son of a market gardener near Edinburgh, settled in Hackney where he started a nursery garden and became a successful author of gardening books which remained popular for the next half century. An extract set out in Table 6 is from *The Hot House Gardener* (1789), in which he describes the forcing of flowers.

In February 1784 Theresa Parker, the young chatelaine of Saltram House in Devon, wrote excitedly of the flowers that had been forced into early flowering in the new 'Peach or Grape House'. As a result the house was 'full of roses, violets, carnations, lily of the valley, minionet and everything that is sweet and delightful'. Minionet, or mignonette – from the French for 'little darling' – *Reseda odorata* was a native of Egypt sent to the Chelsea Physic Garden in 1752. The curator, Philip Miller, likened its scent to fresh raspberries.

Professional establishments such as the Chelsea Physic Garden and Lee and Kennedy's nursery in Hammersmith were the chief recipients of the many new introductions arriving in England. Joseph Banks, for instance, brought plants of *Sophara microphylla* with its yellow pea-like flowers to Lee and Kennedy on his return from his adventurous voyage with Captain Cook on the *Endeavour* in 1771. In turn, after Banks effectively became director of the King's Gardens at Kew the next year, expeditions brought him Banksia species from Australia and *Erica conspicua* and other tree heaths picked up from the Cape on the way home. Another plant to come from South Africa was the curious *Strelitzia reginae* (1773) – the bird of paradise flower named after the Queen, Charlotte of Mecklenburg-Strelitz.

Two of the most important introductions of the eighteenth century – hydrangeas and

Frontispiece to John Abercrombie's *The Hot House Gardener* published in 1789. The gardener proudly displays his pots of plants, with a glasshouse full of more plants in the background.

TABLE 5: Anthony Powell, *The Royal Gardener or Complete Calendar of Gardening*, 1769.

For February
We have winter Aconites, Single Anemonies, Crocuses – yellow and purple, Spring Cyclamen, Spring Daffodiles, Daisies – some double daisies, Hellebore – several kinds, Hepaticas, Hyacinths, Iris – Persian Iris, Snowdrops, Stock gilly-flowers, Wallflowers single. We have in the Green house – Aloes, Geranium, Ficoides [mesembryanthemums], Jessamine – yellow Indian, Laurustinus, Mezerions are yet in blossom, Thalfi semper virens [*Thlaspi sempervirens*, now *Iberis sempervirens*].

For April
Of flowers we have a great variety of Ranunculuses, double Anemones, Auriculas and Tulips, the Crown Imperial still continues to flower, as does also the double Violets, double Hepaticas, and the Polyanthos. We have several kinds of the Narcissus and double Jonquil now in their prime. Several sorts of Iris and Fritillaries with some Hyacinths, Cyclamen and some Stock-gilly-flower.

For June
The flowers are Sweet Williams, Foxgloves, Double Pinks, Sea Pinks, Lilies, Monkshood, Sunflowers, Hollyhocks, African and French Marygold, Amaranthus, Venus-looking-glass, Larkspurs, annual Stocks, Stock-gilly-flowers, Scarlet Beans, Spiderwort, Sweet Sultan, Poppies, Rose Campions, some Carnations and several others. The trees and shrubs in flower are: the Orange, Lemon and Olive, Pomegranate, Sedum, Fritillaria, Rosetree, Honeysuckle, Jessamine, Oleander, Spanish broom.

For September
The flowers are Tuberoses, female Balsam, African and French Marygolds, Convolvulus, Sunflowers, Hollyhocks, Marvel of Peru, Double violets, Colchicums, Amaranthus, Saffron Crocus, Spiderwort, Poppies, Larkspurs, Annual stocks, Candy-tufts, Venus looking glass, Asters of several kinds, Auriculas, Polyanthos, China pinks and Stock-gilly-flowers.

TABLE 6: John Abercrombie, *The Hot House Gardener*, 1789.

A pinery or general hot house, is very convenient in which to forward many sorts of desirable hardy, and other plants, flowers and fruits, to early maturity.... A succession ... of the more curious flowery tribe ... should be introduced in the forcing-apartment every three weeks from January or February till April. They will advance to early perfection in a very agreeable manner ... and succeed one another in production from March or April till June when the natural crops will come into bearing....

Of the bulbous and tuberous rooted kinds ... early tulips, any form of hyacinths, jonquils, polyanthos, narcissus, bulbous or tuberous irises etc. also anemone and ranunculuses, all planted in pots of light sandy earth, one, two, or several roots in each pot according to the size thereof, ... or may also have some of the bulbous kinds placed in root water-glasses, admitted into the forcing house, they will also flower early....

Of annual flowers of several sorts such as sweet peas, mignonette, ten-week's stock, candytuft, larkspurs, balsams, globe-amaranths etc. all sowed in pots and introduced in January, February and March near the glasses they will flower in the spring and early part of the summer.

An eighteenth-century silk embroidery, showing the lady of the house at work in her garden, aided and abetted by her pet dog.

fuchsias – made their first appearances at Kew. *Hydrangea macrophylla*, the parent of today's popular hybrids, was originally known as 'Chinese Guelder-Rose' and came from the Far East in 1789. Its immature green flowers excited curiosity, as did the fact it could produce red flowers one year and blue the next. *Fuchsia coccinea* came from South America in 1792, carried into the garden at Kew by an excited Banks on his head 'not choosing to trust it to any other person'. Alice Coats in *Garden Shrubs and their Histories* relates that *Fuchsia magellanica* was first spotted a year later by James Lee in the window of a poor house in Wapping – the woman's sailor husband had brought it to her from the West Indies. Lee bought it and propagated it in hotbeds with such skill that the next year he had

300 flowering plants for sale. 'Chariots flew to the gates of old Lee's nursery grounds' and in no time at all the plants were sold. Fuchsias became a mainstay of indoor decoration as both pot plants and cut flowers throughout the nineteenth century and beyond.

John Bartram found *Magnolia grandiflora* growing in Bulls Bay in South Carolina and dispatched it to Peter Collinson in London. Its glossy leaves and fragrant creamy flowers ensured that it was treasured by English ladies. In 1744 Bartram came upon scarlet bergamot (*Monarda didyma*) on the southern shores of Lake Ontario, where its scented leaves were used for making tea. In England its scarlet flowers soon found their way into vases, as did the pale purple and blue phlox and the clusters of white flowers edged with red of the shrub kalmia, also obtained from Bartram.

Flowers represented in Chinese paintings and textiles had for years excited the interest of horticulturists. A consignment from Canton, sent to Kew by an officer of the East India Company in 1770, attracted much notice. It included *Daphne odora*, the double pink *Paeonia suffruticosa*, *Osmanthus fragrans* and the hothouse plant *Cordyline fruticosa* (syn. *C. terminalis*), known as the 'Dracaena Palm', which was to come into its own in the mid-nineteenth century, when it became fashionable to have foliage plants indoors.

Another plant from South America that has become invaluable in flower arrangements was *Alstroemeria pelegrina*, the Peruvian lily, discovered in 1753 and named after the botanist, Clas Alströmer. From Siberia, presumably via the Botanic Garden in St Petersburg, came *Gypsophila paniculata* in 1759.

Tropical plants had to be grown in hothouses, but all new introductions were probably cherished in greenhouses of some kind. This accounts for the fact that few appear in contemporary lists of garden flowers grown for the house, even though they probably would have been given pride of place in flower vases.

Despite all these new and exciting arrivals, old favourites for indoor decoration continued, in particular oranges and tuberoses. On 20 August 1748 Mrs Delany wrote to her sister from Ireland, 'My orange trees come on finely; there is but one that has failed and four of them bore prodigiously. All my plants and flowers have done well ... except the tuberoses.'

In 1771 Thomas Anson of Shugborough Hall near Stafford was importing orange trees to add to the collection in his greenhouse. Sir John Dick, British Consul at Leghorn in Italy, wrote to him, 'Inclosed you will find two Bills of Lading, one for Two Casks of Pines [pineapples] & the other for 12 Potts, containing so many of the orange trees which You wanted. I have been obliged to give rather a high freight for the Trees, as they are placed in the Cabbin, and the Master must carry more water on their account, and take extraordinary care of them.'

On 23 March 1767 Mrs Lybbe Powys wrote in her journal: 'Went to see the Queen's Palace ... tho' but in March every room was full of roses, carnations, hyacinths, etc, dispersed in the prettiest manner imaginable in jars and different flower pots on stands.' The palace was Buckingham House, bought in 1762 by George III from the Duke of Buckingham for his new bride, Charlotte of Mecklenburg-Strelitz. Queen Charlotte had her own flower garden in the grounds, where she raised carnations with professional pride.

It is likely that the description of the flowers in her rooms could have applied to many a house of that time, for Queen Charlotte was never a leader of fashion as Queen Mary had been a century earlier. The chance remarks about flowers indoors that appear in diaries and letters, the long lists in gardening books and calendars, the care taken to 'force' flowers and the quantities of vases and stands produced all add up to a picture of rooms filled with an abundance of flowers, both cut and growing.

Horace Walpole, author, antiquary, politician, historian, collector and self-appointed chronicler of his times, liked to have tuberoses and pomegranates growing in the rooms of Strawberry Hill, the unremarkable little house at Twickenham that he transformed into a Gothick fantasy from 1747 to 1753. In August 1773 he wrote to Lady Ossory, 'my house is a bower of tuberoses', and on 12 September 1781 he again wrote to her, encouraging her to get some pomegranate trees: 'You must get some standard pomigranites, Madam. I have one now in this room, above five feet [1.5 metres] in a pot in full blow. At Paris they mix them with their orange trees.'

Lord Edward Fitzgerald, in his constant correspondence with his mother, Emily, Duchess of Leinster, seldom failed to describe the flowers in the room in his letters. The hot-headed idealist, one of the architects of the Irish uprising of 1798, wrote from Frascati, his house at Black Rock near Dublin in May 1793, 'we are now enjoying the little bookroom

ABOVE: *A view from Mr Cosway's Breakfast Room in Pall Mall*, a stipple engraving by W.Birch after William Hodges and Richard Cosway, 1789. Mrs Cosway is shown looking out over St James's Park to Westminster, with an orange tree on a tall plant stand opposite her, and a row of plants in pots on the windowsill.

LEFT: Portrait of George III's queen, Charlotte of Mecklenburg-Strelitz painted by Johan Zoffany in 1771. Queen Charlotte's fondness for flowers is conveyed by the arrangement of larkspur, *convolvulus tricolor* and roses – the cabbage rose (*R. × centifolia*) and the Jacobite rose (*Alba Maxima*) in a silver-gilt vessel of classical form.

with the windows open . . . the plants in the passage are just watered; and with the passage door open the room smells like a greenhouse'.

As yet no English books gave directions as to how flowers should be arranged indoors. Our knowledge of flower arranging at this time derives largely from pictures of interiors, portraits, cartoons, fashion plates and books of furniture design, and to some extent from the decoration on furniture, porcelain and textiles.

The 'glorious irregularity' proposed by Batty Langley and quoted at the beginning of this chapter, applied not only to the manner of placing flowers in a vase. It also meant that in the 1740s and 50s the vase was seldom placed in the middle of a table, but to one side or near the edge. In the homes of the fashionable, the vase would be of a curved or bombé form and the flowers in it often looked as though they had been hurriedly dropped or crammed in. As fashion turned from the Rococo to the neo-classical in the 1760s, so flower vases were made to resemble the urns of ancient Greece and Rome. Now they were placed symmetrically in their chosen positions, though the flowers put in them continued to be arranged as freely, naturally and asymmetrically as before, with a mixture of flowers of every sort, shape, size and colour – including wild flowers – with no thought of a colour scheme or for matching the decoration of the room. This provided an interesting contrast to the neo-classical architects' practice of matching every detail in a room, even down to the keyhole cover.

A recreation of late eighteenth-century flower arrangements took place in 1985 at Osterley Park in Middlesex, in an event called 'Romantic Osterley'. The whole house was filled with the flowers grown there from 1760, when Robert Adam redesigned and redecorated it first for Francis Child and then for the newly wedded Robert and Sarah Child, until 1793, when the estate passed to their granddaughter and thus, on her marriage, to the Jersey family. Robert and Sarah Child's interest in flowers is evident from the lists of rare and expensive flowers they grew in the greenhouses. Many of the flower stands, tables and staging mentioned in the inventories of 1782 are still in the house, bearing witness to the quantity of flowers displayed indoors.

The idea of such a recreation originated at Williamsburg, Virginia, in the United States. In 1699 the capital of Virginia was moved from Jamestown to a village known as Middle Plantation, renamed Williamsburg in honour of the English King. By the mid-eighteenth century it was a thriving and fashionable town, with a Governor's Palace and substantial houses surrounded by their gardens. During the War of Independence many of these houses were destroyed, including the Governor's Palace, and in 1775 British rule ended in Virginia. Five years later, the capital moved to Richmond, and Williamsburg's fortunes went into decline, with the surviving eighteenth-century buildings falling into disrepair. This remained so until the mid-1920s when John D. Rockefeller Jnr. paid a visit and was inspired to finance the restoration of the town as a living recreation of eighteenth-century colonial life. No effort was spared to make all aspects of the reconstruction as authentic as possible, including the gardens and plants grown in them.

It was due to ardent gardener Louise Fisher that flower arrangements became an important part of this recreation and are still to be seen in many of the houses open to the public. She arrived in Williamsburg in 1930 'with one truck of furniture and two trucks of

Flowers in a Porcelain Vase painted *c.*1760 by Jean Baptiste Chardin. This is typical of the small, informal arrangements seen so often in later eighteenth-century interiors. Painted in Chardin's simple realistic style, it contrasts vividly with the earlier, contrived flower-pieces produced by artists like Jan van Huysum (see page 44). The tuberoses, sweet peas and carnations are crammed into a Chinese blue and white porcelain vase of the early eighteenth-century Kangxi period.

An eighteenth-century style flower arrangement by the staircase in the entrance hall at Carter's Grove, a plantation house on the James River seven miles from Colonial Williamsburg. The flowers are arranged in a Chinese export tobacco-leaf pattern *seau*, and include agapanthus, acanthus, lilies, carnations, tulips and chrysanthemums.

flowers'. Two years later the first restored building – the Raleigh Tavern – was opened to the public, and Mrs Fisher became the tavern's hostess. In 1934 she took over responsibility for the flower arrangements in the rooms there, and two years later began to research and organise the flowers in all the most important of the restored buildings. This research continues to ensure the most accurate representation of eighteenth-century American flower arrangements.

Louise Fisher based her choice on the *Gardeners Dictionary*, written in 1731 by Philip Miller, curator of the Chelsea Physic Garden. This book remained popular throughout the eighteenth century, running to eight editions by 1768. She was helped in her researches by the letters and diaries of prominent citizens and enthusiastic horticulturists such as Thomas Jefferson and John Custis, and by the correspondence between John Bartram and Peter Collinson, who exchanged letters and plants throughout their lives. She discovered, for instance, that the tuberose was not successfully cultivated in Virginia until well into the eighteenth century. In 1736, John Custis, member of the Council of Virginia for 22 years, wrote to Peter Collinson bemoaning the lack. Collinson, thinking it 'a pitty you should be without so fine a flower', sent Custis a shipment of bulbs which finally succeeded in flowering in 1739.

In the winter months, dried flowers and fresh greens were used in the rooms in Williamsburg. The globe amaranth was another plant sent by Collinson to Custis, followed by a careful note about its winter usefulness:

I am much delighted to heare you have your amarathoides. It is a Real and may I say perpetual Beauty. If the flowers are gather'd in perfection and hung with their Heads Downwards in a Dry shady Room, they will keep their Colours for years and will make a pleasant Ornament to Adorn the windows of your parlour or study all the Winter. I dry great quantities for this purpose and putt them in flower potts and China basons and they make a fine show all the Winter.

Louise Fisher initiated a cutting garden which eventually provided her with over two hundred kinds of annuals, perennials, bulbs and shrubs. She was able to draw on Colonial Williamsburg's collection of eighteenth-century containers for the flowers. Many of these containers have been reproduced and are now sold at Williamsburg.

From the 1740s 'polite society' on both sides of the Atlantic started to use flower vases made of porcelain from the new European factories as well as the Chinese porcelain and Delftware that had been so sought after in the previous century. In 1710 Böttger at Meissen discovered the secret of how hard paste was made, but artificial or soft paste porcelain was already being manufactured at St Cloud in France.

Hard paste spread from Meissen to other German and Continental factories during the first half of the eighteenth century, while soft paste porcelain was made in France, Southern Italy, Spain and in England. In the 1760s Josiah Wedgwood produced his creamware, marking the beginning of the Industrial Revolution in the ceramic world. Here was a cheap ceramic that undercut the Chinese export market and rendered the Delftwares – which were so much more fragile – virtually redundant. Although soft paste porcelains were more costly to produce, the formula gradually improved and factories such as Sèvres and

A flower holder or bough pot, also called 'flower pot' in the 1770 catalogue of the Worcester factory, where it was produced 1765-70. The sunken top has a large central opening, and pierced holes at either end.

A Sèvres *vase à compartiments* made in 1758 and painted by Jean-Louis Morin. It is now in the Rothschild Collection at Waddesdon Manor.

Chelsea, while they remained in production, produced exquisite flower vases in this material that was so well suited to the naturalistic shapes of the Rococo style.

Waddesdon Manor, built in the late nineteenth century by Ferdinand de Rothschild, houses a magnificent collection of eighteenth-century Sèvres porcelain, including vases. One group of vases for cut flowers and winter bulbs are known as *cuvettes*: all vases made at Sèvres were given names such as *cuvette courteille, à tombeau* and *Verdun*. These were usually made in pairs or garnitures of three or five for displaying on a chimneypiece. The chimneypiece in the Tapestry Bedroom at Uppark displays three matching *cuvettes à tombeau*, a set ordered by Queen Marie-Antoinette in 1773. Many of these shapes continued to be fashionable throughout the nineteenth century, with copies made in English factories.

Vases à compartiments had central partitions dividing them into two, and were made at Sèvres in five sizes. Like *cuvettes* they were used for both flowers and bulbs. *Vases Hollandais* were for growing plants, with the upper part filled with earth; the lower part or stand was filled with water, which was drawn up by the plant through the holes pierced in the hidden base of the upper part. Made from 1754 through to the 1790s, they were sold singly, in pairs or sets of three or five, with differing sizes within the set. They were copied by Minton and other factories in the nineteenth century.

Caisses carrés were miniature copies of the wooden container in which orange trees were grown. They are mentioned in a dinner service ordered in 1752 by Louis XV, so presumably they were originally intended for table decoration. They were made from 1753 and sold in three sizes. Sometimes they were sold with plants in them – heliotrope is mentioned in one account. But mostly they contained miniature orange trees. On 16 July 1765, Lord Holland

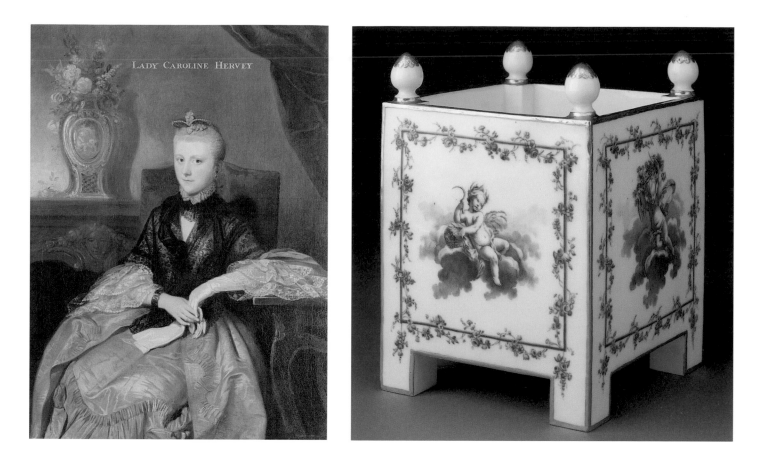

wrote from Paris to his sister-in-law, Lady Kildare, at Carton in Ireland: 'In obedience to your commands ... I sent two square blue celeste orange tubs to the Follys just before I came away.'

Piedestal à l'Oignons were bulb pots made at Sèvres from 1756 to 1773. The pot was filled with water and a single bulb placed on the detachable, gilt-edged tray that fitted into the top. Some had different decoration on each side, which could be revealed as the growing bulb was turned daily to prevent it leaning towards the light. These bulb pots were a far cry from the cheap glass tumblers used by Robert Furber in his pioneering experiments of the 1730s. But bulb glasses continued to be made. In 1782, John Abercrombie wrote, 'Several sorts of bulbous roots may be placed upon glasses of water for blowing [flowering] in the apartments of a house such as hyacinths, narcissuses, jonquiles, early dwarf tulips, etc. The glasses for this purpose are to be had at the seedsman and glass-shops.'

Containers for hyacinth and other bulbs were keenly sought after, and Josiah Wedgwood, sensing a business opportunity, adapted flower bricks for this purpose. He made them in different sizes with rounded cups in which the bulb might rest, and with small holes for supporting sticks. Perhaps his most amusing root container was a hedgehog crocus pot in the natural form of the animal with holes pierced through its bristly body for the bulbs. It was accompanied by a tray for water, and moss or soil was placed inside the hedgehog. This was normally made in 'Black Basalt' but also occasionally in green-glazed creamware.

LEFT: Portrait of Lady Caroline Hervey attributed to Johan Zoffany, *c*.1770. The flower-filled vase on the chimneypiece is typical of many of this period, inspired by Sèvres and made at the Chelsea factory.

ABOVE: One of a pair of white and crimson Sèvres orange tubs made in 1755 and painted by Jean-Louis Morin – with cupids copied from engravings after François Boucher. It is also in the Rothschild Collection at Waddesdon Manor.

An illustration from George Voorhelm's *Traité sur la Jacinte* published in 1773, showing hyacinth bulbs growing in a water-filled glass carafe and an earth-filled Delftware pot.

A flower brick in caneware, adapted by Wedgwood to hold bulbs. These were made from 1770 and were so sought after that three years later they were sold as mantel garnitures in pairs or sets of three, five or seven. Wedgwood made them in three sizes for one, two or three bulbs.

By the 1770s Wedgwood was not only making vases in the soft paste of creamware, but also in hard paste porcelain, reproducing the severe antique shapes of the neo-classical style, then in vogue. His famous Jasperware was particularly suitable for copies of antique vases, but he produced a whole variety of other shapes. A pair of his Krater vases, based on the classical Greek vases for mixing wine and water, stand at either end of the dining-room mantelpiece at Ormesby Hall near Middlesbrough in Yorkshire.

The pyramid vase with spouts, so fashionable in the seventeenth century, continued to be made. On 25 July 1772 Josiah Wedgwood wrote to his partner, Thomas Bentley: 'This morning I have had an opportunity of consulting with Lady Gower & Lady Teignham & their Lords (who have been at the works here and bott. [bought] some flowerpots) upon the subject of Boughpots, & find they prefer those things with spouts, such as the old Delph ones, they say that sort keep their flowers distinct and clever.'

Wedgwood also made versions of the wall pocket, which he called faces and flower horns. These were flower containers that hung on the wall. They first appeared in the sixteenth century in Chinese porcelain, but were made in England and America from the late 1740s to the beginning of the nineteenth century, when they went out of fashion for some years. They were sold in pairs, often made in asymmetrical shapes with right- and left-handed examples.

Two neo-classical vases in Black Basalt, now in the Library at Saltram. Josiah Wedgwood described Basalt as 'a fine black Porcelain, having nearly the same Properties as the Basaltes [rock], resisting the attacks of Acids... and equal in Hardness to Agate or Porphyry', using it for many of his 'Etruscan' style vases.

Wall pocket featuring Flora, the goddess of flowers, made by Wedgwood in creamware in the shape of a cornucopia. Josiah Wedgwood referred to these as 'flower horns' and an entry in his 'crate book' notes that on 18 December 1770 they were for sale at two shillings a pair. The backs were pierced with two holes for hanging.

A bough pot in a fireplace, from a mezzotint by J.G. Haid of Johan Zoffany's *Mr Foote as Major Sturgeon*, 1764. The actors wear early eighteenth-century costume, and the flower arrangement is more reminiscent of this earlier period. By the 1760s, fireplace arrangements were usually smaller and more dainty.

Where were all these pots and vases, in their various shapes and sizes, displayed? As in earlier centuries, furniture was introduced to the centre of living rooms when required. Tripod tables, also known as work-tables and popular from the 1740s, were kept in the corners of the room or were brought in from a passage where they were kept with their tops tipped up against a wall. On them might be placed writing things, and 'work' of various sorts, including knotting and netting and, for 'botanising', a small vase of flowers. Botanising meant the study of flowers, pressing them and making botanical drawings and paintings. This fashionable pursuit was practised by Queen Charlotte and her daughters, of whom Dr Robert Thornton wrote effusively, 'There is not a plant in the garden at Kew ... but has been drawn by her gracious Majesty, or some of the Princesses, with a grace and skill, which reflect on these personages the highest honour.'

Robert Adam designed this chimneyboard for Mrs Child's Dressing Room at Osterley in 1776. The flowers are arranged in a neo-classical vase inspired by the classical Greek vases known as 'Krater vases' and popularised by Wedgwood.

The chimneypiece was still a prime place for the display of flowers and in the summer the empty fireplace or the marble hearth slab could be decorated with bough pots of mixed flowers and greenery or with growing plants in pots. There seems to have been confusion as to the exact use of the bough pot and the difference between it and a flower vase. Josiah Wedgwood found it necessary to make the matter clear to Thomas Bentley in the letter quoted earlier: 'Vases are furniture for a Chimneypiece – Bough pots for a hearth, under a Slab or Marble Table I think they never can be used one instead of the other.' Nevertheless a note written in his commonplace book then suggested that any flower container with a pierced cover, whatever its size, could be referred to as a bough pot, so it would seem a moveable feast.

David Garrick in his play *The Clandestine Marriage*, first performed in 1766, brings a

A caricature of a Macaroni wearing an enormous nosegay, from a late eighteenth-century print. Macaronis were young aristocrats who had adopted Continental manners and fashions as a result of the Grand Tour. The name first appeared in 1764, derived from the Italian pasta dish, and was used to denounce extravagances of dress, including feminine accessories such as nosegays.

RIGHT: James Gillray's cartoon of George III and Queen Charlotte entitled *Temperance enjoying a Frugal Meal*, 1792. On the right he has depicted a flower arrangement in the fire grate.

large bough pot, presumably for a fireplace, into the dialogue when the daughters of the City merchant, Mr Stirling, are showing off to the old roué, Lord Ogle, their fashionable and improved garden, with all its crinkum-crankums, zigzags, twistings and turnings. The younger girl presents him with a bouquet, whereupon the elder exclaims, 'Lord, sister, you've loaded his lordship with a bunch of flowers as big as the cook or nurse might carry to town on a Monday morning to put in the bough pot.' She proceeds to offer him a delicate nosegay comprising a rose and a sprig of sweet briar.

In his *Gardeners Dictionary*, Philip Miller recommends aconitum (monkshood) for the fireplace, 'The flowers ... are commonly brought to market in May to furnish flower-pots for chimneys to adorn Halls and other Appartments being mixed with *Guelder Roses* and other *flowers of the same season*.' Guelder roses, he adds, 'are very proper to intermix with peonies and other large flowers'. For growing in pots, he suggests *Campanula pyramidalis*:

> This plant is cultivated to adorn Halls, and to place before chimneys in the summer when it is in flower for which purpose there is no plant more proper. For when the roots are strong they will send out four or five great stalks, which will rise as many feet high, and are garnished with flowers great part of their length. When the flowers begin to open, the pots are removed into the rooms, where, being shaded from the sun, and kept from the rain, the flowers will continue long in beauty....

In a later edition he suggests that 'if the Branches are regularly spread flat to sticks, it makes a very fine appearance'.

Benjamin Whitwell, gardener at Hoxton in East London, in his *Universal Calendar* of 1726 recommends stock gilly-flower, *Campanula pyramidalis* and scarlet lychnis – 'a beautiful plant ... bearing trusses upon stalks somewhat more than 2 feet [61 centimetres] high'. Samuel Cooke, gardener at Overton in Wiltshire, 'who has practised gardening in many counties upwards of 40 years', in his *Complete English Gardening or Gardening made perfectly easy*, published *c*.1793, agrees about the stock gilly-flower, pointing out 'the double kind, ... a shrub which being transplanted into pots, are for their grateful smell a proper ornament to adorn chimneys'.

Paintings of interiors of this period show bough pots in fireplaces filled with auriculas, cherry blossom, lilies, lily of the valley, morning glories, poppy anemones, roses and tulips amongst other species. As in all arrangements of the time, tall and short flowers were mixed together, even if they appeared rather awkward companions.

The Marchioness Grey of Wrest Park in Bedfordshire wrote querulously in 1770 of the cold she suffered because flowers rather than fires were taking up the fireplaces. 'One May the Dowager Duchess of Bedford gave the newest form of entertainment – a breakfast of cold meat at Bedford House.... There was no fire, the fireplaces being filled with greenery. There was music in the gallery, but even the company present could not warm the room.' Likewise the custom did not please John Byng, later Viscount Torrington, the crotchety traveller and diarist. He complained of dining out on a chilly May evening, 'here were no fires but an elegant assortment of geraniums, and of myrtles, [which] forced you to endeavour to hope that summer was coming'.

From early in the eighteenth century, with the increasing use of coal rather than logs, the

FAR LEFT: Seven Wedgwood Jasperware vases set out in the late eighteenth-century style on a chimneypiece in the library at Osterley.

LEFT: Close-up of the vase on the extreme right. Blooms of Rosa Mundi and other roses, cornflower, nigella, salvia and chamomile have been casually dropped in the vase in the manner often seen at this period.

fire, instead of burning at ground level, was often contained in a free-standing grate which was easily removed in summer to make way for flowers. But in the later part of the century the hob grate became widely popular. Even though this was fixed and immovable, 'deckers' were undeterred and continued to install flowers inside the grate, if rather uneasily. A vase of flowers is usually shown inside the hob grate in the breakfast room at Osterley Park, and another in Mrs Child's Dressing Room.

With the fashion for a wider shelf to top a chimneypiece, there was more space for flowers. The number of vases in a garniture could go up to eleven or even thirteen, the number recorded in the state bedroom at Harewood House in Yorkshire in an inventory taken in 1795.

Throughout the eighteenth century, when new varieties of flowers arrived in Britain from abroad they were greeted with excitement; the different stages of development were

RIGHT: The long gallery at Osterley, which runs the full length of the garden front. It was decorated in the 1750s by Matthew Hillyard for Francis Child. On the marble chimneypieces, designed by Sir William Chambers, are baskets of flowers appropriately placed on the heads of female 'herm' supports.

FAR RIGHT: Close-up of one of the chimneypieces, showing the flower arrangements. The baskets have metal liners with wire netting stretched over the top and pinholders on the bases. The aim was to place the flowers in a natural and haphazard manner. Three tall flowers – all different varieties – were put in first, asymmetrically around the centre, then two at each side to give the shape. Large and small flowers were then added in no particular order, but ensuring that no flowers matched, to achieve 'glorious irregularity'.

Over twenty varieties of flowers were arranged in each basket, including peonies and Canterbury bells, alstroemeria, cornflowers, wild buttercups and ragged robin.

noted with interest and delight – front, back and side views. Small vases set on the chimney-piece were perfect places to put single flowers for observation.

In the long gallery at Osterley the chimneypieces are supported by female or nymph busts on tapering 'herm' or 'therm' pilasters. These provide appropriate pedestals for large baskets of flowers, copies of one found in a potting shed at Petworth. The flowers used in the arrangements are eighteenth-century varieties grown in the walled garden at Osterley.

Occasionally brackets were built into mirrors or picture frames and they could be used for flowers. In Mrs Child's Dressing Room at Osterley, John Linnell, the cabinetmaker, incorporated brackets in the delicate carved and gilt overmantel mirror for the display of vases. At Nostell Priory, over the chimneypiece in the Crimson Bedroom, is a painting in an elaborate Rococo frame, with seven little ledges, ostensibly for candles, but in daytime for flowers. Carved wall brackets also provided places for flowers, as shown in a conversation piece painted *c*.1760 by Henry Pickering, now in a private collection.

As earlier, flowers were placed on pier-tables that stood between the windows, usually with a mirror above them in which the flowers could be reflected. Such opportunities were

RIGHT & FAR RIGHT: The carved and gilded chimneypiece in Mrs Child's Dressing Room at Osterley, designed by the cabinet-maker John Linnell and furnished with little vases of flowers standing on its bracket shelves. The vases are of eighteenth-century porcelain and Wedgwood Jasperware.

The arrangement inside the fire grate echoes a carved one on the top of the mirror. The basket has wire netting stretched across the metal liner and a pinholder in the base. The arrangement is constructed in similar fashion to the baskets in the long gallery (pages 90 and 91),with foxgloves and valerian, *Campanula persicifolia* and aquilegia.

always taken: at night, unshuttered windows could be used for the same effect. They could also be put *under* the tables, as a vacuum was thought ugly. The empty space would be filled with one or more large decorative jars, or with a bough pot. Sometimes carved stretchers incorporated a central platform on which a vase or basket of fresh flowers might be placed. Sometimes a carved vase of flowers sat permanently on the platform as part of the design, as at Nostell Priory where two pier-tables have carvings of two enchanting putti carrying a basket of flowers on a dish.

Cabinet-makers produced flower stands for supporting vases and growing plants. Some took the form of staging; others were like narrow tables. Two charming stepped stages, painted with terracotta decoration on an ivory ground, are at Osterley. They are on

castors, so they could have been moved from room to room. At 'Romantic Osterley' they were dressed with marigolds (the Child family emblem) and pelargoniums in terracotta pots stencilled with decoration to match the Etruscan Room in which they stood.

Flower tables, narrow and rectangular with tray tops, were made to go in the window embrasures of the gallery at Osterley – they are still there. In 1782 they were described as 'two mahogany flower stands'. Since then, three more have been made, so each window has its own table. Sadly no picture exists of them dressed with flowers in the eighteenth century, but no doubt plants from the greenhouses would have been brought in and displayed on them, while Mrs Child and her family and friends watched their progress day by day as they strolled through the gallery. Now, again, they are often dressed with appropriate flowers such as auriculas in pots and hyacinths in bulb vases.

A watercolour painted by Charles Wild in 1817 of the Green Pavilion at Frogmore, one of Queen Charlotte's favourite homes, shows small 'flower tables' in the window, with nine little vases of cut flowers on them, three to a table. From c.1790 tables such as these, called 'quartetti', were made to fit into each other. Now known as a 'nest', they are often thought of as coffee tables, but they were originally made for flowers. The flower tables at Frogmore are still to be seen in the Green Saloon, with their nine vases, though the flowers shown are artificial.

Gilded flower stands were made, similar in form to tall candlestands, 5 to 6 feet (1.5 to 2 metres) in height, and usually topped with fixed, tin-lined baskets or containers. Thomas Chippendale designed four to go in the corners of the Great Drawing Room at Burton Constable in Yorkshire, and his son, Thomas Junior, made six c.1785 for the gallery at Harewood House. A watercolour painted by John Scarlett Davis some 40 years later, and still in the house, shows four of them with flower vases on the platform tops.

The stands and staging, and to some extent the vases themselves, were designed as part of the general decorative scheme. But the *arrangement* of the flowers was not so considered. They represented the one thing in the room that was natural and haphazard. This also

LEFT: A late eighteenth-century staged plant stand in the window embrasure of the Etruscan Dressing Room, dressed with marigolds and pelargoniums for 'Romantic Osterley' in 1985. The terracotta pots have been stencilled to echo the neo-classical design of the room, as recommended by a gardening book of the period.

Tradesman's card with baskets for mignonettes and flowers, and a flower stand, 1796.

India ink silhouette of the
Parminter family at their leisure,
in 1783, ascribed to Francis
Torond. On the left Jane
Parminter is depicted watering
a stage of plants.

applied to pots of growing flowers: violets could stand next to a rose bush. At A La Ronde
in Devon there is a fine Indian ink silhouette of 1783, ascribed to Frances Torond, a master
of the conversation group. It shows the Parminter family at their London house in Greville
Street. Mary Parminter noted on the back that it shows 'My cousin Miss Jane Parminter
watering a stage of plants, Miss Elizabeth her sister netting, Mr Frend reading, Mr John
Parminter her brother playing a mandarin [mandolin], Mrs Frend her sister playing on the
harpsichord'. The simple wooden stage has on it, under it and in front of it different plants
in terracotta pots standing in large saucers.

In the letter quoted on pages 75-6, Lord Edward Fitzgerald goes on to describe how his
wife, Pamela, has 'dressed four beautiful flower-pots, and is now working at her [needle-
work] frame, while I write to my dearest mother; and upon the two little stands there are
six pots of fine auriculas, and I am sitting in the bay window'. Perhaps the little flower
stands to which he refers are similar to the tables at Frogmore. The 'beautiful flower-pots'
dressed by Pamela could well have been filled with the flowers in the garden that he had
earlier described as 'a wilderness of daffodils and narcissi and crocuses, of primroses and
tulips and wallflowers'. A few weeks later, after visiting his mother at Carton in County
Kildare, he was again writing to her: 'The place is now perfection. All the shrubs are out,
lilac, laburnum, syringas, spring roses, and lily of the valley in quantities, four pots full
now in the book room.'

In the eighteenth century the fashion for decorating rooms, particularly long galleries,
with trees was prevalent throughout Europe. In the 1730s at the Court of the Empress
Anne of Russia even in the coldest weather the rooms were kept perfectly warm and
decorated with orange trees and myrtles in full bloom, ranged in rows so as to form
avenues on either side of the room, where company could 'sit out', only leaving space for
the dancers in the middle. The effect of those warm fragrant artificial groves, with nothing
but snow and ice outside the streaming windows, was enchanting.

When William Kent, Capability Brown and their fellow gardeners transformed the

English landscape by sweeping away avenues of trees and replacing them by 'clumps' dotted around the parkland, the arrangement of orange trees indoors reflected the change, and continued to do so for many years. In 1824 the celebrated garden author John Loudon wrote in his *Greenhouse Companion*: 'Sometimes large picture galleries are laid out in imitation of parks in the ancient or modern style, with avenues or with groups and scattered trees.' In 1780, after visiting The Vyne in Hampshire, Mrs Lybbe Powys wrote that she had seen 'two long galleries, one full of whole-length portraits: the other they make a greenhouse of in winter, and they say has a most pleasing effect to walk thro' oranges, myrtles, etc., ranged on each side.'

For a house to contain two long galleries, as at The Vyne, was unusual, but most large houses now had one gallery, often on the first floor where it formed part of the regular circuit of state rooms, and could be used for the balls and assemblies that had become an essential part of social life. Galleries were still used for exercise on rainy days, but came to be used more as living rooms. When Robert Adam in the early 1760s remodelled the Jacobean gallery at Syon House in Middlesex, turning it into one of the most beautiful neo-classical rooms in England, he wrote that it was to be used 'for the reception of company before dinner and for the ladies to retire to after it'.

As well as, or instead of, portraits hanging on the wall, some galleries now contained sculpture brought back from the Grand Tour and shelves of books, so there was plenty to interest and amuse the guests. The flowers would also have provided a diversion. Not only might there be orange and myrtle trees in pots or tubs on the floor, but tall flower stands might bear growing plants or vases of cut flowers standing higher than head level, and on the new flower tables would be displayed the most prized exotics and flowers from the hothouses and garden.

Garden buildings were also decorated with flowers and equipped with various stands. At Osterley in the 1780s the furnishings of a summer-house included two large aloes in tubs, and those of a 'Tea Room in the Garden' included 'circular flower stands'. There was also a flower stage, which could be stored away in winter, brought out in summer and moved from place to place to be decorated with pots of flowers for an outdoor meal or gathering in the garden. It was not unusual for gardens to be decorated with pots of flowers, such as auriculas, on a specially designated stage or theatre. In the corner of the Flower Garden at Calke Abbey in Derbyshire is the last surviving auricula theatre in England. It was installed there in the 1850s for Georgiana, Lady Crewe, an enthusiastic and knowledgeable horticulturist. Today the National Trust provides displays of polyanthus and pelargoniums before and after the auriculas, which only flower from mid-April to mid-May.

From the 1740s every house of any pretension had a separate dining room, more often called an eating room. Grander houses also had a breakfast room, for this had now become a more important meal, to which friends might be invited. Intimate friends, on the other hand, might be entertained to breakfast or dinner in a smaller room – dressing room, boudoir, bedroom, any room thought suitable, or which took one's fancy. On 7 July 1750 Mrs Delany wrote to her sister from Delville, her home in Ireland: 'Lady Caroline and Mr Fox … want to breakfast here … as they are *people of taste* I honour them so far as to permit them to breakfast in the library! It has struck 11 and I hope they will not come till 12'.

The auricula theatre in the north-west corner of Lady Crewe's Garden at Calke Abbey. The auriculas are displayed on shelves painted blue and biscuit brown, the colours of the family's livery.

In the summer meals were often transported to a building in the garden or park: the dairy and even the bathhouse were considered amusing places to entertain one's more energetic friends and now preferred to the more formal orangery. It seems that to be elegant, these meals had to have flowers strewed on the table, no matter where it took place or whether it was for a few friends or for a large gathering. Tablecloths at this time were often embroidered or woven with flowers reflecting this custom. On 30 June 1750 Mrs Delany visited her friend Mrs Vesey and afterwards wrote to her sister: 'Found breakfast prepared for us in Mrs Vesey's dairy, and the table *strewed with roses* … it rained furiously so we fell to work making frames for prints … we dined in the bath…. I mean its antechamber … the coach carried us back to the house for tea and coffee.'

A few years earlier, the enterprising Mrs Delany, who enjoyed being in her garden for as many hours of the day as possible, had written: 'We have discovered a new breakfasting place under the shade of nut-trees, impenetrable to the sun's rays, in the midst of a grove of elms, where we shall breakfast this morning: I have ordered cherries, strawberries and nosegays to be laid on our breakfast-table, and have appointed a harper to be here to play to us during our repast.'

In the dining room chairs were still ranged around the wall when not in use, with folding tables brought in when needed. From 1780 these tables were designed so that they could be put together to make one long table when entertaining on a grand scale. It wasn't until

A basket of flowers from an eighteenth-century embroidery. The flowers in the arrangement include peonies, carnations, convolvulus, lilies of the valley, a hyacinth, auriculas and a white martagon lily

the end of the century that the fashion for having a permanent long table in the centre of the room was introduced. Flower decoration only appeared with the dessert, when the table-cloth was removed. On occasions it was set out on a separate table in the dining room or even in a different room. The decoration was usually arranged on a plateau or *surtout de table* made of porcelain, silver or mirror glass. The simpler board of earlier times, with formal pyramids of fruit and sweetmeats around a vase of flowers, was replaced from the 1740s with much more ornate decoration reflecting the rococo 'taste for nature'. This could consist of numerous small vases of flowers, but an entire make-believe garden might take over the table centre, leaving room for only a row or perhaps two, of the new porcelain dessert dishes on which the fruit and sweetmeats were laid.

The make-believe garden had, of course, to be in the current fashionable taste. In the 1740s it would consist of a parterre of sugar paste hedges, peopled with sugar paste figures, and sometimes sugar paste flowers were preferred to real ones. During the next decade, the parterre was replaced by a miniature landscape of meadows and trees, the sugar paste figures by porcelain figures, first made in Europe at the Meissen factory at Dresden. Accompanying this profusion of ornament there seem always to have been flowers, fresh when available, otherwise of porcelain or sugar paste. Excerpts from M. Massialot's recommended list of flowers for the dining room appear in the previous chapter (see page 62). His book remained popular throughout the eighteenth century, the sixteenth edition

appearing in 1795. In later editions his list of flowers remain the same, but advice has been added. For tables laid for the dessert for eight to ten persons, M. Massialot suggests: 'In the middle a bowl of flowers mounted on a goblet or between two goblets.' For a table for 40 guests, he fancies: 'Fifteen large Bowls or Baskets for the row down the middle, and forty-eight smaller ones for the lesser rows down each side of the table'. Some were for filling with fresh and dried fruits, but all were to be embellished with flowers, leaves and other ornaments following the seasons, as described in his flower list.

In 1748 the Elector of Saxony, who owned the Meissen factory, presented the British Ambassador, Sir Charles Hanbury-Williams, with a 'service for dessart' to take back to

England. As well as dishes, it consisted of a great assemblage of figures for the middle of the table, grouped round barns, stables, farmers' houses and a church, which clearly shows how completely by this date the 'taste for nature' had driven out the grand formal baroque forms of earlier times.

Not everybody approved of this fashion. In 1753 Horace Walpole wrote disapprovingly that the previous 'jellies, biscuits, sugar plums and creams' of the dessert had 'long since given way to Turks, Chinese and Shepherdesses of Saxon [Meissen] china … wandering on the table, unconnected, among groves of curled paper and silk flowers' while 'meadows of cattle of the same brittle materials spread themselves over the whole table, cottages rose in sugar and temples in barley sugar …'.

But Walpole was in a minority. So popular were these Meissen figures 'for dessart' that the Chelsea factory began to copy them. In a sale catalogue of 1755 they dominate the items on offer: 'figures of Pantaloon and Columbine …, a lady and gentleman in hunting dress …, a cook and a fisherman'. Also listed are dishes in the shape of vine, fig and cabbage leaves, sunflowers, pineapples and artichokes, to hold the fruit and sweetmeats. And for flowers, small china flower pots, along with porcelain flowers, mostly roses or tulips.

If a larger flower vase was preferred, it might be in the oval *cuvette* shape produced first by Sèvres, then copied by English factories. Small growing plants might also be introduced, in porcelain orange tubs made by Sèvres (see page 80). Ready-made, all-in-one porcelain pots of flowers were produced by Bow, Derby and Chelsea.

On 18 February 1756 William Farrington, after attending an Assembly at the newly completed Norfolk House in London, wrote to his younger sisters:

> I dined with the Duke and Duchess … it was a very fine affair … I'll give you an account of the Table. After a very Elligant Dinner of a great many dishes, the Table was Prepar'd for Desert, which was a beautiful Park, round the Edge was a *Plantation of Flowering Shrubs* and in the middle a Fine piece of water, with dolphins spouting out water and Dear interspersed irregularly over the Lawn, on the Edge of the Table was all the Iced Creams, and wet and dried Sweetmeats – it was such a Piece of Work it was all left on the Table 'til we went to coffee.

In 1769 the Chelsea factory was still selling 'single figures of all sizes for dessarts' but they added to the sales catalogues 'large and small antique urns' to replace the frivolous rococo flower vases. Greek temples now appeared in the dining-room landscapes, adorned with figures made of biscuit, an unglazed white porcelain resembling the plain marble or stone of the classical sculptures which young noblemen were bringing back from their Grand Tours in Europe.

For those unable to afford the porcelain figures, and disinclined to make hedges of sugar paste or temples of barley sugar, there were shops that sold or hired out everything necessary for a make-believe garden or landscape. Figures, trees, temples, Chinese pagodas, Gothic follies, hedges, serpentine paths, parterres and 'sets' were obtainable in porcelain, silver gilt or enamelled glass, and more cheaply in cartonage (gilded cardboard), with additional artificial grass and gravel. Sometimes, not surprisingly, a hostess confused by the rapidly changing fashions had a mixture of several styles on her table at the same time.

Spectacular recreation of an eighteenth-century dessert setting in the French manner in the dining room at Waddesdon. The service on display was purchased from the Sèvres factory by the Vicomte de Choiseul in 1766, and is accompanied by Sèvres *biscuit* figures and groups from Lord Rothschild's collection. On the mirror plateau, stretching the entire length of the table, a parterre has been created in coloured sugar paste. The fruits are modelled in marzipan and the flowers in sugar paste by Ivan Day.

There is evidence that the flowers were originally displayed in sixteen vases on pedestals set around the plateau, but here just four are used with baskets at either side. The flowers are copied from those decorating the plates, in recognition of the Sèvres porcelain painters' custom of growing their own flowers in the factory garden as examples. A pair of orange trees on the chimneypiece are in the tubs illustrated on page 81.

It wasn't only the grand London houses that boasted this sort of table decoration. In 1783 the Rev. James Woodforde, after dining with the Bishop of Norwich, wrote in his diary: 'A most beautiful Artificial Garden in the centre of the Table remained at Dinner and afterwards, it was one of the prettiest things I ever saw, about a Yard [90 centimetres] long, and about 18″ [45 centimetres] wide, in the middle of which was a high round Temple supported on round Pillars, the Pillars were *wreathed round with artificial flowers* on one side was a Shepherdess on the other a Shepherd, *several handsome Urns decorated with artificial flowers* also etc. etc.'

In 1811 another country parson, the Rev. Talbot, after dining at Saltram in Devon, wrote of 'the table of an immense width with a plateau full of biscuit figures and vases with flowers, etc. the whole length, leaving merely room for a dish at each end of a single row of dishes around'. By this time figures on fashionable dining tables were dwindling: the artificial gardens had had their day.

Flowers were also placed around the dining or breakfast room. In 1780 Le Camus de Mezières, author of *Le Génie de l'Architecture*, advised placing stands with several stages in the dining room, and decking them with banks of fresh flowers. The 1782 inventory at Osterley records that in the Breakfast Room there were 'Two painted flower Stands with Wedgwood Potts on Do.' On special occasions, the sideboard, as in the previous chapter, would have been garlanded with fresh flowers.

During the eighteenth century a lady's dressing room became known as a 'boudoir' – reflecting the influence of French fashion – while gentlemen continued to use a dressing room. In very large establishments a lady might have a dressing room as well as a boudoir. Both boudoirs and dressing rooms were used not only for dressing in and for private activities such as reading and writing, but also became increasingly the setting for entertaining close friends. Contrary to modern ideas about masculine and feminine taste, flowers were just as important a feature of the decoration of the dressing room as they were of the boudoir.

The aim was to furnish the dressing room 'up to the minute', and as well as being decorated with vases of cut flowers, it was often treated as a greenhouse for plants in pots. On 4 October 1800 Elizabeth Freemantle wrote in her diary at Swanbourne in Buckinghamshire, 'I was very busy in taking my plants in, I put them in Freemantle's dressing room, where they look very pretty.' In 1770 the Rev. William Hanbury wrote of sweet rockets, 'Ladies have always been remarkably fond of these plants and have much distinguished them with a place in their bedchambers, dressing rooms and apartments.'

A dressing room at Osterley was decorated in the most up-to-date style, the Etruscan manner, painted and papered to resemble an open loggia with 'Etruscan' terracotta and black arabesque trelliswork against a sky blue background. The floral element is considerable – tazzas full of mixed flowers, and female figures with baskets of flowers, out of which they are filling a tazza. A painted medallion is of damsels entwining garlands round a statue, and the cresting of the mirror is a basket of flowers. In addition, Adam made a design for a painted chimneyboard of a neo-classical vase of flowers for the room, which is now in Sir John Soane's Museum in London, and a needlework screen of a basket of

A hand bouquet in the eighteenth-century style. An elaborate 'language of flowers' had evolved, so that the recipient might understand the sender's message. In this bouquet there is rosemary for remembrance, myrtle for true love, pansy for thoughts, sweet william for valour, lavender for silence, and roses for beauty. The message thus reads, 'Remember me and the true love I bear you, for you are always in my thoughts, be brave and keep silence, my beauty.'

flowers, still at Osterley. For 'Romantic Osterley' the Etruscan Dressing Room was 'dressed up' with pots of garden plants between the chairs all round the walls in imitation of the Uppark Print Room (see page 131). The result was spectacular.

There is plenty of evidence that flowers were kept in bedchambers, and this is reflected at Osterley where flowers in vases are displayed in the bedrooms. Charming little flower containers were made by Mrs Child out of wood covered with paper. Two, in the form of half circles, she painted with tiny swags and flower-heads. Another is in the form of a tall, rectangular flower pot. Filled with silk flowers such as peonies, roses, auriculas and convolvulus, they now decorate the drawing room and bedrooms. A garland of similar silk flowers bedecks the state bed, designed by Robert Adam in 1776. The bed is conceived as a Temple of Venus, and richly decorated with flowers emblematic of fertility. Horace Walpole, who visited Osterley in 1778, found it 'too theatric and too like a modern head-dress, for round the outside of the dome are festoons of artificial flowers. What would Vitruvius think of a dome decorated by a milliner?'

A metal-lined flower container of wood covered with paper and painted by Mrs Child with a delicate neo-classical pattern. It stands in front of a pier glass in the drawing room at Osterley, filled with silk flowers.

Making Garlands

Garlands have traditionally been made for celebrations throughout the year, using available flowers and greenery. Here are late eighteenth-century-style garlands in thick and thin versions, using modern methods and materials.

The thick garland uses unwaxed sash cord and mossing wire, with box foliage, anemones, tulips (esperanto), auriculas, honeysuckle and guelder roses.

1 Wire a loop at each end of the garland, and mark the middle. Place a piece of box over the loop, and wire it with two turns.

2 Place more box onto the rope so that it just covers the wire, and wire it in the same way. Continue down the rope, increasing the width of the box on the outside to give a thickening effect.

3 When the middle is reached, make several turns with the wire and cut off. Start at the other end as before until the middle is reached.

4a

b

4 (a-c) Wire the flowers by pushing a piece straight through the stem or head, then bending the wire back on itself, and twisting the wire twice round the stem, leaving the two ends the same length, though separate.

5

c

5 Stab the flowers at an angle into the garland.

The thin garland uses ribbon and mossing wire, with myrtle foliage, feverfew, forget-me-nots and honeysuckle.

Loop the ribbon and attach with the wire. Place a stem of myrtle over the loop and wire it onto the ribbon. Take a small bunch of flowers and wire them in turn onto the ribbon. Continue in this way, travelling down the ribbon, ensuring that each wired piece is covered with the next foliage or flowers but the effect remains thin and elegant. Reverse the last few pieces so the second loop is covered.

Many eighteenth-century garlands were made by binding single stems of flowers to a ribbon or cord, spacing them apart so that the whole of each flower was clearly visible and separated from the next one. This effect can be seen in the Painted Room at Spencer House (see page 111).

Flower garlands were essential for parties, where they might festoon pictures, statues, doors and window-frames. Mrs Lybbe Powys gave detailed descriptions in her diary of some of the parties she went to, noting the elegant festoons and wreaths of flowers, both real and artificial, that decorated the rooms. At that time a 'wreath' referred to garlands and swags of flowers as well as the modern idea of a round circle. In January 1777 she attended a party at Fawley Court in Buckinghamshire given by her neighbour, Mrs Freeman. The entrance hall was used as a dining room for the evening, and at half past twelve the doors were thrown open 'on which nothing could be more striking … it was illuminated by three hundred coloured lamps round the six doors, over the chimney, and over the statue at the other end'. The tables, running the length of the room, and forming a crescent at each end were ornamented 'with everything in the confectionery way, and festoons and wreaths of artificial flowers prettily disposed; all fruits of the season, as grapes, pines, etc.'

Twenty-five years earlier, Mrs Delany wrote to her sister from Ireland of the astonishing decorations that she had seen at a party organised by her stepson-in-law, Lord Belfield:

> The decorations are really very pretty, though too much crowded. The room <u>represents a wood</u> and there is room left down the middle for thirty couples to dance; at one end is a portico on Doric pillars, lighted by baskets of flowers, the candles <u>green wax</u> so that nothing appears but the flame. On the right hand, from the portico to the end of the stage is diversified by rocks, trees, and caves, very well represented. On the left hand a jessamine bower, a Gothic temple (which is to be the sideboard) trees interspersed, the whole terminates with a grotto extremely well expressed, three rustic arches, set off with ivy, moss, icicles and all the rocky appurtenances; the musicians to be placed in the grotto dressed like shepherds and shepherdesses. The Duke and Duchess of Dorset are to be placed under the portico which fronts the grotto; there is to be a concert, a ball and a supper. The trees are <u>real trees</u> with <u>artificial leaves</u>, but when all is done it will be too much crowded to be agreeable, and most dangerous if a spark of a candle should fall on any of the scenery which is all <u>painted paper</u>!

The arrangements for providing refreshments were as original as the decoration: 'If tea, coffee, or chocolate were wanting, you held your cup to a leaf of a tree, and it was filled: and whatever you wanted to eat or drink was immediately found on a rock, or on a branch, or in the hollow of a tree, the waiters were all in whimsical dress.' It seems that the idea for decorating houses for parties changed little over the next 70 years, for in 1824 John Loudon described the same practice of transforming interiors into caves, grottos and wooded hills.

The Painted Room at Spencer House in London gives a *trompe-l'oeil* impression of how a room could be decked out for a party. Designed and decorated by 'Athenian' Stuart from 1759 to 1765 in the neo-classical style, it is a celebration of the Triumph of Love, and in particular of Lord and Lady Spencer's happy marriage. Round the top frieze alternating wreaths and swags of roses, poppy anemones, guelder roses, tulips, orange blossom and auriculas are attached with bows on to hooks in the form of tiny gilt shells. Swags of flowers bound with ribbon are looped over the tops of picture frames and hung in festoons on either side; others are looped over doors. Gilded garlands are draped over the terms

supporting the chimneypiece. Gilt vases in the shape of amphora balance on top of the projecting dado, and from each rises a tall bacchic 'thrysus' stick entwined with honeysuckle and morning glory, and terminating in a delicate golden pine-cone.

These extravagant Georgian spectacles involved an enormous amount of work, not all of which was done by servants. The Windsor archive contains the diaries of Mrs Kennedy, who lived in the Henry III Tower for 32 years. We are indebted to her for a vivid account of the weeks of activity leading up to a ball given by Queen Charlotte at Frogmore – 'her <u>own</u>, & favourite place' – to celebrate the 1793 anniversary of the King's accession on 25 October.

Princess Elizabeth, third daughter of the King and Queen, was in charge of the decorations, supported by James Wyatt, the architect, who devoted an entire week to helping her. The whole house was to be decorated with garlands of artificial flowers – 1,000 yards (900 metres) was the objective. The Queen, her other daughters, and 'all the Ladys in Windsor' joined in. Mrs Kennedy wrote of their labours: 'Dr Lind, shewd Miss Guard a drawing of the curious Flower lately brought from the Cape, which <u>he</u> called <u>Regina</u> [*Strelitzia reginae*

ABOVE: Detail of the Painted Room at Spencer House in London, designed in the early 1760s for John, 1st Earl Spencer by the architect James 'Athenian' Stuart. *Trompe l'oeil* garlands adorn the frieze and festoon the picture frames, as they would have done on festive occasions.

LEFT: For 'Romantic Osterley' garlands were twined around the Corinthian columns that screen the great staircase. Pelargoniums in pots decorated each tread of the staircase, an idea inspired by an eighteenth-century watercolour.

(see page 70)] he helped Miss Guard to do it.... Miss Gould is Making Scarlet jeranims, in the finest Stile ... Miss Cheshire has also Made some Beautiful Guernsey Lillies, also some Passion Flowers.' While the ladies worked at making these complicated flowers, Mrs Kennedy felt that her old fingers were only equal to tying up leaves. A week later she wrote rather wearily, 'five Mornings I have Sat, from 9 o'clock until 4. Making up Leaves. No More Sent today; so I suppose they have enough.'

Once the flowers and leaves were finished, they were made into garlands: 'P. Eliza makes them all up, and fixes them herself, ... yesterday Princess Elizabeth Tyed up 300 yards [275 metres] with the help of Mr. Wyat, but it is all placed as She Directs, She has the whole Direction.' But the frenzied preparations were interrupted when the unfortunate Queen Marie-Antoinette was guillotined in Paris. The court went into mourning, putting the ball off until 8 November. On the 7th Mrs Kennedy wrote thankfully, 'I have just finished 8 more bunches of Vine Leaves, and I am Rejoiced, they are the Last, for I have worked the Whole Mornings for upwards of 3 weeks past'. All this effort was worth it, for the decorations were vastly admired at the ball. A friend of Mrs Kennedy, who was one of the guests, reported 'the very prettiest Scene they Ever Saw ... the Hall, Staircase and Every Room Decorated with Flowers'. Mrs Kennedy herself was sent tickets to see Frogmore House in recognition of her assistance, 'We all went at <u>Ten</u> and admired our own Works, the most Elegant thing <u>I</u> ever saw.'

Princess Elizabeth, third daughter of George III and Queen Charlotte. A skilled artist, she is appropriately shown 'botanising' in this portrait by P.E. Stroehling, 1807.

CHAPTER FOUR

A Temple of Flora

1800–1850

In 1837 the aspiring politician Benjamin Disraeli attended a banquet given by Lord and Lady Londonderry at their London house: 'It was the finest thing of the season … the whole of the staircase (a double one) being crowded with the most splendid orange trees and Cape Jessamines … the Duke of Wellington and the very flower of fashion being assembled.'

Flowers were now *the* fashion, and visual sources for our information on flower arranging are especially rich. In January 1809 Rudolph Ackermann produced the first issue of his monthly periodical, *The Repository of the Arts*, which aimed to cater for – and indeed to create – a public eager to keep up with the latest styles in furniture and interior decoration. As well as including flower stands among the pieces illustrated in the magazine, some of the colour plates of whole rooms incorporate flower arrangements.

Ackermann shows us the appearance of ideal, fashionable interiors complete with the latest taste in plants and flowers. For information about the flower arrangements that were actually to be found in people's homes we can turn to the art of interior painting, which became particularly popular in the early nineteenth century. Some interior views were commissioned for publication, such as the watercolours for W. H. Pyne's *Royal Residences* (1819), but more often these paintings were produced as private souvenirs, intended to be bound into albums rather than framed and hung. As drawing became a more important element in the education of gentlewomen, young ladies were often coached in the art of watercolour by highly competent professionals. The interior was an ideal subject since it could be undertaken without the vagaries of the weather or the need for chaperonage that would be occasioned by landscape drawing. Homes were thus captured with the rooms arranged for ordinary use – the furniture placed according to the dispositions of light and warmth, the desks covered with writing materials and the flowers arranged for everyday enjoyment.

People could get ideas about what flowers and plants to have in their gardens and houses from visiting public botanic gardens. Liverpool Botanic Garden was opened in 1802, followed by others in large towns and culminating in the Royal Botanic Garden at Kew in 1840. A great attraction at Kew was the Palm House, begun in 1844: visitor numbers rose from 15,114 in that year to a massive 137,865 in 1849 when the glasshouse opened to the public. Another source of inspiration was the ever-increasing number of horticultural societies. The Horticultural Society in London was formed in 1804 with the encouragement of Sir Joseph Banks, and proved so successful that by 1842 there were 200 in England.

Many of the newly discovered plants at this time were found by intrepid plant hunters

The Morning Room at Leigh Court in Somerset, painted by Thomas Leeson Rowbotham, *c.*1840. The picture well illustrates the informal living style that became fashionable from the beginning of the nineteenth century. No longer was furniture set around the edges of the room, but placed permanently in the centre, providing plenty of surfaces for the display of flowers. Here a sturdy predecessor of the later elegant trumpet vase stands on the sofa table positioned in front of a sofa, and a bowl sits on the round table, both filled with mounds of flowers.

sent out by the Horticultural Society. The Scotsman David Douglas made several expeditions to North America between 1823 and 1832, bringing back *Eschscholzia californica*, the California poppy, *Clarkia elegans* and many species of penstemon and pelargonium. Near disasters punctuated his travels, and he finally met his end in Hawaii, having fallen into a trap already inhabited by a wild bull.

In 1823 John Parks was sent to China, then a closed society which put every obstacle in the way of visitors. Nevertheless he managed to return with several varieties of rose (see page 133), the first aspidistra and over twenty varieties of the true chrysanthemum, *C.* × *grandiflorum*, the incurved type that had first appeared in England in 1796. When Britain acquired Hong Kong in 1842, Robert Fortune, often in the guise of a Chinaman, used it as a base for his expeditions. He took advantage of the Wardian case, designed fifteen years earlier by Dr Nathaniel Ward, to transport plants safely in a hermetically sealed atmosphere. The plants were kept alive by the repetitive process of moisture generated by the plants themselves condensing on the glass and trickling down the sides. After its invention, many more plants were able to survive the long sea journeys back to Britain.

Fortune returned home with the Chusan daisy, the parent of the pompom chrysanthemums which are said to have received their name from the bobbles French soldiers wore on their hats. He also introduced the Japanese anemone, *Anemone hupehensis*, 40 cultivars of peony, forsythia, white wisteria and weigela that he found in a mandarin's garden in Chusan. In 1861 he brought back the loose, or recurved, Japanese chrysanthemums.

Independent collectors sent plants to Loddiges of Hackney, the leading nursery during the first half of the nineteenth century. Its magnificent range of hothouses included a Camellia House in which the first *Wisteria sinensis* was reared. The Grand Palm House was completed in 1821 and described by John Loudon as 'the largest hot house in the world'. By the early 1830s it was overflowing with palms, ferns and orchids from Mexico and Brazil; all of these by the mid-century had ceased to be specialist plants and were to be found in many Victorian homes.

When Loddiges closed in 1852, Veitch's nursery in Chelsea took up the mantle. John Veitch, having worked as land steward for Sir Thomas Acland at Killerton in Devon, started the nursery in the 1770s, bringing fame and riches to five generations of his family. His first plant hunter was William Lobb, who went to South America in 1840 and sent back *Lapageria rosea*, the Chilean bellflower, a climbing lily with dangling pink flowers 3 inches (8 centimetres) long, that became indispensable for extravagant table decorations. He also reintroduced *Salvia splendens*, the scarlet species from Brazil, and *Salvia patens*, the sage with clear blue flowers from Mexico.

Two of the most popular flowers of this period were the dahlia and the fuchsia. In 1789 dahlia seeds were sent from the Botanic Garden in Mexico City to the Royal Gardens in Madrid. The flower was admired by Lady Holland, who posted to her husband's librarian in England seeds of *Dahlia coccinea* and of *Dahlia pinnata*, from which most dahlias are descended. In 1829 Loudon proclaimed the dahlia 'the most fashionable flower in England', while the more prolix Henry Philipps in *Flora Historica* described the 'full brilliancy of these floral luminaries' as shining 'as conspicuously in our groves as gas in our towns'. In 1833 the dahlia was decreed a florist's flower (see page 122).

The marriage of James and Maria Bateman was a truly horticultural one, for they were both keen gardeners and distinguished plantsmen. In 1840 they began to create the magnificent garden at Biddulph Grange in Staffordshire, with its concept of a 'world garden' – a series of mini gardens with their own microclimate so that exotic plants might flourish. James Bateman particularly favoured dahlias and built a long stepped Dahlia Walk within a framework of yew and divided into compartments by buttresses also of yew. Within these compartments he planted different kinds of dahlias, some with single colours, some mixed. This walk was rediscovered by the National Trust in 1988 during restoration of Biddulph Grange, and has been appropriately replanted with flowers similar to the cultivars of the early nineteenth century.

The Dahlia Walk at Biddulph Grange Garden, a photograph taken in 1991 before the walk was reconstructed for a second time.

Illustrations from *A Visit to the Bazaar*, a children's book published in 1818. Here the Durnford daughters are shown admiring greenhouse plants and garlands of artificial flowers. The garlands may be more modest than the royal ones described in chapter 3, but Mrs Durnford waxes lyrical 'What can be more beautiful than this *bouquet* of Rosebuds, Myrtle, Geranium, how faithful a copy from nature!'.

While the dahlia's route to England was via high society, *Fuchsia magellanica* arrived in a sailor's baggage, as described in chapter 3. It was soon in great demand as a 'chamber plant'. In 1823 Elizabeth Kent wrote in her book *Flora Domestica or the Portable Flower-Garden*: 'Messrs Loddiges has a very large collection of hardy herbaceous plants in pots'. She extolled the virtues of *Fuchsia myrtoideae*: 'This is a most beautiful little plant; the leaves are of a fine green, their veins tinged with red, the flowers pendulous and of a brilliant scarlet . . . this is an elegant plant for the drawing room or study'.

Between 1824 and 1844 around fourteen more species arrived, including the glorious *Fuchsia fulgens*, with its long tubular flowers, sent from Mexico by a Horticultural Society collector. By 1848, 520 species and varieties were listed, and in the 1880s such was the fuchsia's popularity that 10,000 plants a day were being sold in Covent Garden, some specimens growing to over 10 feet (3 metres) in height.

Another plant that bounded into the limelight was the humble erica – native heathers as well as tree heaths from South Africa. Despite the Napoleonic Wars, the Empress Josephine imported a number from England, increasing her collection from 50 in 1805 to 132 by 1812. By the 1820s some 400 species were cultivated in England, and they were much in use as chamber plants and cut flowers.

The thirst for exotic horticultural knowledge apparently developed early. In a small children's book, *A Visit to the Bazaar*, written in 1818, the following discussion takes place between Mr and Mrs Durnford and their three daughters, Emily, Maria and Caroline:

'How lovely is the Illicium Floridanum with its large red flower!' said Mrs Durnford, 'only smell how delicious is the perfume of its leaves.'

'Delicious indeed!' replied Mr Durnford, 'I must purchase one on purpose that I may enjoy the scent. It comes from Florida. I must also treat myself with one of those

Camellia Japonica, or Japan roses. The blossom is uncommonly fine. Pray what is the name of this tall flower?'

'The Lobelia Fulgens' replied the proprietor. 'It is a native of North America, and is a hardy plant.'

'I should like that pot of china roses, Mamma,' said Emily; 'they came originally, I believe, from China, and are called Rosa sinensis.'

'That mignonette is very luxuriant,' said Maria, 'pray have some, Mamma, the smell is so fragrant. Do they not call it Reseda Odorata?'

'Yes, my love, and it first came from Egypt.'

'Oh, Mamma!, do buy that sweet myrtle,' cried Caroline, 'I am so fond of myrtles and geraniums. What is the Latin term for myrtle?'

'There are eleven different sorts, my dear,' said her mother, 'the common myrtle is a native of the South of Europe and is called Myrtus Communis. Many come from the West Indian Islands, and some from Asia. In the Isle of Wight we have hedges of them.... How lovely is the Convalleria Majalis, or lily of the valley. It is a simple flower, a native of Britain, but the perfume is delightful.'

For those living in large country houses with gardeners, growing plants for the house was obviously no problem. Flower-beds close to the house, banished 50 years earlier by Capability Brown and his disciples, were reintroduced at the turn of the century by the landscape gardener and architect Humphry Repton. His proposals for a flower garden near the house at Uppark included 'a whimsical arrangement of plants ... in such order that a dial or clock was produced by the time of opening and shutting of certain flowers'.

Humphry and John Adey Repton's design for a greenhouse at Gunton Park in Norfolk, 1816. In front of the little neo-classical building is a flower garden designed as an outdoor room with 'furniture' in the form of tall stands supporting baskets of flowers. They seem to be derived from the tripod candlestands which were almost invariably placed in the four corners of a room.

This scheme proved impossible, but with the help of Repton's drawing, Lady Meade-Fetherstonhaugh made the 'Sundial Bed' in 1933. At Osterley, around the year 1800, flower-beds were created in front of Robert Adam's Garden House. Known as the Pleasure Ground, they have recently been restored and filled with the appropriate plants.

Many flowers were grown in greenhouses, conservatories or orangeries – the words are interchangeable. Some were put up especially to house camellias that were first brought from China in 1792 in East India Company ships. When the 1st Earl Brownlow inherited Belton House in Lincolnshire in 1807, a priority was to build a large conservatory. Jeffry Wyatville not only designed the building, but his plans also include the positioning of the flower-beds, along with two aviaries and a statue of Flora. It survives intact, with camellias over 30 feet (10 metres) high, abutilons and fuchsias. The camellias in their season now decorate the rooms at Belton, floating like little rafts in silver bowls.

In 1818 Lewis Wyatt designed a large conservatory for the Egerton family at Tatton Park in Cheshire. This still contains plants introduced to England before 1818, including dracaenas and acacias from Australasia. Originally it was joined to the house by a long corridor.

These are very grand examples of greenhouses. In 1823 A.C. Pugin wrote of 'the rapid improvement that has taken place in the manufacture of cast iron'. This and other technical developments meant that these houses could be heated more cheaply and efficiently with water rather than with flues or steam, and that larger panes of glass could be made. These advances, and the removal of the punitive glass tax in 1845, meant that greenhouses were no longer the privilege of the rich. Even the humblest house could have a miniature greenhouse inside the room thanks to the invention of the Wardian case. Although designed for transporting plants (see page 116), it could be used in a room for displaying decorative plants on a table or on legs of its own. The idea progressed to glass covers fitted over urns and vases, and to larger greenhouse covers attached to the insides or outsides of windows, known as 'window conservatories'.

For those living in suburban villas with smaller gardens, a whole succession of books provided advice not only on what plants to choose and how to cultivate them, but also sometimes where to place them in the house. Walter Nicol published his *Villa Garden Directory* in 1809, John Loudon *The Greenhouse Companion* in 1824, and his wife Jane *Gardening for Ladies*, 1841, *The Amateur Gardener*, 1847, and *The Ladies Flower Garden*, 1848.

Aspiring gardeners could also get ideas from the gardening journals. The indefatigable John Loudon started the *Gardener's Magazine* in 1826 and it continued until his death in 1843. This was widely read by the new owners of suburban gardens. The *Horticultural Journal*, with its results of floral competitions, had a more sophisticated audience. It first appeared in 1833, became the *Gardener's Gazette* three years later, and continued publication until 1847. The first weekly gardening newspaper was the *Gardener's Chronicle*, started in 1841 and seeing out the rest of the century. The leading light in this enterprise was Joseph Paxton, head gardener to the 6th Duke of Devonshire at Chatsworth in Derbyshire, and designer in 1851 of the Crystal Palace for the Great Exhibition.

For those living in the centre of town, battling with pollution from coal fires, cultivating flowers was not so easy. As James Mangles points out in his *Floral Calendar* of 1839, 'The

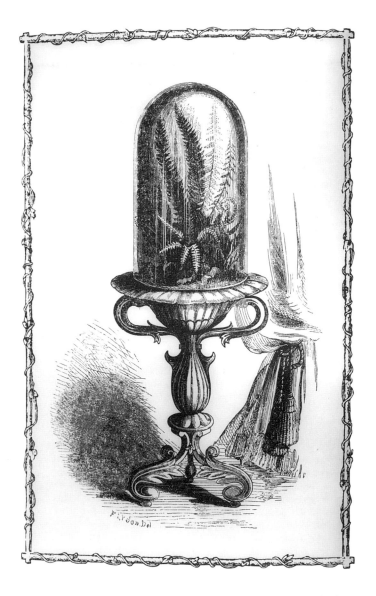

A glass cover over a small plant stand forms a miniature conservatory in which to display ferns; from Shirley Hibberd's *Rustic Adornments for Homes of Taste*, published in 1856.

difficulties which beset the amateur florist in London are great and almost irremediable; day and night he has to contend incessantly with a poisonous atmosphere – no skill or art – no assiduity of care – will protect his plants from the destructive infection of the pernicious blacks; their withering influence will baffle all his precautions.'

To relieve the metropolitan amateur of his troubles, nurserymen hired out plants by the night, the week, the month, or any time that was wanted. The longer contracts included weekly care by professional gardeners who pruned or replaced the plants when necessary. One early example of this service was offered in 1816 by James Cochrane operating from 7 Duke Street on the corner of Grosvenor Square in London. His clientele included the nobility, successful merchants and tradesmen. As well as keeping his customers' rooms regularly furnished, he hired out vast quantities of plants for their routs, fêtes and other parties (see page 146).

The plant seller by Jacques-Laurent Agasse, painted in 1822. The donkey waits patiently with plants set on special staging in his cart, a large white rhododendron and an arum lily to the fore. The salesman conducts negotiations with the children of the house for the purchase of a potted plant.

Bunches of mixed flowers, usually called bouquets, could be bought from nurserymen, from stallholders in city markets such as Covent Garden and from street vendors. As yet there were no florists' shops as we know them today, specialising in cut flowers. The original meaning of the term florist was an amateur who specialised in growing different kinds of a single plant. In the seventeenth century horticultural enthusiasts from the English landed classes joined forces with French Huguenot immigrants to establish florists' societies where they could exchange information and plants, and discuss the finer points of their cultivation. The first was founded in Norwich in 1631, and a society was set up in London's Spitalfields in 1676. The flowers that particularly fascinated them were carnations, anemones, auriculas, tulips, ranunculi and hyacinths, which were thus known as florists' flowers.

By the late eighteenth century, these societies were in decline, to be overtaken in the early nineteenth century by local horticultural societies (see page 115). Meanwhile the term florist was adopted by shopkeepers who sold flowers from their fixed premises. The first and perhaps the most famous of these was Jules Lachaume, who opened a boutique on Chaussée d'Antin in Paris in 1840. In 1897 the establishment moved to the Rue Royale, where it can be visited today.

Lachaume was more than a trader. He created floral compositions, specialising in the art of 'composing wreaths, adornments and bouquets of all kinds for balls and parties'. These works of art were made up by his wife, Adde, with a whole team of female assistants, ranging from the lowly winder up to the 'white' who worked only with delicate white flowers such as guelder roses, gardenias and camellias.

Jules Lachaume also wrote the first book entirely on the subject of flower arrangements, *Les Fleurs Naturelles*, published in 1847. He hoped that his book might be useful for 'les dames Parisiennes and indispensable in the provinces, for no florist I know has had the idea of publishing a manual of his art'. It proved indispensable beyond the shores of France, preceding the first English book of this kind by fifteen years.

As the eighteenth century drew to a close, so the very formal manner of living, maintained through the centuries by the wealthy and privileged, gave way to a more relaxed social style in fashionable households. No longer did people sit in a circle on chairs brought away from the wall for the occasion; instead, they gathered in scattered informal groups, creating 'islands' for different activities around furniture that was now placed permanently in the centre of the room. Sofas were swung out from the walls, often on either side of a fireplace, and cabinetmakers produced new 'sofa tables' to stand beside them, replacing the earlier tripod work tables. Round tables were introduced to occupy the centre of the room. There were now more places to display flowers, and plant stands became so much part of the furniture that the fashionable furniture-makers, Gillow & Co., showed them filled with pots of plants in their room plans.

The number of rooms used for 'living in' increased. Morning rooms were introduced, often sited to avoid the eastern light. Boudoirs were no longer used for dressing, but as sitting rooms for ladies. Rooms that had traditionally been sparsely furnished, such as long galleries and halls, were now also used as sitting rooms, filled with furniture.

Cut flowers continued to be arranged in vases in mixed bunches, still with no attempt to create a colour scheme in the arrangement or to match its colours with those of the room. Greenery was seldom included, and if it was, usually belonged to one of the flowers. The arrangements were still often haphazard or asymmetrical, though the idea of producing a mound or pyramid shape was growing apace.

As earlier, one or two favourite flowers might be displayed alone. In March 1828 the authoress Maria Edgeworth wrote from Ireland to her friend Rachel Lazarus in North Carolina of the anemone which she had been sent from New York:

Mr Prince, proprietor of the Linnaean Botanic Garden at New York, sent me nicely packed in some wet moss some anemones rooted, now all alive! One of them, the

spotless anemone, with a beautiful star-shaped white flower rising from green leaves trefoil shaped, is now standing beside me on our library table and is the admiration of all beholders. It is called in Ree's Encyclopaedia the Rue-leaved Anemone, and I see it is accounted a hardy plant, so I shall take care not to kill it with too much care.

Many of the vases used for early nineteenth-century arrangements were similar to their predecessors – bowls, beakers, urns and vases of baluster, semi-circular, ovoid or decanter shape – but they tended to be larger and more solid. Bowls supported by a central leg or a trio of figures were popular. A ledge resting on top of the vase might be pierced with small holes for single flowers, or with larger ones for growing bulbs in water: sometimes the ledge would have both small and large holes for dual purpose. Some vases had interior metal fittings to hold the flowers in position at top and bottom.

Derby and other porcelain factories made beautifully decorated flared vases in the shape of a modern flower pot. With holes in the bottom and bases to stand on to catch any drips, they were designed for growing plants. The shape which in the eighteenth century was called a bottle or wine glass cooler was now made for flowers and known as a *cache-pot* or *jardinière*. Terracotta pots containing the plants could be hidden inside them.

Bulbs continued to be grown in water in 'glasses' made especially for them by glassware manufacturers. Porcelain factories, including Derby, Worcester and Pinxton, also made semi-circular bulb pots. Walter Nicol in *Villa Garden Directory*, published in 1809, listed

Sir John Soane's 1822 design for a lady's dressing room at Pellwall House in Staffordshire, showing a clock flanked by urns of flowers on the mantelpiece, a characteristic form of decoration of the period.

bulbs that he felt were particularly appropriate for keeping in rooms: *Crinum americanum*, crocus, hyacinth, jonquil (single and double), Persian iris, ixia, lily, narcissus, tuberose and tulips. He advised that those to be grown in water could be put into the glasses at any time from October to January.

The vases and pots were produced in pairs and in sets so that they looked effective when placed symmetrically on mantelpieces (from the nineteenth century the word 'mantelpiece' replaced the earlier 'chimneypiece'). Sometimes a third vase in a different shape or other ornaments were added to the ensemble. In Thomas Hope's design, made in 1807 for the Flaxman Room at his London house in Duchess Street, a large clock is in the middle of the mantelpiece, with a pair of flared vases on either side, filled with low arrangements of cut flowers, and on either side of them, a pair of statues of goddesses. Sir John Soane's design of 1822 for a lady's dressing room at Pellwall House in Staffordshire has large flower-filled urns at either end of the mantelpiece with a clock in the middle, flanked by a pair of ornaments.

Tables in the centres of rooms were particularly good for round bowls or urns, or both together. An illustration of the drawing room at Selsdon House in Surrey, painted by Maria Lushington in 1830, shows two tables and a piano, each decorated with two vases of flowers. One vase is in a tall flared shape, with the rope moulding edge which became popular after the Battle of Trafalgar in 1805. Another is a bowl-shaped vase raised on a central leg. Both are filled with pink roses, and other pink, blue and yellow flowers, in low, slightly rounded arrangements. Further back in the room is a pair of carafe-shaped vases of similar blue, pink and yellow flowers in higher arrangements, standing on a square table.

Design for a flower stand at Belton House in pen and ink with watercolour by Elizabeth Cust, daughter of the 1st Baron Brownlow. The accompanying inscription reads 'Design for *La Citadelle de Flore* being an hors d'oeuvre on each side of the north steps at Belton by E.C. P.O.T., January 12 1818.'

The lady depicted writing letters has moved her desk right into and across the fireplace, so there is no need for flowers to decorate the hearth.

Tables or commodes between windows continued to be a favoured place for flower arrangements. A single vase or basket might be thus displayed, with another put under the table as well. In Ackermann's *Repository* for June 1826, a Gothic patterned basket matches the decoration and furnishings of the room. The pink and yellow roses are crammed in with bell-shaped blue flowers to form a low pyramid. A design by Thomas Hope of 1807 shows a 'flower basket' beneath a table.

The increase in cut flower arrangements was echoed, and indeed overtaken, by the increase in growing plants displayed indoors. Houses now had windows reaching almost to the ground, and French windows opening onto lawns, bringing together the garden and interior. Humphry Repton introduced into England the idea of flower-beds in the form of flower baskets, inspired by the circular *corbeilles* in late eighteenth-century French gardens. As early as 1791 he designed a 'corbeille for flowers' for Lady Wake's flower garden at Courteenhall in Northamptonshire, and in 1808 he proposed a multitude of circular flower-beds framed in basketwork for the garden of the Prince Regent's Royal Pavilion at Brighton.

Repton's outdoor baskets had sides of interwoven metal or wood, and the illusion of bases, and stood on the lawn. His son, John Adey Repton sketched two such baskets in 1823 for reference for Lady Suffield at Blickling. His examples had metal strands resembling the fashionable rope mouldings. It proved irresistible to go a step further and bring these 'flower baskets' indoors. Indoor baskets were made of cane or wire, with solid bases, which could stand on the floor of the room, with pots of flowers growing in them. In February 1827 Prince Pückler-Muskau wrote in a letter from Cobham Hall in Kent, 'I took leave of Lady Darnley in her own room … furnished with delightful disorder … and the floor covered with splendid camellias in baskets, looking as if they grew there.'

John Adey Repton's drawing for a 'Hardenberg Basket', which he appended to a letter to Lady Suffield at Blickling Hall in 1823. The wooden basket, named after Prince Hardenberg for whom he had worked in Germany, was to be filled with roses and form the centre of a parterre. But baskets like these were also being used for flower arrangements that stood on the floor within the house.

Close relations of these baskets were made in solid materials. One of the more unusual examples is in the library at Ickworth in Suffolk. Made in the 1820s, it is of japanned metal with Louis XVI arabesque decoration and Egyptian sphinx feet. Another, possibly in pottery, appears on the floor by a window in a painting by C. Wild of the library at Frogmore in 1817.

The next step was to raise the baskets, now of rectangular or oblong shape, onto legs. There are two examples at Charlecote Park in Warwickshire, consisting of lead-lined, oval cane baskets resting on tripod wooden legs. They are now used to display pots of plants. At Stourhead House in Wiltshire, white painted plant stands in the shape of wooden sarcophagi, designed by Thomas Chippendale Junior, are in every window embrasure of the rooms along the entrance front.

Plant stands of wire and iron were made in a multitude of fancy shapes and designs: they can still be found quite easily in sale rooms and antique shops. Several three-tiered semi-circular examples are stored at Dunham Massey in Cheshire, each tier having a removable metal tray. Shirley Hibberd illustrates one in his book, *Rustic Adornments for Homes of Taste*, published in 1856. 'They can be bought', he says, 'at any of the established makers of wire and iron ornaments.... Where a greenhouse is well managed, there will be no difficulty in furnishing the stands with a succession of Azaleas, Camellias, Calceolarias, Fairy Roses, Fuchsias, Genistas, Geraniums, Heaths, etc, all through the year.' But, he goes on to warn, 'the moment a plant goes out of bloom, it should be removed and its place supplied with another ... as well might the actors dress and rehearse before the audience as

ABOVE: Banks of flowers growing in stands in the form of baskets on legs dominate this Viennese drawing room, painted by M. Grösser in 1843. Even the chandelier has its decoration of greenery.

LEFT: Early nineteenth-century wire plant stand from Dunham Massey, dressed with appropriate pots of flowers, photographed in the entrance hall at Lyme Park. Bottom tier: azalea (modern variety) and eighteenth-century varieties of pelargonium, 'Scarlet Pet', 'Lady Plymouth' and 'Fragrans'. Middle tier: jasmine, gloxinias, hydrangea, pelargoniums. Top tier: stephanotis and gardenias.

A *Country Life* photograph taken in 1941, with a plant in a pot on an elaborate plant stand in the Saloon at Uppark. This stand is described as a 'handsome tripod stand for flowers supported by carved feet' in a bill presented to Sir Harry Fetherstonhaugh by William Summers, a stove manufacturer, in 1835.

a collection of plants be allowed to present themselves in all their preparatory stages to the eye of either visitor or host'.

Flower baskets were displayed on the top of tall, ornate stands. In 1826 Sir Harry Fetherstonhaugh paid Mr Charles Pepper, a London decorator, for painting and gilding various items of furniture at Uppark, including '4 High Tripod Basket Flower Stands with White and Striped frame' and '1 Flower Stand Pink' with 24 flower pots in pink and green. Nine years later, he bought from William Summers, a stove manufacturer in London, '4 handsome tripod stands for flowers supported by carved feet and fitted with 3 sets of brass open galoche work for flower baskets with copper pans inside the top'.

A feature at Uppark is a dressing room decorated as a 'Print Room' with black and white

The Print Room at Uppark showing some of the early nineteenth-century *trompe l'oeil* pots that decorate the walls below the dado. From the door, going left: stock, a rose bush, a peony, and nigella.

prints within ornamented borders stuck on the walls. These were probably put up by Sir Harry's mother, Sarah, in the late eighteenth century. In the early nineteenth century the space below the dado was filled with 22 *trompe-l'oeil* 'cut-outs' of different plants growing in terracotta pots, imitating the many real plants in pots which, as we know from letters and diaries, were kept in dressing rooms. The 22 plants at Uppark include sweet-scented roses, carnations, honeysuckle, stocks, hyacinths, narcissi, lily of the valley and a violet, as well as orange trees and myrtles. When Uppark was tragically burnt down in 1989, by great good fortune the prints and pots were away being restored. They are now back in place, on view once a month in the rebuilt house.

Very large plants often stood directly on the floor. John Loudon suggested 'a few choice specimens of tall plants in fruit or flower should be distributed in the drawing room: the orange, the camellia, the acacia and tree heaths'. The florist Lachaume not only recommended camellias, but also azaleas and rhododendrons, 'which all need warmth and a lot of water'. Rhododendrons feature too in Maria Edgeworth's correspondence. In May 1813 she reported how she had been given 'a fine large one taller than myself (think how tall that must be!) and broader than my two aunts and you and Honora standing close together. It is at this moment standing in our middle bow window with 16 bunches of flowers upon it, each bunch in rich blow. My dear father is so kind as to water it night and morning.' This would have been *Rhododendron ponticum*: a native of Turkey, imported from Gibraltar in 1763 and now regarded almost as a weed; it then, surprisingly, was cherished as a pot plant. The *Botanical Magazine* of 1803 reported that it forced remarkably well and that large numbers were brought to the London markets 'to ornament our houses in the spring'. Later in the century, many other varieties arrived from the Himalayas and China. At Stourhead, it was the custom to display large rhododendrons in the house. They were subsequently planted in the garden, where they flower to this day.

Walter Nicol's *Villa Garden Directory* gave advice to the rapidly expanding middle classes with substantial houses on the outskirts of London and other cities. One chapter focused on 'The Treatment and Arrangement of Shrubs and Flowers in Rooms'. Nicol assumed that 'the finer exotic plants … are purchased of the nurseryman and florists, procured from friends, or the like', so only gives instructions on how to rear 'the more common plants … Campanulas, Rockets, Stocks, Wallflowers and other choice plants in pots … kept out of doors … plunged into the earth … to be carried into the house in succession as they come into flower.'

The plants should then be placed 'on a bench or table … or on small stages fitted to the windows'. The advantage of the stages on castors was that the plants could be moved to catch the light, to appear at best advantage, and be wheeled from one room to another. 'Plants and flowers', he says, 'should be neatly trained to green painted sticks (some like white for the sake of contrast) and should be tied loosely with bits of green worsted or silk – that is, the feeble kinds.' His very useful list of 'The Kinds of Shrubs and Flowers most generally kept in Rooms' is given in Table 7.

Roses in pots were particularly recommended for indoor display. Red and pink China roses (*R. chinensis* 'Semperflorens' and *R. × odorata* 'Pallida') had arrived in England at the end of the eighteenth century, soon followed by Tea roses, so called because their scent

TABLE 7: Walter Nicol's *Villa Garden Directory*, 1809.

Of the shrubby kinds:
Aucuba Japonica
Arbutus, different species
Balm of Gilead
Camellia Japonica, different varieties
Chrysanthemum Indicum
Clethra arborea
Colutea, the scarlet
Coronilla glauca
Daphne, the sweet scented
Erica or Heath, many species
Fuchsia coccinea
Geranium, many species
Hydrangea Arborescens
Hypericum or St John's Wort, many species
Jasmine, the Yellow Indian
Lobelia Cardinalis, or Cardinal Flower
Maurandia semperflorens
Myrtles, broad-leaved, narrow-leaved, variegated,
    and double flowering

Oleander or Rose Bay
Olive-Tree, different kinds
Orange, Lemon and Shaddock Trees
Passion Flower
Polygala myrtifolia, and other species
Roses, the Indian and Semperflorens
Salvia or Sage, different species
Teucrium or Germander, many kinds
Verbena triphylla, or Vervain

Of the Annual, Biennial, and Perennial Flowers:
Amaranthus, the Globe, Pyramidal, and Tricolor
Balsam, double, many varieties
Campanula Pyramidalis
Carnations, many varieties
Cockscombs
Lily of the Valley
Mignonette
Pinks, many varieties

seemed to resemble tea-leaves. In 1819 John Reeves, a tea inspector for the East India Company, imported fifteen of these from nurseries near Canton. Five years later, John Parks, collecting for the Horticultural Society, brought in yellow roses, *R. Banksiae* 'Lutea' and Parks's yellow tea-scented China, *Rosa × odorata* 'Ochroleuca'. The Sawbridgeworth nurseryman, Thomas Rivers, remarked on how these were to be purchased in a market in Paris 'in pots with their heads partially enveloped in coloured paper in such an elegant and effective manner that it is scarcely possible to avoid being tempted to give two or three francs for such a pretty object.' Rivers's *Rose Amateur's Guide* of 1837 contained a section headed 'Christmas Roses' with precise directions for potting the red Bourbon 'Gloire des Rosomanes', so that its flowers 'may ornament the drawing room in that month above all others in which roses are rich and rare – December'.

The favoured shape for plants in pots, as with cut flower arrangements, was the mound or pyramid. William Paul in *The Rose Garden*, first published in 1848, describes how a rose in a pot should be trained 'When the plants are of three or four years growth ... tier above tier of branches may be arranged, each decreasing in circumference in the ascent, 'til it terminates in a point – in a word a pyramid presents the most pleasing object.' He does, however, allow in some instances a round bush 'especially for such kinds as are of lowly growth'.

Pyramid Mound

To achieve a pyramid effect, the Victorians would have used a metal bouquet stand, as shown in an illustration from Shirley Hibberd's *Rustic Adornments for Homes of Taste* published in 1856.

Oasis has been used here instead, carving two pieces to make the appropriate shape. These were soaked and placed in the vase. Two garden canes were stuck down the middle to keep the structure secure. The flowers were then pushed into the oasis, moving from the largest to the smallest.

The flowers that were used in this arrangement were red and blue anemones, guelder roses, tree heath, red pom-pom dahlias, *Fuchsia thalia* 'Timlin Brened', and hydrangeas.

Joseph Nash's watercolour of the Great Hall at Stafford House (now Lancaster House) in London, 1850. The magnificence of the setting is reflected by the massive flower stands that flank the grand staircase and the high vases of flowers set precariously on slender columns. In contrast, to accord with the fashion of the day as described by Lord Ronald Gower, the Duchess of Sutherland's brother, the hall has been 'converted into a most commodious sitting room', with armchairs surrounding tables decorated with simple vases of flowers.

Entrance halls were made to look welcoming with flowers and plants, whether in stately homes or suburban villas. In a watercolour painted in 1850 by Joseph Nash of the Great Hall at the Duke of Sutherland's London house (now known as Lancaster House) every aspect of the architecture and contents is formal and symmetrical, and the flowers follow suit. Pairs of massive flower stands crowned with mounds of cut flowers flank the entrance and the staircase, and stand in the corners of the half landing. Two surprisingly small arrangements of cut flowers are placed on each of the six tables that furnish the hall. When Mary Elizabeth Lucy from Charlecote Park attended a reception held by the Duke and Duchess of Sutherland for the Grand Duke Constantine of Russia in the summer of 1847, the hall presented a very different appearance, with 'perfect showers of roses and garlands hanging from pillar to pillar'.

The architect and designer J.B. Papworth in 1818 gave his original and very different ideas for the decoration of the hall in a *cottage orné* – a medium-sized house with the attributes of a cottage, such as a thatched roof. He decreed that the hall and staircase be decorated with 'trellising composed of light lath and wicker basket work ... painted a dark green'. To this were attached brackets on which 'the most elegantly beautiful flowers' could be displayed in green porcelain pots. As if this wasn't enough, in 'the parlour, the music-room and the lobby ... upright flower-stands of basket work are placed in each angle of the room, and the verandah is constantly dressed with plants of the choicest scents and colours'.

An illustration from the *Journal of Horticulture* of April 1862 showing the massing of flowering plants that became the style for entrance halls and staircases. Pelargoniums trimmed into pyramids stand on the brackets: sometimes at night they alternated with candelabra. Beneath them, for contrast, hydrangeas grown with a single stem and round bushy tops alternate with climbing plants of *maurandya* neatly trained to tall rods.

Both A.C. Pugin and Ackermann designed rather cumbersome stands for entrance halls that incorporated lamps and goldfish bowls as well as shelves, brackets and bowls for flowers. Eighteenth-century Chinese porcelain bowls that used to accommodate goldfish were now brought into service as *cache-pots* – at Wallington there is one in the saloon on a stand, and likewise at Belton.

An early nineteenth-century watercolour by Nicolas Condy of the hall at Antony in Cornwall shows a vast arrangement of cut flowers in the fireplace. They are in a large tub that had perhaps been brought in from the garden, or perhaps it is a variation of Wedgwood's 'Devonshire Flower pot', first produced in 1778. Always the canny marketing man, Josiah Wedgwood used to name lines after leading members of high society, and decided to name these particular pots, which were rather a dull brown hooped with green, after Georgiana, Duchess of Devonshire – an irony as she was the outstanding beauty of her day. In the Antony painting the tub stands on the hearth, and flanking it, on either side of the chimneypiece, are two urns on solid stands.

Flowers overflowed from indoor rooms into conservatories attached to the house. A magnificent example was built for the Prince Regent at Carlton House in London in 1807 to the designs of Thomas Hopper, modelled on Henry VII's chapel in Westminster Abbey. This vast and ornate room lasted less than twenty years before being demolished along with the rest of Carlton House, but in that time was used for the Prince's lavish parties.

In Russia conservatories were known as winter gardens. They were used for balls and

BELOW: Drawing by Emma Trevelyan of her sister Beatrice in the Saloon at Wallington in 1827. In front of her is a large *famille rose* bowl, used in the eighteenth century as a fishbowl but by now for the display of plants, set on a gilt stand. The plants shown are probably red hot pokers, while a *cachepot* on the right, in blue and white ware, contains cyclamen.

RIGHT: Thirty-two years later, when William Bell Scott painted Sir Walter Calverley Trevelyan's portrait, the venerable bowl was planted with arum lilies and set on a table.

entertaining, and were kept warm with huge stoves. A watercolour from the 1830s of the Winter Garden at Pavlino, shows it decorated with pots of hydrangeas, climbing roses, clematis and a pergola of bamboo canes supporting ferns and delicate climbers such as white jasmine and plumbago. A profusion of plants indoors helped Russians to endure the long, freezing winters. On 29 September 1836 Lady Londonderry during her travels in Russia noted with interest in her diary that at the Winter Palace in St Petersburg: 'They have excellent contrivances for flowers ... large stands for filling up corridors and fireplaces and recesses and a particularly pretty manner of portioning off corners or posts

Nicholas Condy's watercolour of the hall at Antony, painted in the 1830s. While the Carew estates are being pointed out to admiring visitors at the front of the picture, the fireplace in the room beyond is shown filled with a large tub of flowers.

[parts] of rooms by railing or *Treillages* on which creepers are trained having their roots in a box on the ground.'

In 1820, after visiting Badminton in Gloucestershire, Maria Edgeworth wrote to her sister Honora to tell her of conservatories being attached to houses: 'How this luxury of conservatories added to rooms and opening into them has become general – enlivening old thick-walled mansions as well as new built boxes.' At Elford in Staffordshire she found that the dining room had 'glass doors into a jewel of a little greenhouse … thus December seems the middle of summer'. At High Wycombe in Buckinghamshire she wrote 'we met in the library, the most agreeable room I ever was in, opening into a conservatory full of roses and flowers of every hue in bloom'.

Conservatories added to libraries seem to have been particularly popular. Henry Edward Kendall made a watercolour design *c.*1842 for a splendid conservatory to be attached to the library at Wimpole Hall in Cambridgeshire. Palm trees, flowering shrubs and plants are shown in 'flower-beds' sunk into the floor, while antique urns are raised high on plinths. The oil chandeliers would have made it easier to use the conservatory after dark, and it was used as a 'sitting out' room during the great balls given by the 4th Earl of Hardwicke who entertained Queen Victoria and Prince Albert here in 1843. A second design shows the large potting ground backing onto the blank back wall of the library. This serves as a reminder of the huge amounts of plants constantly being brought in and out of the house

A Russian Winter Garden, c.1835–38, a watercolour attributed to Vasily Semenovic Sadovnikov. Pots of hydrangeas, roses, clematis, camellias and other flowers are massed in groups round the walls and columns. The bamboo pergola, furnished with *chinoiserie* cane seats, is covered with delicate climbers such as plumbago and jasmine, and crowned with waving ferns. Large squares of parquet have been laid on the floor in preparation for a ball. The winter garden was in a wing of Pavlino, the eighteenth-century house owned by Prince Wittgenstein, probably on his estate near St Petersburg.

and conservatory, and in need of repotting. A small lobby between the library and the potting ground was used as a collection point for indoor servants and gardeners.

One of the Prince Regent's spectacular parties in his conservatory at Carlton House took place on 19 June 1811 to celebrate George III's Golden Jubilee. Over two hundred guests sat down to dinner at supper tables 200 feet (60 metres) long stretched down the conservatory, out into the garden and under marquees. In front of the Prince Regent, at the grand supper table, was a basin of water, with an 'enriched temple' in the centre of it; and from this fountain, down the whole length of the table, meandered a stream which was bordered with moss, and aquatic flowers, spanned by three or four fantastic bridges, and filled with frolicking gold and silver fish.

Tom Moore, author of the popular *Irish Ballads*, was enchanted: 'It was in *reality* all that they try to imitate in the gorgeous scenery of the theatre.' Fellow poet Percy Bysshe Shelley, maybe because he was not invited, took a much dimmer view: 'What think you of the bubbling *brooks* and mossy *banks* at Carlton House, the *allées vertes* etc?' he asked a friend the next day. 'It is said that this entertainment will cost £120,000. Nor will it be the last bauble which the nation must buy to amuse this overgrown bantling of Regency.' The invoice submitted to the Prince Regent by Curtis and Salisbury, Nurserymen at the Botanic Garden, Brompton, gives a long list of plants supplied, including 'Fine Palms'. This is an unusually early reference to palms being used for indoor decoration, twenty-five on the grand staircase, sixteen in the Grecian Hall, and twelve standing on the sideboard.

Edward Kendall's watercolour design for a conservatory at Wimpole Hall, *c*.1842, built for the 4th Earl of Hardwicke so that he could entertain Queen Victoria and Prince Albert in a suitably grand manner. Like many early nineteenth-century conservatories, it leads directly out of the library, and has taken on the furnishings of a sculpture gallery. Colza-oil chandeliers enabled it to be used for evening parties. Sadly the conservatory was demolished after the Second World War.

Soon after this party, the popularity of artificial gardens for dining rooms went into decline. The plateau continued to run down the middle of the table during the dessert course, but now it was likely to be decorated with vases of fresh flowers. The hallmark of this period was the pyramid-shaped flower arrangement, with the flowers held in place in special contrivances. In 1830, after dining with Lady Londonderry, Disraeli wrote that there was 'a bouquet by every guest and five immense pyramids of roses down the table'. The decoration had to form a line down the centre of the table. In Flaubert's novel written in 1857, the ambitious Madame Bovary, when dining with the Marquis d'Andervilliers, took careful note that 'bouquets were placed in a long line the whole length of the table'.

Pots of growing shrubs or trees, sometimes bearing ripe fruit, were often placed in silver wine coolers or porcelain *cache-pots*. John Loudon in his *Greenhouse Companion* of 1824 recommended:

> In select entertainments . . . during dinner a few pots of fruit-bearing shrubs, or trees with their fruit ripe, are ranged along the centre of the table, from which, during the dessert, the fruit is gathered by the company. Sometimes a row of orange trees, or standard peach trees, or cherries, or all of them, in fruit, surround the table of the guests; one plant being placed exactly behind each chair, leaving room for the servants to approach between. Sometimes only one tall handsome tree is placed behind the master, and another behind the mistress; and sometimes only a few pots of lesser articles are placed on the side-board, or here and there round the room.

In France it was customary to have baskets of cut flowers on the table, a custom taken up in England in the 1860s (see page 169). In 1847 Lachaume wrote: 'In general, cut flowers are preferable on the table to flowers with roots growing in pots which should be kept to decorate other apartments. In some big houses it is the custom to decorate the tables with baskets of flowers which are put in place at the beginning of the meal, and which are distributed to the ladies after the dessert.' He thought camellias were particularly appropriate, surrounded by heather and leaves twining around the handles of the basket. A pineapple might be placed in the middle of a basket of flowers. And 'sometimes one pays the ladies a compliment by placing a pretty bunch of flowers in their drinking glasses'.

In the 1840s in the grandest establishments it became fashionable to display a large ornate centrepiece, usually of silver or silver gilt, sometimes of porcelain, in the middle of the table. Often this piece was presented in commemoration of an event – Prince Albert designed one for Queen Victoria which included four of her favourite dogs. At Charlecote, one of the two large pieces of table silver that still adorn the dining-room table displays a palm tree, serpent and native figures. It was given in 1842 to Thomas Williamson by the inhabitants of the Provinces of Bombay for his work as a humane administrator.

These complex structures often incorporated dishes for sweetmeats and a vase or tazza at the top for flowers, when they would be known as epergnes. Thomas March, writing in the 1860s (see page 180) disparaged these structures: 'I object to seeing flowers "in the garret" looking down from a perilous height upon the heathen mythology.'

In 1816 the Duke of Wellington was given an elaborate silver and parcel gilt centrepiece by the Portuguese government in gratitude for his help in freeing the country from the

Painting by Louis Haghe of a banquet in the Picture Gallery at Buckingham Palace on 28 June 1853, following the christening of Queen Victoria's fourth son, Prince Leopold. The Queen is seated on the far side of the table, with her son's godfathers. In front of her is the christening cake topped by a pedestal raising on high a fashionable pyramid of flowers. On either side of the cake a silver-gilt plateau runs down the centre of the table decorated, in the fashion of the time, with tall trees and shrubs standing in gilt wine coolers.

clutches of Napoleon. This was used every year at Apsley House, his London home, at a banquet to celebrate the battle of Waterloo. In 1836 William Salter painted a picture of the banquet, showing silk garlands made of narrow pointed leaves with tiny flowers at intervals, linking together the upraised hands of the maidens dancing on the plateau.

For the banquet in 1853, the centrepiece made its annual appearance, but this time flanked on either side by tall trees, nearly 6 feet (2 metres) high, standing in silver wine coolers, and rising out of moss or greenery. The base of trees and shrubs continued to be hidden in this way throughout the century, whether they were standing on a dining-room table, or anywhere else in the house: indeed, even in the garden, trunks of trees were often surrounded by a ring of flowers, the horticultural equivalent of clothing legs of furniture.

We get an idea of the incredible lengths that fashionable society was prepared to go to create magnificent gardens in rooms for parties from the 'Fashionable World' column of the *Morning Post* and from the six daybooks meticulously kept by James Cochrane, a nurseryman, florist and plant contractor.

The *Morning Post* for 30 July 1821 described a party given by the duc de Grammont to celebrate the coronation of George IV:

> The Promenade Saloon ... represented an enchanted grove.... The finest flowers in every species bloomed in beds of a semi-circular form along the sides; and behind them arose, in great abundance, the most beautiful shrubs and orange trees, growing in a state of nature – there were forty waggon-loads!! All above were enlivened by festoons of artificial flowers intermixed with 670 wax-lights, placed in fanciful girandoles.

Kissing Bough

This bough is made up every year at Christmas to hang in the kitchen at Fairfax House in York. Because it is in place for several weeks, artificial apples are used, but real apples are preferable.

2 Fill the basket with yew and pull some sprigs through the wire to cover it. Pile high to give a ball effect.

1 The hanging basket is wired with tubes for candle holders, and has hooks for the apples at the bottom and a chain for hanging. Hang the basket at shoulder height for easy management.

Collect a good mix of variegated and plain holly, preferably with berries, bunches of green and golden yew or another dense evergreen, a bunch of mistletoe. Buy false berries if natural ones are not available, eight large red apples, and four church candles, 1 foot (30 centimetres) high, and 1 inch (2·5 centimetres) in diameter.

3 Cut holly into sprigs and push into basket from the outside to fill out the ball. Push the mistletoe into the bottom of the basket so that it hangs down a little.

4 Push apples securely onto wire hooks and place candles in holders. Take care to balance the arrangements. Hang from the ceiling hook just above head height, light candles, and kiss lover.

For the 'beau monde' in the Season, James Cochrane hired out enormous quantities of flowers and shrubs from his shop in Duke Street. He grew plants in his nursery at Paddington, supplementing them with supplies from neighbouring nurserymen. Not only did he supply the plants, but set them up with his team of gardeners, earning much praise from the 'Fashionable World' for his 'happy disposition' of plants at routs and fêtes. The most popular plants leased out for the night were a combination of mignonette (*Reseda odorata*), stocks (*Matthiola incana*) and heartsease (*Viola tricolor*). Other favourites were verbena, pelargoniums, myrtle, pinks, heaths, sweet briar and orange trees. Cochrane also supplied laurel, wreaths and boughs of evergreen to decorate staircase balustrades and passage walls, and vases of cut flowers to fill fireplaces.

Not everyone employed professionals to set up for them. A young Irish visitor to London, Miss Sydney Owenson, already a successful novelist, gives an amusing account of the preparations for a rout at the Duchess of Gordon's house in 1810. Sydney arrived to find the footmen, porters and pages scurrying about half dressed. As she sauntered through the rooms:

> a loud hammering induced me to look back, and there mounted on a step-ladder stood a bulky lady, in a dimity wrapper and a round eared cap, knocking up a garland of laurel over the picture of some great captain of that day. . . . As I took the elderly lady for a housekeeper, I asked her if the Duchess was still in her dressing room? 'No child' said the elderly lady, 'the Duchess is here, *telle que vous le voyez*, doing that which she can get none of her awkward squad to do for her', and down sprang the active lady of seventy, with a deep inspiration of fatigue, ejaculating, 'Gude God, but this pleasure is a toilsome thing'. So saying, she bustled off, and in less time than can be imagined reappeared in the brightest spirits and the brightest diamonds.

Garlands of greenery have traditionally been used at Christmas. The way in which they were employed in the late eighteenth and early nineteenth centuries can be seen at Fairfax House, built in the 1760s by Viscount Fairfax and now looked after by the York Civic Trust. Every year from the beginning of December until Twelfth Night, the rooms are decorated. Garlands are draped over the frame of a portrait above the dining-room mantelpiece, in imitation of those described in a diary account in the Woburn Abbey archive. George Gent's *Sketchbook*, 1820, noted that the 'heroic ancestor' of his host had been venerated in this way for the Christmas celebrations.

At Fairfax House garlands are also spread along mantelpieces, round columns and festooned above the sideboard in the dining room. Sprigs of holly appear in every available container and, inspired by late eighteenth-century engravings, decorate the windowpanes. Pendants made of medallions of greenery attached to ribbon decorate the hall, and a kissing bough hangs in the kitchen.

It was during the late eighteenth century that Christmas trees probably first appeared in Britain. They were introduced by Queen Charlotte, who would have enjoyed them as a child in Germany where the custom was prevalent. Our first reference to them comes in the diaries of the Hon. Georgina Townshend, State Housekeeper at Windsor Castle, recorded in 1799:

The Queen entertained the children here, Christmas evening, with a German fashion. A fir tree, about as high again as any of us, lighted all over with small tapers, several little wax dolls among the branches in different places, and strings of almonds and raisins alternately tied from one to the other, with skipping ropes for the boys, and each bigger girl had muslin for a frock, a muslin handkerchief, and a pretty necklace and earrings besides. As soon as all the things were delivered out by the Queen and Princesses, the candles on the tree were put out . . .

Adelaide, consort of William IV, was also a German princess, from Saxe-Meiningen. She had a decorated tree at her Christmas parties for children in the Dragon Room at Brighton Pavilion. Queen Victoria, too, had one as a child, but it was not until she and Prince Albert initiated their family Christmas celebrations that trees became generally popular in Britain.

At Saltram in October 1810, Lady Boringdon wrote to her sister-in-law, describing the success of a ball: 'The Saloon was prepared for the dancing and looked quite brilliant and beautiful – We lighted it by hanging lamps over the windows and putting a quantity of candles over the doors, the places in which they were fixed being concealed by large wreaths and festoons of leaves and flowers beautiful to behold. . .'. Wreaths and garlands of flowers, then as now, were useful for covering up anything unsightly, often in combination with candles and lamps.

John Loudon provided valuable advice to his readers in his *Greenhouse Companion* on how to arrange their plants at routs:

[They] must be tastefully arranged individually by rods and threads. The soil should be covered with moss, and the pot either cleaned and painted in any appropriate body colour, or chalked, or covered with coloured paper. An earthen brown with black and gray lines is among the most suitable colours, whether for the temporary painting, chalking or papering. Where they are to decorate the apartments for two or three days in succession, they should be set in saucers on a little gravel, and over the gravel the saucer filled brimful with moss or fine turf.

He goes on to advise on the decoration appropriate for the different rooms, including a quincunx (arranged in the pattern of five spots on a dice) of orange trees in the drawing room, with cages of nightingales and canary birds in the branches, and groves, caves and grottoes for the picture gallery. His advice is echoed by Lachaume's *Les Fleurs Naturelles*, where he has a chapter headed '*Decoration de bals et soirées*': 'For the most successful parties it is necessary to launch out and have flowers everywhere. From the hall to the boudoir, every room must be covered with flowers on the day of a reception and become a Temple of Flora.'

CHAPTER FIVE

A Pleasing Air of Sprightliness

1850-1890

When 'one of Her Majesty's Servants' wrote an account of life in Queen Victoria's household in 1897, her preference for simple flowers was noted. The Queen's private sitting room at Osborne House, her retreat on the Isle of Wight, gave the impression 'of extreme simplicity and homeliness … on the broad mantelshelf are four vases containing flowers, some half-dozen cartes-de-visite in frames, and a pair of five light candelabras, and two small white busts.... A large round table bears, amid a host of minor objects, a huge vase of flowers which as often as not are from the fields and hedgerows.'

The home life of the Queen may have been simple, but the horticultural arrangements for her palaces certainly were not. At Frogmore a vast walled garden was laid out for her. Surrounded by two miles of high brick wall, it was divided into eight portions, each under a foreman responsible to the head gardener. It supplied not only Windsor Castle, but all the other royal residences as well – Buckingham Palace, Osborne House, Balmoral Castle in Aberdeenshire – with flowers, fruit and vegetables all the year round. Flowers for special occasions were also supplied to the Queen's wide family circle. In 1858, 3,304 boxes of cut flowers were dispatched.

'Her Majesty's Servant' described the hierarchy of staff ensuring the flowers reached their various destinations. At Windsor Castle:

> The vast daily orders of fruit, flowers and vegetables required for the castle consumption are received by Mr Thomas [the head gardener] from the various departments every morning. The Clerk of the Kitchen, the chef, and the Table Deckers whose business it is to arrange Her Majesty's board, all state to him what they want. Certain other servants are deputed to change the great plants and palms that stand in the Grand Corridor, while an entirely separate order is given for flowers wherewith to decorate Her Majesty's private apartments.

This elaborate organisation, positively medieval in its hierarchy, was reflected on a slightly more modest scale in the mansions of Britain. For these families this was a time of great prosperity, enabling many to enlarge and transform their reasonably sized classical houses into variations of St Pancras Station, and others to start from scratch, building on a grand scale. Technological developments and a huge labour force of servants ensured the height of comfort for the privileged and the wealthy.

A photograph of Queen Victoria with her youngest daughter, Princess Beatrice, in her private sitting room at Windsor Castle, 1895. The room is full of vases of flowers.

A late nineteenth-century photograph of the interior of the Palm House at Cragside, taken for the catalogue of the manufacturers, Mackenzie & Moncur Ltd of Edinburgh. On the right, stephanotis, plumbago and passion-flowers rampage up the columns of the building. On the left, a large *Agave americana* is surrounded by flowering plants, while the head gardener can be seen standing beside a kentia palm.

RIGHT: Interior of the Orchard House at Cragside, showing some of the revolving pots that allow the fruit to ripen evenly. Although this ingenious invention was probably Sir William Armstrong's, it was his wife Margaret who was responsible for much of the planning of the various glasshouses, and who corresponded with Mackenzie & Moncur about the heating apparatus. The fruit is still grown in the nineteenth-century Cragside manner, with nectarines, peaches and pears trained as pyramids, apples on U cordons, grapes on the rod and spur system, and oranges in bush form.

One such was Sir William Armstrong, later Lord Armstrong, a successful industrialist, who in 1863 bought land in the wilds of Northumberland and started to build his house, Cragside. He also created a magnificent garden out of the bare hillside and rugged crags. His walled kitchen gardens were added in 1870, including hothouses which enabled fruit and flowers of the highest quality to be produced throughout the year, despite the harsh Northumbrian climate. There were houses for forcing, and cold-frames for 'holding back'.

The Glasshouse Range consisted of, first, a Palm House which, in addition to palms, had stephanotis climbing up the pillars and other exotic flowers, all of which were cut for indoor arrangements. Next came a Tropical Fernery, which contained ornamental leaved plants, in particular begonias. The Temperate Fernery housed quantities of maidenhair fern (*Adiantum capillus-veneris*) and ladder fern (*Nephrolepis cordifolia*) grown as pot plants and for cutting. Last came the Orchard House, the only one to survive intact. One hundred feet (30 metres) long, it was divided into three compartments to contain enough fruit to supply the house for the entire year – peaches, nectarines, apricots, pears and mulberries trained to grow as pyramids, grapes and apples on trellis frames, and bush figs.

All these grew, and still do so, in large pots made from giant water-pipes designed by Sir William, a skilled engineer and chairman of the Whittle Dene Water Company. At a touch of the hand they would swivel round so that the fruit could be perfectly ripened on all sides. The fruit was as decorative as the sweet violets, passion flowers and other flowers which also flourished in the warmth of the Orchard House.

Many houses, large and small, had a fern house or fernery; the latter term also applies to a collection of ferns growing in the open air. Such a collection can be seen at Sizergh Castle

ABOVE: The Fernery at Tatton Park, designed by Joseph Paxton for the 1st Baron Egerton in 1859, to house the family's collection of tree ferns from New Zealand. The collection includes *Dicksonia antarctica* and *Cyathea* species, and plants of *Woodwardia radicans*, a semi-hardy fern that, interspersed with clumps of agapanthus, covers the floor. *Ficus pumila* (creeping fig) covers the walls.

RIGHT: Maidenhair fern in an oriental pot on an ornamental stand. This detail from a watercolour is one of several painted by H. H. Emmerson and J. T. Dixon for an album presented by the people of Rothbury to Sir William and Lady Armstrong after the visit to Cragside of the Prince and Princess of Wales in 1884.

in Cumbria, where over a hundred varieties of hardy fern grow in the large rock garden. One of the few fern houses to survive is at Tatton Park in Cheshire. It was designed by Joseph Paxton for the Egerton family in 1859 to house the tree ferns collected in New Zealand by Captain Charles Randle Egerton. Their rapid growth necessitated the raising of the roof at the end of the century.

The Victorian fern craze reached dizzy heights in 1851 when Wardian cases filled with ferns were exhibited at the Great Exhibition in the Crystal Palace in Hyde Park. Those on a modest income could keep half a dozen pots under a glass bell, and in 1866 John Smith, the Kew expert, pronounced that 'ownership of a fernery extended even to the hardworking mechanic'.

From the 1830s they had been collected by keen botanists. On 12 December 1834 Pauline Jermyn had won the heart of Walter Calverley Trevelyan by presenting him with a species of his favourite maidenhair fern 'from a locality near St Ives', and on that day they became engaged. Both were botanists, probably brought together by their passion for collecting ferns. They later inherited the great house of Wallington in Northumberland.

Fern mania was swiftly followed by foliage mania. The prolific gardening writer Shirley Hibberd published *The Fern Garden* in 1869, but the next year he produced *New and Rare Beautiful-Leaved Plants*, illustrating some of the newly introduced varieties with their splashes, stripes and variegations in the brightest of colours. 'It is but recently', he wrote, 'that the beauty of leaves has been fully recognised and the passion that has arisen for collecting and cultivating fine foliaged plants is one of the newest.' But, he reassures readers, 'Beautiful leaves will not elbow flowering plants aside, but will enhance their beauty by contrast'.

Queen Victoria was an ardent admirer. At Windsor Castle in 1881 one of her foreman gardeners, probably Mr John Jones, noted in his daybook that he was kept busy potting up these dazzling plants from the Far East – dracaenas, crotons, begonias – and from South America – caladiums and coleus. Regularly, the day before the Queen arrived at Windsor, he was 'filling in with plants at the castle'.

The head gardener at Cragside not only had to supply the house across the valley with perfect displays every day, but also ensure that fresh flowers and plants were sent to the Armstrong house in London. The northward spread of the railway made it possible for him to send plants and flowers on an almost daily basis. Cut flowers were wrapped in spinach leaves and tied with raffia. Each bunch was labelled with the name of the room and the vase in which it was to go, then they were packed in hampers amongst moist sphagnum moss. Flowers were never mixed with fruit and vegetables, which produce ethyelene gas that could age them. The hampers were then taken by horse and cart to Rothbury Station and put on the night train for London so that the flowers could be in the vases before the family arose the next day.

The fashion at this period was to cover every surface within a house with cut flowers and growing plants. A flat surface would look quite undressed unless it had at least one, and often several vases of flowers on it, and there were many flat surfaces as rooms became cluttered with items of furniture. Flowering and foliage plants and palm trees in pots crowded

Some of the brilliantly coloured coleus leaves, from plants that can be seen in the Decorative Display House at West Dean Garden.

Photograph taken in 1887 by
Lady Gore Booth of Lady Erne
and her sister, Lady Alice Cole,
in the Blue Drawing Room at
Crom Castle in Co. Fermanagh,
Northern Ireland. The room is
crowded with plants and flowers,
including a pot of flowers atop a
draped sculpted figure, a trumpet
vase on the mantelpiece, and
huge palms in basket containers.

the rooms still further. It is not surprising that the garden designer Gertrude Jekyll was impelled to write at the end of the century: 'There comes a point where the room becomes overloaded with flowers and greenery. During the last few years I have seen many a drawing room where it appeared to be less a room than a thicket.'

The important task of supervising the arranging of this large quantity of flowers was usually allocated to the head gardener. Indeed, he often arranged the flowers for the dining room and main living rooms himself. At Cragside, the head gardener sorted out his flower vases in the Flower Room, in the group of buildings in the walled garden attached to the Glasshouse Range. Nearby was the Cane Room, where canes for supporting the flowers were stored, and raffia for tying them. Beside it was the Basket Room. All these were situated half a mile from the house, so the filled vases were carried there on a flower cart, which has recently been purchased by the National Trust and returned to Cragside. It was carried like a sedan chair with a man at each end. Holes in the boards ensured the vases didn't wobble about, and sides and a cover could be attached if necessary to protect the flowers from wind or rain. The journey was not easy, going down one side of a valley, crossing over the Iron Bridge and up the other side. Finishing touches in the butler's pantry were vital before the vases were placed in the rooms.

Edward Luckhurst, head gardener at Oldlands Hall in Suffolk, wrote about the equipment required for a flower room in the *Journal of Horticulture* in 1881: 'It should contain a table close to the window, another large table or two, a sink with a water tap, a large lofty cupboard with plenty of broad shelves for vases, and a broad shelf or two along any convenient part of the walls.' He advised keeping a supply of charcoal so that a single piece might be placed in every vase to keep the water sweet, while a single drop of gum arabic dissolved in water could be dropped in the centre of a flower to prevent it shedding its petals.

It wasn't always the head gardener who arranged the flowers. Ladies of the house tried their hand too. Mary Gladstone, daughter of the Prime Minister, seems to have arranged the flowers in all her father's homes. On 20 May 1872 she wrote to her cousin Lavinia Lyttleton from Downing Street, 'about a dozen huge boxes of flowers arrived [from Hawarden Castle in Cheshire] ... wildest confusion ... arranged some in jugs, some in basins, some in pots.... The dinner a huge success, rooms lovely, brilliantly lighted, and one mass of flowers.'

Competitions for independent flower arrangements, or table decorations as they were then described, came to be a regular feature of flower shows, enabling professional and amateur gardeners to keep up with the latest fashions in this field. The first such competition was held by the Royal Horticultural Society in 1861, and it was not long before horticultural societies in towns and villages throughout Britain were following suit, encouraging people of all walks of life to take an interest in the subject.

Inspired, no doubt, by these competitions, head gardeners began to contribute articles to the gardening journals describing the indoor decorations they had created, as well as exchanging ideas on how best to cope with the exotic plants flooding into the country that were used in displays, and which were the best varieties to grow. The leading gardening journal, the *Gardener's Chronicle*, was now rivalled by the *Cottage Gardener*, founded in 1848. One authority quipped that the latter was 'more suitable for a double-coach-housed cottage of gentility than for a labourer's cottage', and in 1861 its name was changed to the *Journal of Horticulture*. Magazines such as *The Queen* and *The Illustrated London News* sometimes gave details of the flower arrangements at grand society balls, while *The Lady* and *The Daily Graphic* were amongst the publications that included articles and letters on what had become an increasingly important subject.

Another effect of the flower-arranging competitions was the appearance of the first English books to be written entirely on the subject. Mr March, who achieved fame when he carried off the top prize in the first competition at the Royal Horticultural Society with his ingenious flower stand (see page 178), published his book *Flower and Fruit Decoration* in 1862. In the same year Miss Maling from Norwood published *Flowers for Ornament and Decoration and how to arrange them* and its companion volume, *Indoor Plants and how to grow them*.

The number of flower-arranging books grew, and began specialising in certain areas. In 1877 John Perkins, having worked for 24 years as head gardener to 'the late and present Lord Henniker' at Thornham Hall in Suffolk, published *Floral Decorations for the Table*. Large coloured plans and keys revealed some of his most successful arrangements. Mrs Beeton, or rather her husband Sam, included colour plates of table arrangements in editions from 1888 of the famous *Book of Household Management*.

Ideas about both the style of gardening and of the way flowers and plants should be displayed in the house developed rapidly during the second half of the nineteenth century.

The Ribbon Border at
Peckover House in Wisbech,
Cambridgeshire, planted with
the bands of colour that were
fashionable both in the garden
and in flower arrangements for
the house. In this border the
planting is of busy lizzies, thrift
and London pride, with cotton
lavender and bronze cordylines.

And the style of flower arranging paralleled the style of gardening. By the 1850s, old-fashioned hardy flowers and shrubs had been pushed out of the flower-beds round the house in pursuit of the craze for 'bedding out'. Bedding out involved filling the beds with low-growing, half-hardy plants that had to be wintered indoors and planted out after the frost. This meant banishing not only hardy flowers, but spring bulbs too. Henry Kingsley wrote in *Argosy* that gardeners 'are discontented unless they have their beds brown and bare for six months, and for the other six filled with formal patterns of geraniums, caleolarias and lobelias'. These were planted in thousands in bands or ribbons, or in patterns resembling oilcloth.

Some of the hardy flowers were exiled to the walled garden for cutting. At Biddulph Grange, Maria Bateman was not prepared to do without hardy plants, and Edward Kemp, the landscape gardener, was delighted to find growing in her 'private garden', hidden by tall yew hedges and only visible from the window of her boudoir, 'all the beautiful Delphiniums, Phloxes, Penstemons ... which the modern style of gardening has almost banished from our gardens'. Today they flower there again.

At Wallington the Trevelyans consoled themselves with paintings of their banished hardy plants. In 1852 they decided to roof over the central courtyard of the house and open up the walls to create arcades, transforming the centre into a saloon filled with tropical plants. When Calverley realised that many tropical plants would not survive as the temperature was inadequate, the idea was abandoned. Instead, it was decided that Pauline and their artistic friends should paint their favourite flowers on the pilasters between the arches of the arcade.

The result is an entrancing depiction of mainly 'old-fashioned flowers' painted by members of the Pre-Raphaelite circle on their frequent visits to Wallington. William Bell Scott, a disciple of Rossetti, who was commissioned to paint scenes from Northumbrian history on the spandrels, found time to produce common iris and martagon lilies. Arthur Hughes painted dog rose and sweet briar. Laura Capel Lofft depicted hollyhocks and foxgloves. John Ruskin decided to paint oats and corn cockles, but on being criticised for producing blue cornflowers instead of reddish purple corn cockles, refused in high dudgeon to finish his work.

Now was the time when exotic flowers discovered in the Southern Hemisphere came into their own. Those with enough money could provide the hothouses of varying temperatures essential to their survival, and employ dedicated gardeners with the skill and time to cherish them, and to arrange them indoors in the current fashion, where they showed to advantage on the new flower stands.

From South America came a member of the amaryllis family, a species of *Eucharis* found in Colombia in 1854, and two vigorous climbers that provided masses of blooms for indoor decoration, the yellow-trumpeted *Allamanda cathartica* 'Grandiflora' from Brazil and *Lapageria rosea* with its pendulous tubular red flowers from Chile. The heliotrope had been introduced from Peru back in 1757; now a variety appropriately named 'Beauty of the Boudoir' was much used for cut flowers and as growing plants.

From South Africa came two other amaryllis relations, valotta – *Cyrtanthus elatus* (the Scarborough lily) in 1774, and *Clivia miniata* in 1854. *Stephanotis floribunda*, the Madagascar jasmine, twined up to 10 feet (3 metres) or more, providing quantities of flowers for cutting. From Egypt came *Nymphaea lotus*, the pink-tinged waterlily, so useful for floating in bowls.

Of hardy plants, the most popular introductions were the Japanese *Lilium auratum* in 1862 and pampas grass from South America, which arrived in the mid-nineteenth century. The long plumes proved a favourite indoor decoration.

By the second half of the century, orchids were esteemed above all other flowers. The first tropical orchid to flower in England, *Bletia verecunda*, had been sent from the Bahamas to Peter Collinson in 1731. Loddiges nursery seems to have been the first to cultivate them commercially at the beginning of the nineteenth century, offering three hundred species for sale in 1831. For James Bateman of Biddulph Grange orchids were the 'master passion of his life', and he was recognised as an international authority on them. In 1833, when still a student, he persuaded George Ure Skinner, who had a trading company in Guatemala, to look for orchids. Among the plants he received were *Cattleya skinneri* and *Lycaste skinneri*; most of the 40 orchids described and illustrated in Bateman's *Orchidaceae of*

FAR LEFT: William Bell Scott's contribution to the decoration of the central hall at Wallington, 1856. His painting is of a common flag iris with giant sedge, herb robert, saxifrage and cocksfoot. The paintings flanking the pilaster are of scenes from Northumbrian history, also painted by Scott.

LEFT: The library at Oxburgh Hall in Norfolk, a photograph taken in the late 1880s. On the mantelpiece, and on top of a bookcase behind a member of the Bedingfeld family are oriental-style vases filled with pampas grass, then a very fashionable plant for indoor decoration.

Mexico and Guatemala (1837-43), the largest botanical book ever published, were collected by Skinner. When Bateman moved into Biddulph Grange, his treasured orchids remained in a range of hothouses at Knypersley Hall, his parents' home two miles away. They were brought over for arrangements in the house at Biddulph, particularly for dining-room table decorations.

Within the house, a revolution took place in the style of flower arranging. Previously displays had used mixed flowers, often crowded together in a low pyramid or mound. Seldom had greenery been used, and no thought of a colour scheme. The 1850s represent a time of transition: flowers were still mixed, but becoming less crowded. A rage for ferns was underway, and they began to make their appearance amongst the flowers. Lachaume's recommendation to have 'light and airy leaves, such as those of the iris and the pancratium' or 'leaves disposed to hang down' were particularly effective for the trumpet-shaped vases now becoming fashionable.

In the next decade the ribbon effect of the garden beds was being echoed in the use of flowers within doors. Arrangements became much flatter, with shorter stalks, sometimes so short that for the first time some flowers were 'wired'. The flowers, usually no more than two kinds, or at the most three, were arranged in bands of the same variety and colour to provide a contrast for each other. Sometimes they were separated by bands of greenery, particularly the climbing fern, *Lygodium scandens*, and the creeping club moss, *Selaginella kraussiana*. The colour scheme within a vase had become an important consideration.

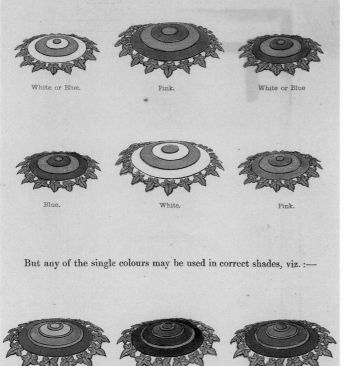

White or Blue.   Pink.   White or Blue

Blue.   White.   Pink.

But any of the single colours may be used in correct shades, viz. :—

Orange shaded off to Light Yellow.   Dark Purple shaded off to Mauve.   Crimson Damask shaded off to Light Pink.

LEFT: 'Table shewing what colours will agree when three flower groups are placed on one table, a single colour being used for each decoration.' Thomas March's recommendations for decorating the table, from *Flower & Fruit Decoration*, 1862.

BELOW: A banded flower arrangement from Peter Henderson's *Practical Floriculture*, 1869.

Banded Dish

This spectacular arrangement is taken from Peter Henderson's *Practical Floriculture* published in the United States in 1869. It uses the bands of colour which were so fashionable at that period.

The base of the arrangement should be a hump of damp sand covered by a thin layer of moss, but if your container is too delicate to take the weight, use a half and half combination of sand and oasis.

The flowers used here are fuchsias 'Winston Churchill', tuberoses, violas, phalaenopsis (moth) orchids, bouvardia and camellia leaves.

The fuchsias and tuberoses were individually wired (see page 107 for the method) but this is not necessary if their stems can reach the damp sand or oasis. The camellia leaves were also wired to ensure they drooped gracefully, but they can be allowed to droop naturally as in Henderson's arrangement.

Start in the centre and move gradually outwards.

When Henderson's *Practical Floriculture* was published in the United States in 1869, the style took off there too. Peter Henderson had been trained in the gardens at Melville Castle in Scotland before emigrating to America and setting up a market garden in Jersey City, New York. He soon became the leading American expert on floriculture and flower arranging. He advised against:

Table bouquets made in the fashion of the confectioner's stiff pyramids of macaroons.... Better a thousand times to have half the quantity of flowers decently arranged ... the more loosely and unconfused the better. Crowding is particularly to be avoided, and to accomplish this readily a good base of green is required, to keep the flowers apart.... Sprays of delicate green are indispensable to the grace and beauty of a vase bouquet.

But the horticultural tide was once again on the turn. The young garden designer and author William Robinson initiated in the 1860s a campaign against bedding out with its serried ranks and blocks of bright and dazzling flowers. Instead he proposed gardens of roses, shrubs and hardy plants, with flowering creeper covering the walls in the tradition of cottage gardens – a tradition that in general has been maintained in British gardens to this day. These ideas were proclaimed in his book *The Wild Garden* published in 1870, and in the weekly journal *The Garden* launched by him the following year.

In 1875 Robinson met Gertrude Jekyll, who developed his ideas into natural looking but carefully planned 'herbaceous borders'. Ladies in the grandest houses now welcomed back into their flower-beds the old-fashioned flowers. Daffodils and spring bulbs cast onto rubbish heaps or surviving in meadows and orchards were now dug up and brought back. In 1875 the *Saturday Review* published a rather condescending article entitled 'Queen Anne's Flowers' by Mrs Loftie, a cousin of the author Robert Louis Stevenson:

It is often amusing to trace a fashion as it percolates downwards. By the time it has reached the far away sleeping country villages, something quite new and entirely opposite is the rage among the upper thousand. Cottagers would try to fill their little plots with geraniums and calceolarias.... meanwhile the lady at the Court is hunting the nursery grounds ... for the fair tall rockets, the cabbage roses, and the nodding columbines which her pensioners have discarded and thrown away.

Helen Allingham's paintings of cottage gardens, Myles Birket Foster's watercolours and Kate Greenaway's illustrations of children in cottage gardens all contributed to the revival of old-fashioned gardens. In June 1875 Mary Gladstone recorded her visit to the studio of the artist Edward Burne-Jones. After tea they 'strolled about the pretty, old-fashioned garden and picked roses'.

The effect on flower arrangements was to make them more 'natural, light and graceful' with grasses 'springing' out of the lower flowers. In *The Garden*, William Robinson wrote a column each week headed 'The Garden in the House', in which he described and often illustrated vases indoors that included wild flowers and the old hardy garden flowers, sometimes mixed with the newly imported exotics, to which he had no objection for they did not displace the old garden flowers, but were grown in hothouses. He also advised

Helen Allingham's watercolour of Gertrude Jekyll's main border in her garden at Munstead Wood in Surrey, reproduced from M.B. Huish's *Happy England*, 1903. Helen Allingham gave a detailed description of the border, explaining that 'Miss Jekyll does not entirely keep to her arrangement of masses of colour; whilst, as an artist, she affects rich masses of colour, she is not above experimenting by breaking in varieties.'

having greenery amongst the flowers, best of all the flowers' own leaves, 'Each fine blossom or cluster of blossoms ought to have some quiet background to set it forth. Green foliage in delicate sprays or handsome leaves is according to nature's plan.'

Those who considered themselves the avant-garde went even further in their desire for the natural, or the aesthetic, as they put it. Taking as their heroes the Pre-Raphaelite painters and William Morris, they believed in the 'cultivation of beauty in every area of life'. In their uncluttered houses, some went for simple cottage-style flower arrangements, others strove to copy the refreshingly simple and artistic style of Japanese arrangements that were being revealed to the Western world.

By the second half of the nineteenth century not only had many houses increased in size, but in some the number of living rooms had again expanded: drawing rooms, saloons, libraries, morning rooms and boudoirs for ladies, smoking rooms for gentlemen. Halls and galleries were now often filled with armchairs, sofas and tables, and conservatories were regarded as extensions of the general living space. The amount of furniture proliferated too: pier-tables, pembroke tables, sofa tables, occasional tables, writing tables, secretaires, commodes. All these surfaces were then filled up with objects, including vases of flowers. Added to this were pots of plants, including palm trees. Photographs of interiors in the 1860s and 70s show a bewildering clutter.

Living screens of plants might be used to divide the rooms. These screens, known as 'treillage' had been noticed by Lady Londonderry at the Winter Palace in St Petersburg in

An arbour of yuccas, New Zealand flax, palms and ivy around a sofa, recommended for the drawing room by F.W.T. Burbidge in his *Domestic Floriculture*, 1875.

James Wyatt and his grandaughter, 1849, by John Everett Millais. On a bracket between the windows is an arrangement in an urn, a vase going out of fashion. The style for the future is represented by a sturdy forerunner of the trumpet vase. A bowl in which flowers might float, like the one on the left, became a mainstay from now on.

1836 (see pages 138-9). By the 1870s, they were the fashion in Britain. *The Garden* on 7 September 1872 reported:

To have living screens in drawing rooms and saloons is a favourite practice at Trentham, Cliveden, and other large houses, and they might advantageously be used generally. Upright trellis covered with ivy green or any other suitable climber, and springing from oblong boxes, the soil being placed in narrow troughs, which are placed within ornamental ones of various materials and patterns . . . and the whole so arranged that they may be desired, are elegant and useful ornaments in large drawing-rooms and saloons . . . where a person reading or writing may desire to be cut off from the general glare or openness of the apartment.

Another form of 'living screen' was on occasion erected around a sofa, creating an arbour. This custom continued into the twentieth century, when Lady Ashbrook remembers that in the large drawing room at Arley Hall, her home in Cheshire, pots of tall *Campanula pyramidalis* towering above hydrangeas were raised upon stands and placed around the sofa.

For flower arranging, two kinds of vases predominated in the second half of the nineteenth century: trumpets and bowls. A portrait of James Wyatt and his granddaughter by John Millais, painted in 1849, shows the development of the style of vases themselves. On a bracket placed high up on the pier between the windows is an urn-shaped vase with a display of mixed flowers, a style that was soon to become outmoded. On the table in the window embrasure are a trumpet and a bowl, the fashionable vases of the future. The trumpet, filled with dahlias, roses and other flowers, is still rather heavy. Its base is surrounded by a rope of flowers that appear to be laid on the table, looking forward to the flower stands, where these flowers would be in a lower dish. Flower stands were essential features of flower arranging of the 1860s and 70s.

A watercolour of the saloon at Erddig, also painted in 1849 by an unknown artist, shows a more elegant trumpet vase standing on a small round table by the window. It contains a low bunch of mixed flowers. Three other small tables in the centre of the room have flowers on them, and there are also two plant stands, one rectangular, the other round.

Miss Maling claimed to have designed the first two-tier flower stand, a trumpet rising

The Salon at Erddig, a watercolour dating from *c.*1849. The room is decorated with several flower arrangements including, on a table in the window, a posy in an unusually early tall and elegant trumpet vase that is still in the house. There are vases on the other three tables in the centre of the room, and two flower stands, one rectangular, the other round.

Miss Maling's two-tier flower stand of frosted glass from *Flowers for Ornament and Decoration* published in 1862. The lower dish is decorated with fruit resting on its own leaves, topped by a few ferns, while the trumpet contains ferns, roses and other flowers that provide 'a graceful waving shade without interrupting the view across the table, which is such a great discomfort'.

out of a dish. She explains that it was 'so much liked by Messrs Philips that they have manufactured the vase for sale in their establishments in Oxford and Bond Street'. Mr March, winner of the Royal Horticultural Society competition in 1861, would have begged to differ on who was first (see page 176), and the pictures show that the idea was forming before Miss Maling's *coup*, but she pressed her claim regardless. Though primarily designed for the dining room, she thought that 'the vases, being simply made of glass, are also very pretty for the drawing room table when entirely filled with flowers' and in fact this is where they were most used. A small one could be concocted by standing a champagne flute in a saucer. Miss Maling's suggestions for summer and winter flowers suitable for new flower stands are given in Table 8.

Trumpet vases came in a variety of sizes and shapes. Small specimen vases were generally 6 to 9 inches (15 to 25 centimetres) high, and intended to contain a flower or two. Annie Hassard who published *Floral Decorations for Dwelling Houses* in 1875, recommended 'a Rosebud, a spray of Stephanotis, an Orchid, or any other effective flower, backed by either a spray of Selaginella or a small Fern frond'. These were made in plain, coloured or frosted glass, and by the 1880s in iridescent and crackled glass too. They could be used in the drawing room, or on the dining-room table, where one was placed before each guest.

Larger single trumpet vases were advocated by F. W. T. Burbidge in his book *Domestic Floriculture* published in 1875: 'various kinds of these, to suit all tastes, can be obtained at most glass-works or warehouses, in all sizes from 9 inches [25 centimetres] to 3 feet [90 centimetres] in height. They are graceful in outline, and require but few flowers to fill them effectively.' Miss Maling's remedy for keeping awkward flowers in place was to put 'a branch of Rose leaves or a bushy piece of Myrtle in the centre'.

Miss Maling and Mr March's stands were both illustrated in Annie Hassard's *Floral Decorations*. But she preferred a stand, apparently of her own design, which incorporated the elements of both, rising to three tiers with a trumpet rising out of the top dish. She also liked a much more complex structure, of three trumpets curving away from and surrounding a taller central trumpet. She gives suggestions for these two stands and for Miss Maling's stand (which she calls a trumpet vase) for each month of the year, some of which are listed in Table 9.

TABLE 8: Miss Maling, *Flowers for Ornament and Decoration and how to arrange them*, 1862.

For summer:

In the trumpet: Graceful blue and white bell-shaped flowers, such as the Campanulas and beautiful Lily tribes.

In the dish: Wisteria and Acacias (Mimosa), exquisite for leaves and flowers if laid in large fan-like layers all around it.

And for winter:

In the trumpet: Rose coloured and white Camellias or Heaths and red Poinsettias, or Hyacinths and red Tulips.

In the dish: Hyacinths with Snowdrops, Moss and Bluebells.

LEFT & CENTRE: Two sizes of trumpet vases from Mr Burbidge's *Domestic Floriculture*, 1875. In the large trumpet he suggests inserting a few fern fronds, and adding 'two or three distinct richly-coloured flowers'. A small trumpet could contain 'a flower or two, as a rosebud, a spray of stephanotis, an orchid, . . . backed up by either a spray of selaginella or a small fern frond'.

RIGHT: A compound trumpet stand from Annie Hassard's *Floral Decorations*, 1875. Her suggestions for flowers in different seasons are provided in Table 9.

Mr Luckhurst waxed lyrical on the other fashionable shape of the period, the bowl:

There is nothing better than large china bowls filled if possible with fragrant flowers. What is more liked than a bowl of Sweet Pea blossom, or Mignonette, Honeysuckle, Lily of the Valley, Harebell, Roses, Violets or Primroses? All are welcomed in their seasons. Depend upon it, it is not the costly Orchid or other rare flowers requiring expensive glass structures for their culture that are most often in favour, even in a palace. There is a craving for the 'old fashioned flowers' of our childhood, and only a selection of those of the most easy culture are needful to carry on the work of decoration well.

But bowls and trumpets were not the only containers used. Dishes of flowers were also popular. Miss Maling recommended 'A large glass or china dish, about 2 inches [5 centimetres] deep . . . in form like a gigantic saucer or a common soup bowl' that could be placed on a side-table. She suggested filling it with bands of lilies and roses, lilies and geraniums, or water lilies within a belt of cactus. She also suggested growing flowers in these dishes, again in bands: 'Hyacinths in the centre, Bluebells or scillas next, and round the edge Snowdrops drooping their graceful heads over a green mossy edging.'

In the 1870s, when bands were no longer so fashionable, Annie Hassard liked to arrange violets alone:

Take an ordinary saucer and fill it with fresh looking moss . . . build up the moss in the form of a little mound in the saucer . . . round the edges Fern fronds should be arranged so as to hide the china. . . . Take the violet blooms, make them into bunches – say eight or ten in each bunch – and bind their stems together . . . when a sufficient number of these little bunches have been made, they should be dotted over the ground-work of green Moss.

TABLE 9: Annie Hassard, *Floral Decoration for Dwelling Houses*, 1875.

MARCH

Marchain Vase

LOWER TAZZA – Stephanotis, pink Pelargoniums, double white Primulas, pink Heaths, Cyprus alternifolius, and Maiden-hair; round the edge fronds of Pteris serrulata and Pteris cretica albo-lineata.

UPPER TAZZA – White Carnations, pink Azaleas, Lily of the Valley, and Maiden-hair, fronds of the same drooping round the edge.

TRUMPET – Lily of the Valley, pink Heaths, and three sprays of Solomon's Seal, a few fronds of Maiden-hair being arranged round the mouth.

Vase with Curved Trumpets

IN EACH OF THE CURVED BRANCHES – a spray of Solomon's Seal, some deep blue Cinerarias, Deutzia gracilis, and Maiden-hair.

IN TOP TRUMPET – Three sprays of Solomon's Seal, some Lily of the Valley, a few sprays of Cineraria, Maiden-hair, and Lygodium scandens.

Trumpet Vase

TAZZA – Yellow Roses, Neapolitan Violets, Lily of the Valley, and Maiden-hair; round the edge, mixed varieties.

TRUMPET – Lily of the Valley, Cyclamen, and Maiden-hair.

JULY

Marchain Vase

LOWER TAZZA – White Water Lilies, Kalosanthes coccinea, white Rhodanthe, Maiden-hair, and wild Grasses; round the edge fronds of Pteris serrulata.

UPPER TAZZA – Blooms of Eucharis amazonica, scarlet Pelargoniums (the same shade as the Kalosanthes), white Rhodanthe, Maiden-hair, and Grasses; round the edge drooping fronds of Maiden-hair.

TRUMPET – Scarlet Pelargoniums, white Rhodanthe, wild Grasses and Oats, Maiden-hair and Lygodium scandens.

Vase with Curved Trumpets

RISING OUT OF CURVED BRANCHES – Blooms of Lilium longifolium, pink fancy Pelargoniums, white Rhodanthe, and Maiden-hair.

TOP TRUMPET – White and pink Rhodanthe, and wild Grasses.

Trumpet Vase

TAZZA – Water Lilies, blue Forget-me-nots, Rhodanthe, and wild Grasses; round the edge fronds of the common Brake Fern.

TRUMPET – Blue Forget-me-nots, white Rhodanthe, and wild Grasses.

OCTOBER

Marchain Vase

LOWER TAZZA – White Asters, double scarlet Pelargoniums, Clematis, and Maiden-hair; round the edge fronds of the Brake Fern.

UPPER TAZZA – Scarlet Pelargoniums, Clematis, white Sweet Pea, and Grasses.

TRUMPET – Scarlet Salvias, Clematis, Grasses, and Maiden-hair.

Vase with Curved Trumpets

RISING OUT OF CURVED BRANCHES – Pink Heaths, Eucharis amazonica, pink Begonias, and Maiden-hair.

IN TRUMPET – Pink Heaths, Begonias, Clematis, Grasses, and Ferns.

Trumpet Vase

TAZZA – White Campanula, blue Agapanthus, Ferns, and Grasses

TRUMPET – Filled to match.

A round flat glass basket might be substituted for the shallow bowl. Mr March recommended them for 'Roses, Geraniums, or Delphiniums with white stocks, Water Lilies with blue Iris and they are well adapted for Gloxinias and for variegated hot-house leaves such as Caladiums, Maurantas and Begonias.' He advised putting the basket on a plain dark cover of cloth or Utrecht velvet, 'which does not confuse the effect of leaves and flowers'. Peter Henderson explained to his American readers what to do with the handles: 'having doubtless been originally designed to carry; the handle invariably interferes with the general effect, and can only be tolerated when beautifully trimmed with flowers and fine greens'.

Wicker baskets could be bought ready arranged from the flower market during the summer months. For those who wanted to arrange their own, Peter Henderson gave instructions:

> Flower baskets are lined with tinfoil, then filled with sawdust, rounding above, damped and covered with wet moss: a border of arbor-vitae, then bouquet green (Lycopodium) is set around to support the overhanging flowers. The flowers, stemmed on pieces of match stick or twigs are now inserted with moss between them. The more common method is to insert bouquet green over the whole surface, and arrange the flowers therein without any moss packing.

Illustration from *The Garden*, 13 November 1875, showing how an arrangement in a dish, called here a 'flat tazza', can be created. 'Large flowers are best for this style of arrangement, light varieties being left for trumpet-shaped and similar vases.' Recommendations include water-lilies, lilies of all kinds, roses and camellias. The hole in the middle can be used for a small palm.

Emboldened by the success of Thomas March's stand at the Royal Horticultural Society (see page 178), his daughters produced flowers in baskets with glass handles to their father's design. These, too, won a first prize – for 'Drawing Room Decoration' in 1862. The central basket is arranged with lilies of the valley, white lilac and narcissi. The basket on the left contains purple gloxinia, and the one on the right, roses 'De Meaux'. The foliage is fern and sprays of club moss.

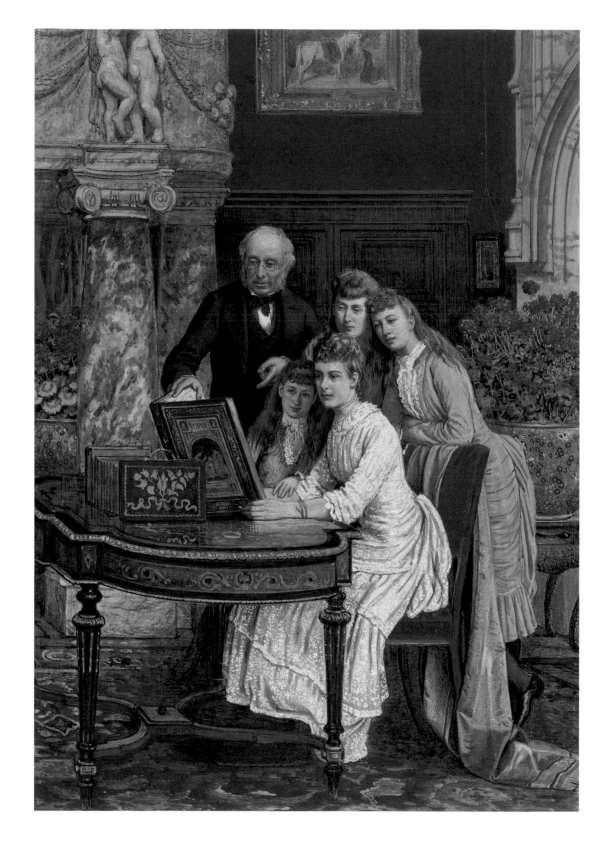

Princess Alexandra and her daughters with Sir William Armstrong in the Drawing Room at Cragside, 1884, from the commemorative album illustrated by H.H. Emmerson and J.T. Dixon. Huge oriental pots, mounted on stands and filled with pelargoniums can be seen behind the group.

Even gold and silver racing cups were brought into use for flowers. An entry for 13 May 1881 in Mr Jones's daybook at Windsor Castle reads 'filling a Goodwood Cup with *Ericas ventricosa* for centre, Lily of the Valley round it with Selaginella'. A keen racing man, he noted that the inscription on the cup read 'The Goodwood Cup – 1829, won by His Majesty's mare, Fleur de Lis.'

In her description of a dish of violets, Annie Hassard referred to 'groundwork'. By the 1870s this had become an established method of flower arranging, using the large heavier flowers as the groundwork with lighter, longer stemmed flowers and grasses, fresh or dried, springing out of them. Simple arrangements of this kind were described by Mr Luckhurst. He used 'bold scarlet single blooms of Vallota for a groundwork, out of which springs a few white [Japanese] anemones, also single, yet with the flowers gracefully clustering', but thought 'nothing can be more lovely than a groundwork of pure white roses with Pelargonium Manglesii flowers mingled with and springing out of it'.

This type of arrangement could be done in any vase, but Mr Luckhurst's favourite was a glass fish bowl, which he would put in the centre of a round table. The edge would be fringed with fern fronds, on which rested circles of 'Gloire de Dijon' roses in clusters and white flower spikes of *Ligustrum japonicum* projecting irregularly between them, 'two or three being made to droop downwards upon the green fringe'. The centre was filled with spikes of larkspur, principally blue but with a mixture of pink, and clusters of dried quaking grass (*Briza minima*) 'springing irregularly' out of the central flowers imparting 'a pleasing air of sprightliness and finish to the whole'. Mr Luckhurst was so taken with fish bowls that he thought every flower-room cupboard should contain a complete set, a dozen of each size 'down to those that will not contain more water than a teacup . . . for using in groups in a variety of ways'.

For halls, corridors and staircases he recommended 'gigantic vases two or three feet [60 or 90 centimetres] high' standing on the floor, preferably of terracotta, Wedgwood, maiolica or oriental ware. If tables were available, then large china bowls should be used, with the most fragrant flowers to waft their scent through the house. It was particularly important to decorate the hall with flowers, for this provided a guest's first impression of the house, and was a room through which they frequently passed. William Taylor, head gardener to the Marquess of Bath at Longleat, used oval containers to decorate either end of the hall. In these he would place *Campanula pyramidalis*, ten or twelve pots, each containing seven plants. 'It lasts good in the house for two months, it might not look so well in a small house, but in our stately apartments it is very imposing'. The newly introduced *Lilium auratum* provided an alternative, and for Christmas and shooting parties in the winter he grew tall poinsettias and chrysanthemums in two or three distinct, bright colours.

With the spreading popularity of the Arts and Crafts Movement, and its rebellion against the fussiness of house interiors, a new simplicity in flower arranging emerged. In 1880 the movement's leading exponent, William Morris, described in his lecture entitled *Beauty of Life* the 'simple necessities' that ought to furnish a room. First a bookcase, then a table, chairs and pictures, and finally 'we shall also want a vase or two to put flowers in, which

The Japanese Garden at Tatton
Park was created for the 3rd Lord
Egerton in 1910. To the left of the
arched bridge over the pool is a
Shinto temple, brought from
Japan. On the left of the temple
are pink rhododendrons, and on
the right yellow azaleas with
yellow iris beneath them.

latter you must have sometimes, especially if you live in a town'. The 'vase' was likely to be
a simple jug, or, in the case of growing plants, an undisguised terracotta pot. Carl Larsson,
an enthusiastic adherent of the Arts and Crafts culture, painted a watercolour of one of his
rooms in his house in Sweden in the 1890s, now in the Nationalmuseum Stockholm. It
shows terracotta pots of carnations, fuchsias and other plants lining the window-sill.

Another simplifying influence was the Aesthetic Movement, to which flower arranging
was of central importance, and which looked for inspiration primarily to Japan. For
centuries Japan had isolated itself from the rest of the world, so that when the country was
opened up in the 1860s the style of life and art came as a sensational revelation to the West.
Japanese gardens were introduced into English country houses, complete with bridges, tea-
houses and Japanese flowers.

At a Japanese Exhibition at the White City in London in 1910, Allen de Tatton, like many
others, was captivated by the gardens laid out complete with tea-houses and pavilions with
painted backdrops. Probably he was further inspired by a book by the English architect
Josiah Conder, *Landscape Gardening in Japan* (1893), which gave exact plans and instructions. In any event, a Japanese garden was soon created at Tatton Park by gardeners
brought over from Japan. It is now one of the few to survive in England, as after the Second
World War many things connected with Japan were destroyed. The osmunda ferns (the
royal fern of Japan), cryptomerias and other Japanese introductions, including auratum

Adelaide Talbot, Countess
Brownlow, painted by Frederick
Leighton in 1879, holding a
bunch of roses. She and her
sisters were known as the 'three
ghosts' because their artistic
inclinations impelled them to
dress only in white.

Nina Cust reclining on her day-bed in the library at Chancellor's House in Hyde Park Gate; a painting by Florence Seth, *c.*1894. Nina's decor made her seventeenth-century London home seem like a house in the country. Her vases of long-stemmed peonies and magnolias are typical of the natural, single-flower arrangements loved by the 'Souls', a style of arranging soon to be taken up by the Edwardians.

lilies, still flourish there. It was the custom to keep the tea garden unclipped or controlled so that there were plenty of branches available to make arrangements inside the tea house.

Liberty's of Regent Street, opened in 1875, specialised in artistic goods, including Japanese blue-and-white porcelain vases and bamboo furniture such as plant stands. Eager purchasers could draw upon a lecture given by G. A. Audsley on Japanese art, reported in *The Gardener's Chronicle*: 'The Japanese delight in bouquets of flowers and branches, with which they ornament the interiors of their simply ordered apartments on all festive occasions.' He went on to describe dwarf trees and clusters of giant flowers in asymmetrical arrangements, sometimes with bamboo rising vertically from the midst of the flowers, but English arrangers did not venture so far.

In 1891 Josiah Conder published *Flowers of Japan* and *The Art of Floral Arrangement*, later revised and reissued as *The Floral Art of Japan*, with illustrations by Japanese artists. Arrangements of twigs, leaves and branches in huge oriental pots started to appear in the houses of the 'artistic' set, and must have seemed very stark and barbaric to their friends of less advanced tastes.

This striving to be artistic could reach odd heights. Constance, Lady Lothian surrounded herself at Blickling with everything white: cattle, ponies, pigeons, peacocks and presumably flowers. She and her sisters, Gertrude, Lady Pembroke and Adelaide, Lady Brownlow, were known as the 'three ghosts' as they dressed only in white.

Lord and Lady Brownlow were on the fringes of the 'Souls', an elite group of high-minded, idealistic and intellectual aristocrats whose inner band included George Curzon, Arthur Balfour, Margot Tennant and Lord Brownlow's cousin and heir, Harry Cust. The group is said to have been named at a dinner party given by the Brownlows in 1888, when

My Aesthetic Love by A. Concanen, 1881. This popular song satirised the attitudes and excesses of the Aesthetic Movement. From a floral point of view, this meant that the subject of the song is lost in admiration for a single lily in a vase, while cradling a sunflower in her lap.

Lord Charles Beresford mocked their intensity, saying, 'You all sit and talk about each other's souls'. At Belton House, home of the Brownlow family, hangs a painting of Nina Cust, the long-suffering wife of Harry, a compulsive womaniser. She is shown in their drawing room at Chancellor's House in Hyde Park Gate in London, where the flowers are long-stemmed and naturally arranged: peonies in one vase, and branches of magnolia in a round bowl on a porcelain stand, one of several still at Belton.

The artist George du Maurier was quick to satirise 'artistic' pretensions. When asked to describe an aesthetic interior for a stage set, he advised 'here and there a blue china vase with an enormous hawthorn or almond blossom sprig … on mantelpiece, pots with lilies and peacock feathers wanted'.

Enthusiasm for the new simplicity of style was sometimes translated into moral terms. In

February 1882 Mary Gladstone wrote: 'On hindlegs all day ... arranged a million snow-drops from Hawarden, they overspread all the rooms and looked angelically pure in this atmosphere moral and physical, if there is such an expression.'

During the latter half of the nineteenth century families wealthy enough to do so entertained on a very grand scale. In new houses, the dining room was usually one of the largest rooms in the house, and for older houses changes had to be made. At Castle Howard in Yorkshire in 1882 a large dining room was created by knocking three rooms into one. At Ormesby Hall in 1871 the large, south-facing saloon on the central axis of the house was turned into the dining room and extended with a broad shallow bay.

Dining-room tables too became larger, both in width and by extensions in length. For smaller family meals the 'ends' could be put together to form a round or square table. In some great houses it was the habit to seat guests at a series of small tables, as though in a restaurant. Mary Gladstone commented on this when she was staying with Lady Brown-low at Ashridge in Hertfordshire in December 1875: 'To dinner with Mr Compton. All in small tables.' She evidently didn't like the habit much, for she added 'Bored rather.'

However large or small the table, it was now covered with a white damask tablecloth reaching nearly to the ground that remained on the table throughout the meal, including the dessert. The whole style of dining had changed. In the old style, now known as *service à la française*, dishes were brought to the table simultaneously in a series of main courses, usually two but more for grand events. These were followed by a dessert course when the cloth was removed. This was now superseded by *service à la russe*, so called because the custom in Russian society was to have the courses handed round by servants rather than putting the dishes on the table for people to serve themselves. The idea, introduced to Paris in 1810 by the Russian ambassador, gradually took hold in England, first for grand banquets, and by the 1860s most homes of fashion served food in this manner.

This left the centre of the table, previously cluttered with joints, pies and puddings, available to be decorated with flowers throughout the meal, instead of just during the dessert course. Flowers looked better, and stood out more, against the sparkling white of the cloth. Annie Hassard wrote: 'The finer the damask the better the floral arrangement will appear. Beautiful designs are now woven in damask of groups and bouquets of fern fronds, with wreaths of the same, and ivy round the border, which are quite in keeping with the floral display arrangements in the vases.'

Just as the dining style completely changed in the 1860s, so did the style in table decoration. The heavy epergnes, tall trees and pyramid arrangements of fruit and flowers now disappeared. In their place came the flower stand. Thomas March, who was not a professional gardener but worked in the Lord Chamberlain's Office, designed an ingenious two-tiered stand for flowers that consisted of two shallow glass dishes, the larger one on the table, the smaller held about 2 feet (60 centimetres) above by a slender glass rod rising out of the centre of the bottom dish. Mr March entered a group of three of these flower stands in the first Flower Arranging Competition held by the Royal Horticultural Society as part of the inauguration of the Society's new garden at South Kensington in June 1861.

Mr March's exhibit, in which the flowers were thought to be arranged by his younger

Second and third prizes at the Royal Horticultural Show of 1861, demonstrating the lumpish heaviness of table decorations before the arrival of Mr March.

sisters, not only carried off the first prize but caused a sensation. A letter from an unnamed girl was published in *The Gardener's Chronicle*:

> I forget the 2nd and 3rd prizes, indeed in the crush I am afraid I was pushed past without seeing them, but the moment my eye rested on one group, I said, 'Oh, there is the best of all' and was lost in admiration of the exquisite arrangement of the three pieces. I was delighted to see on the card at the foot, 1st Prize, for it was my idea of the perfection of refined taste.... They were decorated with the Maiden Hair Fern, a ring of Forget-me-not, and a centre of Lilies of the Valley, and Lycopodiums creeping up the pedestal; not as much crammed in as the vessels would hold, but each flower and each leaf producing its own effect – not one too many, not one too few. In one of the stands, instead of Forget-me-nots, there were Pansies, Rosebuds, and small bunches of Grapes were introduced here and there: it was the most exquisite thing of the kind I ever saw.

For the next few weeks *The Gardener's Chronicle* enthused about the lightness and slenderness of Mr March's exhibit, referring to the second prize winner as lumpish, and to the few who objected to the winning arrangement as 'those who cannot perceive how superior graceful form is to mere heaps of colour'. Not surprising, therefore, that the new stands were in demand. By July Messrs Dobson & Pearce of St James's Street were manufacturing and supplying them to customers under the name 'March Stands'. They were easily taken to pieces for packing and transporting. The top and bottom dishes could be used separately, and could be sent to Covent Garden for dressing with flowers. Mr March suggested that if transporting one in a jolting cab, hairpins could be used to keep flowers in place.

Thomas March's prize-winning flower stands at the Royal Horticultural Show, 1861. In all three stands the lower dishes have a wide fringe of simple bracken or fern, while the upper ones are fringed with maidenhair ferns. Club moss twines up the glass rods. On the left stand both tiers have a band of forget-me-nots surrounding a clump of lily of the valley; on the right stand bands of pansies surround rosebuds. The central stand has just grapes and their leaves.

March Stand

Thomas March's flower stand caused a sensation when he revealed it to the world in 1861. Within the month Messrs Dobson & Pearce of St James's Street were manufacturing and supplying March stands for their customers. Flowers arranged elegantly in March stands were now all the rage and preferred to the 'lumpish' arrangements that had been fashionable.

The real March stands are now almost impossible to find, so this one was ingeniously created using a cake tin for the upper dish and a metal tray for the lower dish, curtain rail ends and a glass rod. It is very important that metal is used for the trays, as plastic is insufficiently rigid. The upper tray is 8 inches (20 centimetres) in diameter, the lower tray 20 inches (50 centimetres) in diameter. The rail ends have been stuck onto the dishes with superglue. The glass rod is 2 feet (60 centimetres) in length.

This decoration consisted of peonies 'Sarah Bernhardt' and lilies of the valley, with maidenhair, leather leaf fern, plus a honeysuckle trail.

The trays were filled with damp sand, covered by a thin layer of moss. The ferns were put in first, next the peonies,

and then the lilies of the valley. The arrangement was completed with a stem of honeysuckle wound up the glass rod to the upper tray.

Flower stands remained indispensable to most households for the next twenty or thirty years, giving rise to numerous variations. Miss Maling claimed to have invented one in her book of 1862, which has been described in the section on living rooms as that was where it was most used (see page 165). Mr March very shrewdly made the point that his flower stand could be used in any room, including on staircases, but it appeared to its best advantage on the dining table. On rectangular or oblong tables three stands were most effective, with the tallest in the centre, separated from the lower two by candelabra. One was enough for a round table.

Detailed instructions for the management of flowers in the stands were provided in Thomas March's *Flower and Fruit Decoration*, published in 1862. It was praised by the *Journal of Horticulture* as one of the essential texts for any gardener to study. First, he explained how to keep the flowers in place: 'Flowers have hitherto been arranged almost exclusively in tall vessels filled with water only, but it is different with wide shallow vessels where damp sand and clay must be used ... then you have the power of planting each flower-stalk and leaf by itself in the exact position and at the precise height you choose.' To give the impression that the flowers are springing out of the tablecloth, he advocated hiding the dish with ferns or moss. The latter had been difficult to obtain in town – only one variety of moss out of the two hundred grown in Britain was available at the flower market in Covent Garden. But Mr March was creating a revolution, and moss became much more widely available as a result of his strictures. Sand and clay covered with moss continued to be used until displaced by the present-day 'oasis', making the flower arranger's life so much easier.

Next he showed how the flowers were to be arranged: 'The surface to be filled is large, and it will not suffice to crowd in a quantity of different flowers with no relationship to each other ... this may captivate the "good gracious" people, but for people who have correct and refined taste, it will be necessary to adopt some definite design or leading idea, which must be adhered to more or less throughout the arrangement.' Mr March's designs were influenced by the banding arrangements then in vogue in garden beds, and by the style of bouquets sold in Paris shops and markets, consisting of only one colour, or of two colours in bands.

As for flowers Mr March, unusually for the time, preferred ordinary garden flowers to orchids or other hothouse flowers. He took as a compliment an old gardener's objection to his winning exhibits because 'the flowers might have come out of a ditch'.

Table 10 reproduces some of his suggested arrangements. They are for stands where the lower dish is 12-15 inches (30-38 centimetres) in diameter, and the upper one slightly smaller. The dishes are both 1 inch (2.5 centimetres) high, and when fern fronds are fanned out around the edge of the lower dish, the diameter is increased to 2 feet (60 centimetres) or more. The arrangements are also suitable for a single flat dish for the drawing room. First both vessels must be filled with damp sand and covered with moss, then the fringe of fern or other leaves is put in.

For foliage Mr March preferred ferns of various kinds, ivy and oak leaves, though many others are mentioned. His one warning was that laurel was too stiff and pointed. With carnations and camellias he liked using maidenhair fern to contrast with the deep green

1 Large Flowers of a Rounded Form

Generally 7 flowers in lower circle and 5 in upper, equidistant from each other, as close as possible to the edges of upper and lower dishes and rather overhanging them and inclining outwards from the centre.

Several flowers and buds required to form a cluster at the base of the glass stem and the same for the centre of the upper glass, but these should be of another kind. Then a spray of jessamine or cobea twined round the stem.

List of Large Flowers of a Rounded Form to go Round Edge

Using their own foliage when it is graceful or any other which may be liked.

Azalea	Kalmia
Cactus	Lilies of all kinds
Calceolaria	Pansy*
Camellia	Passion Flower
China aster	Peony
Christmas Rose	Petunia*
Chrysanthemum*	Phlox
Cineraria	Poinsettia
Dahlia	Primrose, Primula – these
Double Poppy	should be arranged to
Double white narcissus*	look as though plants
Gardenia*	growing
Geranium in large trusses	Rhododendron
Hollyhock – the double	Rose
flowers must be	Tulip
cut off and used for	Verbena
the circle	Water-lily
Iris	Zinnia*

* These being smaller may be more numerously inserted, although still in circles and at regular distances.

List of Flowers which are useful to form a Cluster round the Stem and in the Centre of the Upper Glass encircled by some Other Flower

Ageratum	Iris, smaller kind
Azalea	Ixia
Campanula	Lilac
Crocus	Lilies, of different kinds
Cyclamen	Lily-of-the-valley
Delphinium	Lobelia
Deutzia	Oleander
Flowering Currant	Rose 'de Meaux', Banksian
Foxglove	rose or small climbing rose
Fuchsia	Salvia
Geranium	Snowdrop
Gladiolus (for large	Spirea
sizes only)	Solomon's Seal
Harebell	Sweet Pea
Heath	Syringa
Heliotrope	Veronica
Hyacinth, when small	Violet

2 Drooping Flowers like Wisteria or Fruit like Grapes

The long pendant flowers or heavy bunches of fruit should hang down from the edge of the upper glass and be fastened with wire or ribbon round the glass socket in the centre, the stalk being pinned into the moss and sand at the edge of the glass to keep it steady. The sand and moss in the lower glass should be heaped up well to give the flowers or fruit an arched form.

Suitable Flowers

Acacia, white and rose

Currants

Grapes – purple and green alternately with vine leaves in between

Hops

Laburnum 6, 8 or 10 bunches

Large hanging fuchsias

Fruit as plums, pears, cherries, etc, which with a little management may be made to droop from the upper glass with very good effect.

Some kinds of berries

Wisteria 3, 4 or 5 bunches

leaves. To climb up the glass stem by way of introduction to the upper glass, he suggested jessamine, passion flower and lycopodium.

As with living-room arrangements, dining-table flower displays lightened up in the 1870s, and bands gave way to more natural arrangements, with grasses mixed with the flowers. Popular hothouse flowers were *Eucharis amazonica* and vallota, (*Cyrtanthus elatus*, the Scarborough lily). Mr Burbidge in *Domestic Floriculture*, 1874, describes how he arranged a three-tier stand for the dining room:

> The base of the stand is concealed by a fringe of large fern fronds on which is laid flowers of the snowy Eucharis and the fiery Scarborough lily alternately. The effect of the lower part is further enhanced by the judicious use of graceful ornamental grasses. The tier above is fringed with Maidenhair Ferns beneath which hang blooms of the rosy and white flowered lapagerias. The other flowers are the same as below. The trumpet shaped vase above is filled with spikes of Scarlet Penstemon and light grasses.

Mr Burbidge reminded his readers about the effect that artificial lighting had on the colour of the flowers. Under gaslight the range of blue, mauve and purple looked grey and dingy. 'Preference should always be given to large flowers of decided shades of red, or to those of pearly whiteness. These show well, and never fail to please when tastefully set off with fresh green ferns.' Electricity was first used domestically at Cragside, where Sir William Armstrong, with his interest in the latest technology, installed a hydroelectric system in 1878. But still the blue range of flowers did not look their best.

When flowers were scarce, particularly from September to March, pots of growing flowers, or the newly fashionable variegated foliage plants, or even fruit trees could be used as centrepieces on the table. As with the flower stands, they were placed in a line down the centre of the table, alternating with candelabra. Sometimes each centrepiece might consist of a group of five or seven plants, with the tallest in the centre. When Baron Lionel de Rothschild dined with Benjamin Disraeli and his wife Mary Anne at Hughenden Manor in Buckinghamshire in 1859, he brought his own fruit which was laid out on the table around a lemon tree.

John Robson, head gardener at Linton Park in Kent, writing in 1871 recommended plants no higher than 20 inches (50 centimetres) with small roots that did not require a large pot. The size of the roots was always a worry as the pots had then to fit into silver wine coolers or porcelain *cache-pots*. In a crisis, plants could be turned out of their pots and bits hacked off their roots. According to Mr Iggulden, head gardener at Marston Hall in Suffolk, such rough treatment 'did not harm the plants very much'.

Edward Luckhurst spelt out one of his favourite arrangements for the dining room at Oldlands Hall, using quantities of vases in ingenious patterns. For slender trumpets 'four sprays of Selaginella put in so as to be gracefully pendant and most of it long enough to rest upon the tablecloth, then come six or eight of the small pink Pelargonium Manglesii trusses, two or three very choice little fronds of Maidenhair, and half a dozen clusters of dried Briza. Sufficient slender glasses must be so dressed as to form a double chain around a cup or whatever is used for the centre of the table.' Sometimes he would link the glasses with a garland made of 'two sprays of Selaginella twined together so as to gracefully connect the glasses'.

At the beginning of the 1870s came a new fashion for putting flowers into zinc troughs to encircle the centrepieces and dishes of desserts. They could spread all over the table in a myriad of patterns 'for the eye to look down upon'. Mr Robson described his method: 'We frequently make use of a set of troughs of zinc about 2″ [5 centimetres] wide and about ³/₄″ [2 centimetres] deep and made in half circular form so that when two are placed together they form a perfect circle or ring.' The sides were painted green, and the troughs were filled with sand and dressed with flowers – roses in the early summer, later geraniums, and chrysanthemums in autumn. It was preferable to hide the edges with ivy or rose geranium rather than ferns. 'I would not advise more than one kind of flower or perhaps two, while only one kind of foliage is wanted.... The semi-circular troughs are capable of being placed in a number of forms – but one of the most pleasing is a set of scallops all around the tables – and enclosing dessert dishes or something of that kind.' He also liked them in a serpentine form, and for a border around the table he had straight troughs and curved corner pieces. If flowers were scarce, he substituted garlands of greenery and used them to create the same effect.

Sometimes Mr Robson put large sheets of mirror glass down the centre of the table. These measured 5 feet (1.5 metres) long and 2 feet (60 centimetres) wide, and he would surround the edges with straight troughs of flowers or evergreens, perhaps even sticking in some little sprigs of pampas grass. At Christmas holly could be used for good effect. Besides the flower stands in their usual places, he put small baskets of flowers on the glass, but 'it should not be so thickly studded with objects as the cloth might be'. For a modern recreation of this, tiles of mirror glass can be bought. At Joseph Chamberlain's dinner parties in London, mirror glass was surrounded with green painted troughs containing orchids in moss lightly veiled with maidenhair fern.

John Perkins went a step further, dispensing with troughs and laying flowers directly on the tablecloth for his employer, Lady Henniker at Thornham Hall. His book *Floral Decorations for the Table* (1877), written in his retirement, shows 'at a glance how a Dinner Table for from eight to one hundred persons should be decorated' with greenery or ornamental leaves dotted with flowers. This he calls 'tracery', weaving its way in patterns all over the cloth, around pots and vases of flowers, candelabra, dishes of fruit and sweetmeats, leaving just room for the place settings around the edge. He compares it to a flower garden which 'when looked down upon from some distance above its own elevation is far more pleasing to the eye than otherwise', adding that 'Dinner "à la Russe" has within the last ten or fifteen years become so fashionable and popular that to have a dinner in these days without the accompaniment of Cut Flowers, Plants, Ornamental Leaves, etc, would be like dessert without wine'.

John Perkins' book contains 24 detailed plans in colour of tables for dinners, luncheons, breakfasts, a wedding, harvest supper, a hunt breakfast, a cricket luncheon and Christmas. The fashion spread. At Cragside the head gardener found it easier to construct his scrolling patterns of tracery for the table with a pliant garland made of flowers tied at intervals to long strands of smilax.

Design no.14 for a dining table from John Perkins' *Floral Decorations for the Table*, 1877. Mr Perkins recommends using golden variegated ivy and white chrysanthemums for the inside wreaths, and small-leaved ivy with *Smilax mauritanica* for the outside wreaths. The numbers refer: (1) lamps; (2) plants; (3) fruit; (4) confectionery; (5) small glass dishes with cut flowers; (6) small vases with a single panicle of pampas grass; (7) glass tubes, 8in (20cm) high for cut flowers; and (8) glass tubes 8in (20cm) high filled with dried *Agrostis pulchella* (now *Sporobulus pulchellus*) and maidenhair fern.

RIGHT & FAR RIGHT:
A recreation of Mr Perkins' design no.14 in the dining room at Lyme Park.

The entire centre of the table is occupied by flower decoration and dishes of fruit and confectionery. The magnificent Sèvres dinner service, presented by the French government to the Foreign Secretary, Lord Liverpool, to mark the Peace of Amiens in 1802, has been loaned to Lyme by his descendants.

Mr Perkins' instructions have been varied a little, in that the central wreaths are composed of variegated ivy dotted with marguerites, and the outer ones of sprigs of box with red carnations. The taller trumpet vases contain maidenhair fern with freesias or *Eucharis amazonica*, and the smaller ones violas. Sèvres meat juice pots have been put to use to mark the angles of the wreaths, filled with forget-me-nots, daisies, cornflowers and sweet sultan. The silver ice buckets contain maidenhair fern, while a large ladder fern decorates the central epergne.

Design no.6 from John Perkins' *Floral Decorations*, the Wedding Breakfast Table. For the lower part of the wreath he recommends myrtle with cyclamen blooms and 'pips' of white hyacinth. But, he sagely points out 'As interesting events, such as Weddings, are likely to take place at all seasons of the year, it is advisable that Gardeners have a good Stock of white flowering plants always in store.'

(3) and (4) are fruits and confectionery; (5) glass tubes 8in (20cm) high with *Eucharis amazonica* and maidenhair fern; (6) glass tubes 4in (10cm) high with white roses, camellias, stephanotis and lily of the valley. *Eragrostis elegans* (now *E. tenella*) surrounds each tube.

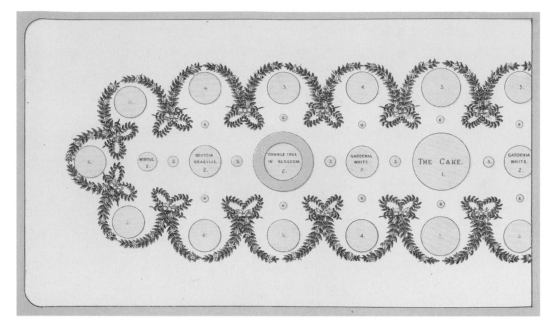

Mr Robson was of a conservative disposition, but even he could indulge in novelties. For one summer event at Linton he installed two table-top fountains, with water pumped up from the kitchen below. As the pipework had to come up through the dining-room floor into a specially constructed table leaf, it is not surprising to learn that 'there was a lot of trouble'. But he took comfort that 'its order affording good space for a floral display, while the mechanical parts could be varied', the fountain could be reused on different evenings. Mr Burbidge meanwhile used blocks or obelisks of sparkling ice to enhance his dining table, 'wreathed with fresh trailers and well lighted, they are very handsome'. But he warned that great care must be taken to arrange for a receptacle to catch the drips.

Trees 'growing' through the dining-room table was another challenge taken up by the Victorians. Visitors to an exhibition held in 1870 in the Crystal Palace at Sydenham were astonished to see a palm tree as the centrepiece of a table decoration. This was the first time such a thing had been seen in England, though Lady Londonderry had observed a similar sight at a ball in St Petersburg some thirty years earlier. Now the idea took off, and in 1872 the Duchess of Devonshire employed the device at Chatsworth for the visit of the Prince and Princess of Wales. Lady Frederick Cavendish noted in her diary for 17 December: 'Cavendish and I went down to Chatsworth with the lovely Princess and the fat but apparently blooming Prince.... Dinner very fine, with feathery cocos palm springing out of the table and overshadowing us.'

Annie Hassard explained to her readers the secret behind this phenomenon:

As nowadays dinner tables are never uncovered, a leaf can be made of common deal for the centre or the ends of the table, with a circular hole in its centre and beneath it will be placed a wooden box or stand to hold the plant. Or keep the leaves of the table an inch or so from closing, leaving room for the narrow stem of a palm. This causes no difficulty for I constantly practise it. My tables both at South Kensington and Birmingham had plants put through them.... Imagine the striking effect which young tree ferns or palms have in such positions; their elevated fronds shading from the glare and blaze of light the smaller arrangements of flowers and fruit laid here and there on the snowy damask below them.

Not only palms and tree ferns were sunk through tables – any tree or plant could be treated in this way and apparently there was no limit to the number. A letter to the *Garden* of 3 April 1875 describes a dinner party for 26 where the construction of the table permitted ten plants of dracaena to be put through its leaves 2 feet (60 centimetres) from the edge and at intervals of 3 feet (90 centimetres). Round each plant were zinc trays filled with white azaleas, crimson pelargoniums and fronds of maidenhair fern. In the centre of the table, gleaming gold dessert dishes of varying heights were admirably set off by the crimson, white and green of the plants and flowers, and filled with dull coloured fruit that did not detract from the colour scheme – russet apples, dried figs, 'Easter Beurre' pears, almonds, filberts, walnuts and olives.

If one was not prepared to cut a hole in one's dining-room table, Mr Burbidge explained that 'The pots may be concealed easily enough by draping them with common small leafed Ivy, Selaginella, creeping jenny or Periwinkles (vinca) or with Fern fronds pressed into the soil and gracefully bent over the sides.'

On 2 July 1885 *The Lady* described a Maypole Decoration, to be done at any time of the year, as long as a carpenter and other helping hands were available. Once the pole, 2-4 feet (60-120 centimetres) in height, was erected, a disc of wood was firmly nailed to its top.

The coming-of-age party of the Marquess of Stafford, given by his parents the Duke and Duchess of Sutherland at Trentham Hall in Staffordshire, from *The Illustrated London News*, 5 January 1850. Trees are shown 'growing' through the tables in one of the reception rooms.

White and dark red ribbon was plaited to the mast, and long garlands of flowers, preferably moss roses and pinks, were hung from the disc to the corners of the table 'where their ends can be fastened by knots of ribbon to the candlesticks, which must be tolerably high and preferably of the pillar form'. A stout nosegay was tied to the top of the pole to crown the festoons, and hoops of flowers and ribbons were hung round the maypole about 6 inches (15 centimetres) apart. The wooden base was heaped with moist sand and hidden with flowers and ferns.

The arrival of the vogue for using shades on candles, thus diverting light downwards, meant that tall stands were no longer satisfactory. Instead dining-room tables were decorated in the most extravagant fashion of all, with the entire surface covered by an imitation of a mossy bank, a flower-bed, or even a field with a crowd of trees, plants and flowers supposedly growing out of the moss, sand or grass, leaving no room at all for the dishes of dessert, which had to be handed round like the other courses.

In some houses the 'growing field' went too far, and on 27 July 1878 the *Garden* received a furious letter complaining that:

> table decoration ... is now ridiculously overdone.... Only a year or two ago a lady, high in rank and social influence, drove home from a grand dinner at a neighbour's house and ordered mutton chops, as she had not dined, and could not, as both Lady L's flower garden and conservatory seemed crushed onto the table .... No longer is it possible to dine in comfort with abundance of good talk to aid digestion, for now there are rocks, lakes, streams, waterfalls, ponds, glaciers, dense masses of foliage and flowers, tanks of moss, zinc dishes and glass dishes innumerable – all piled on the table to swamp the dinner and prevent the diners from either seeing each other, or their dinner, or indeed, anything save the decorations.'

Mrs Panton (see page 203) took a different view of the 'growing field' fashion. For those with 'little money and no experience' she suggested a flat wicker basket covered with moss, with flowers stuck in as though growing, and low groups of flowers and ferns in pots to look as much like a bank of flowers as possible. Candles with shades to match the prevailing hues of the flowers should stand on the tables, and the dessert should be handed round after dinner.

As a reaction to all this, the 'artistic' set in the 1880s began to decorate their tables in a very different way. When the Gladstone family stayed with Lord and Lady Aberdeen at Haddo House near Edinburgh in 1884, the table had a scattering of autumn leaves down the centre, surrounding the centrepieces of ferns in silver wine coolers, the candelabra and the fruit dishes. In the same year Lady Monkswell dined at a similarly decorated table when she stayed with Sir Julian Goldsmid, a distinguished banker and MP at Somerhill, his country house in Kent. She noted in her diary, 'the dinner table was exquisite with rows of different coloured leaves'.

Mary Gladstone, too, went in for 'artistic' arrangements at Downing Street. In 1880 for a particularly large dinner party attended by the Prince of Wales, there had to be tables in two rooms. One she arranged artistically with 'masses of flowers' sent up from Hawarden, 'covering it with chestnut and may, quite lovely and all done in an hour', while 'the great

Mentmore gardener [from Baron Mayer Amschel de Rothschild's home in Bucking-hamshire] took eight hours over the other, and it was not half so pretty'. The latter was probably decorated in a more conventional and formal way, so this juxtaposition is very interesting. For a dinner party two years later Mary Gladstone's decoration resembled 'one big cowslip field'.

For special occasions arches of flowers arose over the dining-room tables. In 1875 Annie Hassard described how she constructed a simple arch of wire secured in zinc pans, painted it all green and filled the pans with damp sand. Next she covered the arch with the creeping fern *Lygodium scandens*, using two plants with their roots transplanted into the pans of sand. Then through the lygodium she twined sprays of *Lapageria rosea*, or its white-flowered variety. A central flower stand and several trumpet vases surrounding it were filled with pink and white flowers, ferns and grasses and, with rosebuds and forget-me-nots in the pans at each end of the arch, the table was complete.

Illustrations in the gardening journals and in Mrs Beeton's *Household Management* show how arches of garlands were hung over tables (see page 224). At Cragside this custom continued right up to the beginning of the Second World War. The garlands were made of small roses, pinks or forget-me-nots attached at intervals to a string or fine wire

Dinner at Haddo House, by Alfred Edward Emslie, 1884. Guests include Lord Rosebery, extreme left, and William Gladstone, right foreground. In reaction to all the profusion of flowers and plants, the decoration of the table is limited to an artistic scattering of autumn leaves down the centre, and two centrepieces of ferns in silver wine coolers.

A dinner table with an arch decoration, as recommended by Mr Burbidge in *Domestic Floriculture*, published in 1875. He suggests covering the arch with *Lygodium scandens* (now *L. microphyllum*) and putting pink cacti, water-lilies, forget me nots and rose buds in the pans at either end.

covered with smilax or asparagus fern, with any joins hidden by a bow or a ball of foliage. The arch was formed by hanging them from the chandelier to the candelabra at the corners of the table. Sometimes circular garlands were hung round the table corners. In some houses, garlands were hung in swags around the edge of the table, but not at Cragside.

Garlands, sprays or single flowers were sewn onto dresses, supplied by the head gardener and applied by the lady's maid. Gardenias, stephanotis, pinks and border carnations stayed fresh for a long time without water, but other flowers had to be put into silver holders with just that degree of moisture to see them through four or five hours of the evening. When Alexandra, the Princess of Wales, stayed at Cragside in August 1884, she and Lady Armstrong were portrayed in a watercolour wearing dresses covered with fresh flowers (see page 196). At fashionable parties, ladies resembled perambulating herbaceous borders, with flowers in their hair, on their bosoms, sewn onto their dresses, while they carried gigantic bouquets.

Garlands of flowers were much in use for birthday and Christmas celebrations. Every year from 1846 a room was specially decorated for Queen Victoria's birthday on 24 May. A watercolour of her birthday table at Osborne House, painted in 1861, shows how garlands were placed everywhere, along the cornice, hanging in swags around the room, outlining the panels and mirrors, and along the top and bottom of the table. In addition, vases thought to have been arranged by her children are in front of the mirror, on the window-sill, on a table and on plant stands, while plants both large and small are massed on the floor around the room.

Mr Jones, the foreman gardener at Windsor Castle, decorated birthday tables for all the royal children. For Prince Arthur, Duke of Connaught's thirty-first birthday on 1 May 1881, an entry in the daybook reads 'Making wreaths [garlands] for Prince Arthur's Birthday to go round a table', and the next day with a hint of complaint, 'Sunday morning had to turn out at 4 to make Bouquet for the Prince'.

For the wedding in 1881 of Prince Leopold to Princess Helen of Waldeck at Windsor, so many flowers were required that even the vast garden at Frogmore could not provide enough and more were brought in from Veitch's nursery in Chelsea. The daybook records that on 22 April the gardener collected the plants ready for the Queen to inspect and approve. The following day he began arranging them. On the 25th he made '8 bouquets and 3 wreaths'. On the 26th there were eight people working on the displays: 'I arranged the Punch Bowl in the Private Dining Room with Fuchsia and Azaleas, etc.' On the actual

Queen Victoria's Birthday Table at Osborne House, 24 May 1861, painted by James Roberts. The room is full of flower arrangements and massed pot plants, as well as magnificent garlands. In the foreground the artist has laid a long, thick garland bound with ribbon and inscribed with names of countries, towns and houses which may refer to some of the places visited by the royal family in the previous year.

wedding day, the working party went up to twelve, and Mr Jones was gratified to see the procession of Prince Leopold's marriage.

For the coming-of-age of the Marquess of Stafford, held at Trentham in Staffordshire on 5 January 1850, the architect Charles Barry supervised the decorations. Garlands were used to decorate the temporary supper room erected in a courtyard – thick ones of flowers linked the capitals of the columns surrounding the room and thin ones of evergreens were twined round each column. *The Illustrated London News* reported that 'the ceiling was composed of crimson and white drapery ornamented with wreaths and festoons of evergreens' and that an arch of flowers surmounted the entrance to the drive.

Garlands of greenery, in greater profusion than ever, provided decoration for Christmas. For those in need of inspiration as to how to use them, magazines such as *The Lady* provided imaginative ideas, including geometric patterns and letters for overdoors and blank walls, with diagrams and instructions.

Encouraged by Prince Albert and Queen Victoria, Christmas trees were no longer the preserve of the royal family, but were appearing in many homes. The Hon. Eleanor Stanley, a maid of honour to the Queen, wrote to her mother on Christmas Day 1847 describing the scene in the Oak Room at Windsor Castle on the previous evening, when the ladies in waiting received their gifts. The Queen and the Prince stood by a large table, covered with a white cloth, in the middle of which was a decorated fir tree surrounded by presents. The royal children, like the ladies, shared a tree, but Queen Victoria, Prince Albert and the

ABOVE: The Grand Banquet at Lord Stafford's coming-of-age party from *The Illustrated London News*, 5 January 1850. Garlands are festooned around the room, and encircle the pillars.

RIGHT: *An American Dining Room on Christmas Eve*, a pencil drawing by Lucy Ellen Merrill, *c*.1870. Greenery has been used on every conceivable surface, including the chandelier, the corner cupboard and the message of prayer and greeting at the end of the room.

FAR RIGHT: Victorian Christmas decorations set out in the eighteenth-century dining room at Tatton Park. On the table, the epergne contains red carnations with a fringe of ruscus. Tracery and garlands made out of a mixture of foliage, including ivy, ruscus, holly, laurel, gaultheria, camellia leaves, asparagus fronds and sprengeri ferns, are spread over the table and mantelpiece, creating a spectacular effect.

Duchess of Kent (the Queen's mother) had one each as usual. Miss Stanley thought she had never seen anything prettier.

Queen Victoria strove to spread the custom by presenting trees to barracks and schools where large Christmas parties took place. On 16 January 1865 she wrote to Major (later Sir) Howard Elphinstone, 'She rejoices to think that the Prince and herself are the source of Christmas trees being so generally adopted in this country.'

The custom spread to America. A pencil drawing of *c*.1870 of an American dining room on Christmas Eve shows not only a tree laden with decorations and candles, but also to what extent garlands of greenery were used in the room. Here they trace round the cornice, the windows and all around the corner cupboard and its shelves. They entwine the chains or cords from which mirrors, pictures and chandeliers are suspended, and a large festoon of greenery hangs from the chandelier. They even form the words of prayer and greeting at the far end of the room, and demarcate each place setting in front of which is a pile of presents.

Many National Trust houses now try to recreate Christmas decorations and customs of the period. At Tatton Park in Cheshire, for instance, all the rooms are decorated in late nineteenth-century style, while the dining-room table is laid out as for a Christmas meal.

Peter Henderson in his *Practical Floriculture* gave advice for flower decorations for American parties: 'Balls of flowers, like hanging baskets, are best displayed from the centre of an arch or folding doors, and with festoons of flowers looped from centre to sides the effect is greatly heightened.' Descriptions of these decorations were followed with great interest in Britain. *The Journal of Horticulture* in 1874 noted that 'the profuseness with which flowers are used in New York is fairly a subject of extraordinary comment'. It went on to describe how festoons of smilax looped with rosebuds were arranged along the

Watercolour from 'A Memorial of the Marriage of H.R.H. Albert, Prince of Wales', an album compiled by Sir William Howard Russell in 1863. This scene shows Princess Alexandra arriving with the Prince at the Bricklayers Arms Station in London, to find the station covered in garlands of laurel and white and red roses, and plants massed around the base of statues borrowed for the occasion.

cornices, draperies of roses and smilax hung between the windows and the mantels divided into three beds of flowers, with violets in the centre, daphnes and roses on each end and groundwork of lycopodium and ferns. In the wide doors between drawing rooms, there was a canopy of flowers shaped like a parasol and supporting nine balls made of different kinds of flowers. Walls were transformed into beds of flowers with wire frames supporting great fields of heliotrope, camellias, roses, tuberoses and carnations, edged with ferns, smilax and the scarlet leaves of poinsettia.

Such an extravagance of flowers might cost $2,000 for one evening, and similar sums are quoted for parties in Britain. In 1871 Sir Edward Scott 'gave his house up into his florist's hands for three full days, with carte blanche orders, regardless of expense, the only stipulation being that the handsomest decorations possible should be produced'. The result was apparently so novel and beautiful that afterwards 'everyone who gave great entertainments followed in the track which he had pointed out'.

For great entertainments the staircase often could be a decorative focus. Mr Burbidge recommended covering it with crimson baize which looked 'very beautiful fringed on each side with Palms, Ferns, Isolepsis and flowering plants such as Begonias, Liliums, Vallotas, Chrysanthemums or Spireas'. Ferns could provide a useful screen. In her memoirs, Lady Monkswell remembered how her engagement took place on 29 June 1874 at her future mother-in-law's London house in Eaton Place: 'Behind the ferns on the stairs my dear old Bob committed himself . . . I was struck dumb.'

Ivy was one vital ingredient of parties. In 1874 John Wills, a leading London decorator, supplied two tons of ivy and 2,000 blooms of 'Maréchal Niel' roses to drape the pictures, mirrors and walls at the Mansion House for a ball. At a similar event given by the Marquess of Bristol six tons of ivy was used to give a castellated effect to the bare walls of an improvised ballroom.

Another important ingredient was ice, sometimes in the form of obelisks wreathed with ivy, *Lygodium scandens*, etc. At a ball given by the Princess of Wales in honour of the Csarina of Russia in the large conservatory of the Royal Horticultural Society at South Kensington 'ten tons of the finest ice were employed in building an illuminated rockery which, draped with drooping ferns, surrounded by crimson baize and illuminated from within, was strikingly effective and much admired'.

On important occasions flower decorations could spill out into the streets. The arrival in England of the young Danish princess, Alexandra, a few days before her marriage to the Prince of Wales on 10 March 1863 is recorded in an album compiled by Sir William Howard Russell and illustrated with watercolours. After a rough crossing on the royal yacht, she was cheered to find the pier, station and streets of Gravesend decorated as though for a ball:

Festoons of roses, disposed in regular series in the same order of colour were suspended across the street from tall masts so that from one extremity the spectator saw . . . what seemed a colonnade roofed in with curved lines of bright garlands . . . the windows and even the dead walls of the houses were draped with wreaths of flowers and evergreens . . . one was tempted to think all England must have laid tribute to furnish the display.

At the end of her train journey to London, she found the Bricklayers Arms Station decorated with 'an affluence of flowering exotics . . . sweet and odorous. . . . The roof of the Terminus . . . was transformed into an enormous inverted flower garden, from which laurels, white and red roses and a forest of evergreens, arranged so as to form distinct patterns of colours, sprang downwards, and through their tendrils, festoons and garlands clustered all over the naked beams and joiners' work aloft.' With classic understatement, another observer wrote, 'the station had assumed an aspect quite unlike that of its very ordinary everyday look'.

Unreal Loveliness

1890–1930

'The character and cost of flower decoration changed completely. Orchids replaced Begonias, Malmaisons replaced Petunias … outsize orchids, outsize Malmaisons, outsize lilies … the flower scents were stifling.' This is how Sonia Keppel, daughter of Alice, one of Edward VII's mistresses, recalls the early years of the twentieth century.

The actual reign of Edward VII lasted from 1901 to 1910, but his influence on society and fashion was already paramount in the ten years leading up to his accession, and prevailed until the outbreak of the First World War in 1914. In some of the grandest establishments the extravagant lifestyle continued unabated into the 1930s.

Quantities of the most beautiful, perfectly formed flowers were required for rooms at all times of the year. In 1896, Arthur Beavan described the household of the Prince and Princess of Wales in *Marlborough House and its Occupants*. Of their flowers he wrote:

> From three hundred to four hundred vases of cut flowers, constantly changed and kept fresh, are used every day in the various Royal apartments, necessitating the employment of two men exclusively for this work. It is somewhat difficult to decide as to which are the Princess's [Alexandra's] favourite flowers – everything from the lowly wild flowers to the regal lily is welcome to her, but probably roses, carnations, lilies-of-the-valley, tulips of all colours, and violets command her greatest attention.
>
> … In their lavish use of flowers, the Royal owners of Marlborough House, apart from personal liking, are only adapting themselves to the universal fashion of the day. Nothing is more remarkable than the immense increase of florists' shops in London during the last 40 years; and the amount of money expended in fashionable circles upon indoor flower decoration is prodigious.

At one stage, the King decided that he must economise, and so went round inspecting the floral arrangements. He found that the only saving he could make was one small vase with three roses from Queen Alexandra's boudoir. The Queen indignantly ordered this to be put back, and that was the end of the matter.

At Waddesdon Manor in Buckinghamshire, built by Baron Ferdinand de Rothschild between 1874 and 1889, over 40 glasshouses were needed to achieve the required floral delights. Grouped around an enormous palm house, they covered most of the four-acre walled garden and included separate houses for orchids, agaves, camellias, crotons, anthuriums, Malmaison carnations, pelargoniums, azaleas, and sweet peas. Sadly all these glasshouses were demolished in the 1960s when it was realised that their deterioration had reached a dangerous level.

Princess Alexandra, Lady Armstrong and guests in the drawing room at Cragside; a watercolour by H.H. Emmerson from the album compiled to commemorate the visit of the Prince and Princess of Wales in 1884. The Princess is a living flower arrangement, with bouquets sewn onto her dress, and a bouquet held in her hand.

ABOVE: Interior of the Cool Fern House situated on a north-facing wall in the garden at West Dean. The staging on either side of the brick path is covered with plants of streptocarpus (pink 'Gloria' and blue 'Falling Stars'). Amongst them is a collection of nineteenth-century ivy cultivars and behind are lilies: 'Casa Blanca', 'White America' and *speciosum* var. *album*.

RIGHT: Clumber Park in Nottinghamshire was the country seat of the Dukes of Newcastle until 1938, when the house was demolished. The extensive walled gardens and their superb nineteenth-century glasshouses have survived, however, and are being restored. This photograph, taken in the 1920s, shows the central palm house and one of the long wings in the background, and in front the cutting garden filled with plants for decoration of the house.

But at West Dean in Sussex, a Jacobean house bought by William and Evelyn James in 1890 and their home until 1912, the glasshouses put up during their tenure have recently been skilfully restored and appropriate plants are again flourishing in them. The Decorative Display House contains a large collection of coleus and nineteenth-century cultivars of fuchsias, pelargoniums and Malmaison carnations. The Temperate House, Stove or Tropical House, Orchid House and a small Fernery also contain plants that would have decorated the rooms of the house.

Mr Smith, who supervised a staff of twenty gardeners, was interviewed by *Garden Life* in August 1904. Under glass he listed 1,000 chrysanthemums (the Japanese incurved and bush varieties), 1,000 tree carnations, 300 border carnations, 150 coleus, 150 poinsettias, 600 heliotrope and 100 *Exacum affine* (Persian violet). For Goodwood Race Week in July, when Edward VII joined the James's house party, 200 campanulas and 36 humeas had to be 'in blow'. The Malmaisons were flowering then, too, and 150 dozen were cut for the house between March and August. Winter-flowering begonias filled an entire glasshouse, ready to decorate the house for Willy James's famous shooting parties.

A cutting garden, or 'reserve garden' as it was then called, has been recreated at West Dean. Gertrude Jekyll advised that the reserve garden should consist of 'narrow beds set apart for the purpose. Four foot is a convenient width for the beds'. It was usually situated in the kitchen garden, and could be bounded by flowering shrubs which provided blossom for vases. Other flowers were picked from double borders that often lined a walk through the walled garden, hiding the vegetables from view. At West Dean, not only does a photograph of such borders survive, but also a description of the flowers in them, given by Mr Smith: 'Roses, Clematis and Jasmine are grown on the trellis behind, and the border

Nineteenth-century conservatory filled with chrysanthemums at Sibalds Holme on the Peckover Estate in Wisbech. On the left of the open doorway is an aspidistra plant, and on either side of the old lady are cordyline or dracaena plants of upright aspect with long, lance-shaped colourful leaves. The right hand one is overshadowed by a kentia palm.

Begonias in the orangery at Peckover House in Wisbech. These plants were extremely popular with Victorians and Edwardians, who valued their brightly coloured flowers for decorating the house in winter.

includes Delphiniums, several varieties of Phlox, a quantity of Tree Paeonies, Campanula latifolia, Salpiglossis in variety, Scabiosa caucasica [a soft lilac-blue shade], Asters in variety, the old Scarlet Lychnis, Alpine Pinks, and a number of single Hollyhocks'.

Other flowers could also be picked from the numerous flower beds dotted on the lawn outside Mrs James's morning room, and on other lawns surrounding the house. Contemporary photographs show that many beds contained flowers of only one kind. One large bed consisted of 800 phlox, another of the orange *Lilium henryi*, 9 to 10 feet (2.75 to 3 metres) high, one of Belladonna delphiniums and another entirely of asters.

Gertrude Jekyll's borders were filled with 'groups' of one kind of flower massed together and carefully positioned to harmonise with its neighbouring group. In due course not only beds, but whole gardens within gardens were devoted to one colour: Lawrence Johnson's Red Garden at Hidcote Manor in Gloucestershire and Vita Sackville-West's White Garden at Sissinghurst Castle in Kent are famous examples. This was echoed indoors, where it was the fashion to have one kind of flower in one colour in a vase.

Introductions of this period were, generally, species of plants already known rather than new varieties. Probably the most important was a new species of lily, *Lilium regale*, found on the borders of China and Tibet in 1903 by Ernest Wilson, collecting for Kew and the Veitchs. From China too came the cherry tree, *Prunus sargentii* (1893), which led to the introduction of many other species of Chinese and Japanese cherries and to the fashion for displaying vases full of their blossom.

This was a time of hybridisation and specialist breeding, carried out by nurserymen, plantsmen and private gardeners. The first 'waved' variety of sweet pea was raised by the gardener to the 5th Earl Spencer at Althorp Park in Northamptonshire, and named 'Countess Spencer' in 1900. The aim was to increase the number of flowers on each stalk, and the variety of colours of this very popular flower.

At Eaton Hall in Cheshire, home of the Duke of Westminster, there was a specialist orchid breeder in residence. Loelia, Duchess of Westminster, explained how this came about: 'The very first visit of all I made to Eaton, I went round the wonderful greenhouses, and I idly remarked "You haven't got any orchids".... When I went back to Eaton after our honeymoon, I found a whole conservatory or greenhouse full of orchids – not only that, but there was a laboratory with an orchid specialist in a white coat, mixing up pollen for new species.'

When being wooed by the Duke, Loelia received almost daily deliveries of flowers: 'He always sent South African chincherinchees, then a rarity. They arrived in wooden boxes and had waxed ends to the stems which had to be cut off. Then one put them in the dark for three days and when they finally emerged, they lasted for ever.'

Malmaison carnations vied with orchids to be the favourite flowers in the grandest houses. Jim Marshall, who holds the National Collection of Malmaisons, notes that although they originated in France, their cultivation was perfected in Britain. 'Old Blush' or 'Souvenir de la Malmaison', so called because it resembled the flowers of the Bourbon rose of that name, first came to Britain during the 1860s. By the end of the century a number of cultivars were being grown, and they had become the flower of fashion for the London Season, sought after for their distinctive fragrance of cloves.

The White Garden at Barrington Court in Somerset. The planting of the garden at Barrington was designed by Gertrude Jekyll for Colonel Lyle in 1920. She was in her late seventies, with very poor eyesight, so the plans and samples of garden soil were sent in biscuit tins to her home in Surrey. Her Rose and Peony Garden was replanted as a White Garden in 1986 as a result of rose sickness: it was designed by Colonel Lyle's grandson, Andrew, using Miss Jekyll's *Colour Schemes for the Flower Garden*. Strongly Edwardian in character, its planting includes antirrhinums, cosmos, gypsophila and silver stachys.

A single flower of the Malmaison carnation 'Princess of Wales' in a champagne flute. Edwardian ladies would have received such a flower on their breakfast tray in the privacy of their bedroom.

Consuelo, Duchess of Marlborough, recalled in her memoirs the visit of the Prince and Princess of Wales to Blenheim Palace in the 1890s: 'the long suite of reception rooms filled with orchids and malmaisons looked to me truly palatial'. One night, the dining room table was decked with a profusion of huge pink malmaisons and the next, with a display of soft mauve and white orchids.

Where high society led, a newly enriched and expectant professional class followed. In 1893 a contributor to the *Pall Mall Magazine* wrote: 'The houses of the great, the decoration of their tables, their dinners, their dresses, their carriages, all are followed by every other class, with a fidelity only limited by their pecuniary ability . . . with passionate fervour the whole community follows the example set by the coterie [the set surrounding the Prince of Wales], simply because it is the highest in the land.'

Newspapers and periodicals of the day reported on the flower arrangements at grand balls and parties, but it was a group of pioneering ladies who gave detailed advice in a

series of books called *Art at Home*. Mrs Panton wrote a weekly column in the *Ladies Pictorial*, answered letters privately for 7s 6d, and would travel anywhere to give advice for a guinea and her expenses. Her book *Nooks and Corners* published in 1889 was 'to assist the timid and those who lack confidence in their own tastes, and furthermore who may live in distant country places, where nothing new penetrates even in these days of parcel posts and illustrated newspapers'. Nothing is left to chance in her advice:

> In the richest households there are many things which should never be left to servants if one wishes the house to look like the abode of a lady ... the principal one in my eyes being the arrangement of the flowers. The best gardener in the world has only a gardener's ideas.... The first duty a girl should undertake is that of going round the rooms the moment breakfast is over, to decide which plants are to be removed and which vases should be refilled. In the country the gardener should wait her orders,

The Library at Polesden Lacey. This was Mrs Greville's favourite room and, as in her day, the flowers have been chosen to go with the white walls and yellow furnishings: white lilies and narcissi, yellow gladioli and freesias, orange freesias and blue *Brodiaea laxa* to harmonise with them. Many of the vases are blue and white Kangxi *c.*1700, and they are filled with just one kind of flower with a little asparagus fern, as was the fashion in the early twentieth century. Mrs Greville's desk is covered with vases of flowers and framed photographs of her guests, 'all with signed inscriptions testifying to their friendship for this popular hostess'.

and have the flowers gathered dry and before the heat of the sun is on them, and should himself exchange the plants, the position of them being determined by his mistress as the arrangement of the flowers should be left to her alone. If done systematically in the manner here indicated, all the house will look fresh and nice.

Having discovered the enjoyable pastime of arranging the household flowers, Edwardian ladies required somewhere to carry this out. So instead of, or sometimes in addition to, the flower rooms in the walled gardens for the convenience of the head gardener, a special room was required in the house itself. In *Leaves from a Housekeeper's Book* (1914) the indefatigable Mrs Panton insists that: 'Flowers should not be "done" in the drawing room. A young mistress should take all the vases and plants out of the room when she thinks they require attention, and should have a place set apart for that purpose, and neither haste nor laziness should allow her to depart from that rule.'

At Rockbeare Manor, built in 1740 near Exeter in Devon, this need was fulfilled in 1914 when charming cupboards were built on either side of a passage leading to a door into the garden. Shelves above hold the vases, while on one side the lower part of the cupboard consists of a table which can be pulled out on which to arrange the flowers, and in the cupboard on the other side is a basin with taps. When Coleton Fishacre, also in Devon, was built in 1926 for the D'Oyly Carte family, a flower room was incorporated. On entering the hall, it is the first room that one comes to, conveniently situated opposite the saloon. A pretty room, with a window looking out onto the forecourt, it has the usual sink and cupboards – it also doubled as the 'telephone room' and still has its original telephone.

Mrs Panton reckoned that the arrangement of flowers should occupy the lady of the house for at least an hour each day, 'after which [she] should sit down for a steady read at some standard work, or else to sewing work'. Cecil Beaton in *The Glass of Fashion* (1954) looked back at the central position flowers held in his mother's life:

> Like any other hostess of the period my mother gave luncheons or dinner parties. The day of these events she would be too busy to give any but the most cursory attention to her personal appearance, though the flowers were always tastefully arranged on all the occasional tables. The masterpiece of decoration, most usually sweet peas, was saved for the centre of the dining table.

The development of refrigeration made it possible for a wide range of flowers to be available all the year round. But fashion dictated that flowers in an arrangement should nearly always be of the same kind. Lady Ashbrook's Edwardian aunts told her that it was 'very vulgar to mix flowers'. Not only was it unfashionable, but people might think you could not afford to grow enough of one kind to fill the vase. Only with the publication of Constance Spry's first book, *Flower Decoration*, in 1934 did the idea of 'mixed' flowers become acceptable again, and even then they were frowned upon by the older generation, who considered it a rather racy, not to say common, way of arranging flowers.

Not only were the same flowers displayed in one arrangement, but they could also provide the whole theme for the dining room, where the flowers on the table, on the sideboard and on the mantelpiece were often all the same. There was considerable debate

about the ideal greenery accompaniment: foreign versus own foliage. In one gardening journal a correspondent 'from a great house in the county of Lincoln' wrote that in his opinion 'Lycopodium and Ferns for flowers to rest on are the outcome, to say the least, of a depraved taste. Avoid above all things foreign foliage … only use foliage cut with the flowers as inseparable.' He liked to fill silver wine coolers with Roman hyacinths, or lily of the valley *en masse*. A letter soon came back in response: 'For those as myself, who have to do without costly vessels for the arrangement of flowers and plants, I frequently find a simple arrangement of foliage and flowers affords much pleasure. Some foreign foliage is essential, and ferns are essential for orchids, flowering as they do without foliage.'

Palms were used everywhere, placed on tables or on stands of every size, shape and

height, some practically touching the ceiling. Their roots were crammed into various pots or baskets, or were wrapped around with a piece of material. This style of decoration has been recreated at Waddesdon where tall kentia palms in eighteenth-century porcelain bowls on stands, underplanted with maidenhair fern, decorate the galleries and other rooms. By 1914, however, Mrs Panton had to defend her affection for palms in the face of their waning popularity: 'Personally I find palms a great resource in London, though I am told by hypercritical folk that they are only to be seen in restaurants nowadays. I do not care in the least. Flowers in London are much too expensive, and had I not some of the kindest friends on earth who continually post me flowers from the country, I should never have any in the house.'

The development in style of flower arrangements continued towards the more natural, as noted in the previous chapter. Instead of a few blooms resting on the top of a trumpet vase, it would now be filled with long spreading stems, such as montbretia, gladioli, chrysanthemums, lilies or Solomon's seal, which was particularly recommended by Robert Felton, a leading florist of Hanover Square in London. For a softening effect, gypsophila or asparagus fern might be mixed with the flowers. Branches of blossom were also popular. The vases themselves were taller, sometimes of such a height that they stood on the floor. As well as trumpet vases, there were containers in the shape of cylinders, such as those used in Japanese flower arrangements, or of variations of cylinder, including simulated pieces of bamboo. Violets and lily of the valley were put in bowls, water lilies floated in shallow dishes, and roses and sweet peas were provided with special vases of their own.

Mr Felton detested the 'prim dwarfed bunches of flowers' seen in homes half a century earlier. In 1910 he published *British Floral Decoration*, in which he advised those in doubt to 'ask themselves where and how the flowers with which they might be dealing originally grew' and then 'endeavour to arrange them in as nearly similar positions as possible. . . . Thus, if you have robbed a Laburnum in the garden of one of its branches, see that it is put in a high vase on the tallest pedestal in the house, so that it may be looked up to; or, if you wish to get the best effect from a great bunch of roses, arrange them in a rose-bowl on a low table where you can look down into their very hearts.'

'It is advisable', he continues, 'when decorating to employ one kind of flower, or at most two. Gertrude Jekyll in *Flower Decoration in the House*, 1907, also allows that two-flower arrangements can be tolerated with the proviso that 'they should only be attempted by those with a keen and well trained colour eye'. For those without her skill, she makes suggestions: poets narcissus with sweet briar – a charming association both for sight and smell; blood red wallflowers with white tulips; . . . *Eryngium giganteum* (the silver thistle) mixed with white foxgloves, delphiniums or five stems of *Campanula lactiflora*, 5 feet (1.5 metres) high with its large heads of a pyramidal outline of pretty bell flowers.

For noble rooms in great country houses, she suggests pampas plumes on stems 8 feet (2.5 metres) high, carefully placed in tall Nankin jars on either side of a marble console, on which is a jar of wider shape, filled with the silvery pods of honesty, cut in whole plants 3 feet (90 centimetres) high, with great handfuls of the red berried pods of *Iris foetidissima*, and the scarlet Chinese lanterns of the large physalis.

Among her favourite single flower arrangements are: rose 'Madame Alfred Carrière' cut

The Jacobean Corridor at Polesden Lacey. A very tall glass trumpet vase, with an arrangement of lilies, stands on the floor just to the left of a portrait of Mrs Greville, painted by Carolus-Duran at the time of her marriage in 1891. Palms in pots are ranged all along the Corridor.

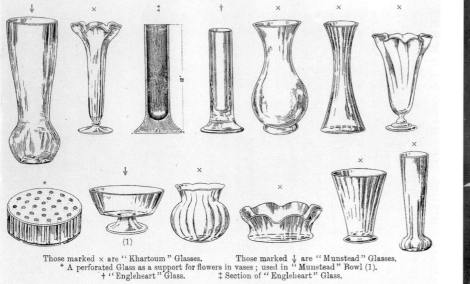

Those marked × are "Khartoum" Glasses.   Those marked ↓ are "Munstead" Glasses.
* A perforated Glass as a support for flowers in vases ; used in "Munstead" Bowl (1).
† "Engleheart" Glass.   ‡ Section of "Engleheart" Glass.

ABOVE: R.P. Brotherston's recommendations of vases for cut flowers in *The Book of Cut Flowers* published in 1906. On the left, lower row, is a perforated glass to support flowers within the 'Munstead' glass.

RIGHT: Two arrangements in Munstead glasses recommended for June in Gertrude Jekyll's *Flower Decoration in the House*, published in 1907. On the right, flag iris and artichoke leaves, on the left, stock 'White Cloud' and stachys.

with stems 3 to 4 feet (90 to 120 centimetres) long; iris and artichoke leaves, which need a complete immersion with the cut end split open to make them last; brilliant coloured gladioli, tiger lilies, sunflowers and 'the new tall variety of snapdragons'. In wide bowls, she recommends whole sprays of sweet peas, or pansies 9 inches (25 centimetres) high. For silver bowls, lily of the valley, Christmas roses or white hyacinths. And to scent a whole room, little blooms of wintersweet, floating on a shallow dish of water.

Rooms used for 'living in' during the Edwardian period remained the same as during the second half of the nineteenth century – drawing rooms, libraries, morning rooms, galleries and halls. Boudoirs were the domain of ladies, smoking rooms, also known as studies, of men. On the whole, rooms were now furnished more sparsely and decorated more plainly, with most of the clutter removed.

However, there were distinctions in style. Houses of the old aristocracy, where the furnishings had been built up through successive generations, were conspicuous in their resistance to change. Three such houses, now in the care of the National Trust, show how the prevailing fashions were interpreted in very individual ways, and provide different aspects of Edwardian flower arrangements.

At Lyme Park in Cheshire, Lord and Lady Newton liked their flowers to be flamboyant and showy. This is evident from pictorial records – watercolours painted by Lord Newton's sister, Dulcibella (known as Sybil) in 1898, and photographs of the rooms taken in 1900 and 1904. These are backed up by written accounts: *Treasure on Earth*, a description of an idyllic family Christmas in 1906 by their youngest daughter, Phyllis, and the memories of gardeners and estate workers employed at Lyme between 1898 and 1946 that have been preserved in a book entitled *Cricketer Preferred* – the words included in every advertisement for new staff, such was the importance of the Lyme cricket team.

Under the tenure of Thomas Legh, 2nd Lord Newton, Lyme enjoyed an Indian summer in the years before the First World War. Lady Newton, proud of the fact that the Leghs had lived at Lyme for five hundred years, allowed few changes. For instance, the family continued to dine *à la française* when 'fashionable society' was enthusiastically embracing *à la russe* (see page 176). But her vivacious nature found expression in exuberant arrangements of flowers that decorated every room.

Some of the greenhouses that supplied the flowers were remembered by Dora Addison, whose father Joseph was head gardener from 1907 to 1922. 'There was a malmaison house … and two or three pit-greenhouses, sunk in the ground. They were kept very hot for orchids and things like that.'

Oswald Stokes describes his time as one of three gardeners who slept in the bothy. Every third week they had to take their turn at being 'duty man' to keep the greenhouse boilers going continuously:

You used to start the duty 12 o'clock Saturday right the way through to 12 o'clock the next Saturday, and when that snow was there you used to have to stoke the greenhouse boilers all night long. You were up there at 10 o'clock, then 12 o'clock, then 3 o'clock … and 5. The duty man had to keep going. And of course all the laundrymaids and the housemaids and that were out tobogganing! … The orangery used to be full of camellias, and you've never seen such a sight in all your life.

The orangery, designed by Lewis Wyatt in 1815 and finished by the 1st Lord Newton in 1862, still stands on the top terrace near the house, with camellias covering an entire wall – providing an unforgettable sight in spring.

Lord and Lady Newton's daughter-in-law, Helen, must have ruled her garden staff with a rod of iron, for the memory remains that the head gardener was terrified to death of her. 'He'd be smoking a pipe, you know, and somebody'd say, "Mrs Legh's coming". "BY GOD MAN, WHERE?". Pipe would go in his pocket – I've seen him throw it in the pond.'

In due course both Joseph Addison and Oswald Stokes were promoted to arranging the flowers in the Bright Gallery that runs round three sides of the inner courtyard and is so called because of the light from its many deep-silled windows. On each sill stood a metal tray (they still exist), which had always to be furnished with large terracotta pots of flowers. Dora Addison used to help her father: 'sometimes lilies, sometimes chrysanthemums, three pots to a window. You had to put a dustsheet down, bless you, and you had to have a sponge to mop up the water from the tray, and be off the corridor at eight o'clock. By gum, we did see life!'

Oswald Stokes remembered the flowers used: '400 plants to decorate those windows. … In the summer we had pelargonias … before that there was all the specials like begonias, lorraines [winter-flowering begonia 'Gloire de Lorraine'], poinsettias and tuberous begonias. It was a very interesting job because you weren't really rushed. You just had time to grow all these things in preparation for the time when the people came there.' Like many landed families, the Leghs divided their time between London and the country.

A photograph taken of the Bright Gallery in 1900 shows three pots of giant white tobacco plants (nicotiana) on the metal tray on each sill – the scent must have been

ABOVE: The Bright Gallery at Lyme Park, a photograph taken in 1900, showing pots of giant white nicotiana in trays on the windowsills.

entrancing. A photograph taken a few years later shows spreading palms or ferns balancing on each newel of the grand staircase. Another, again of 1900, shows the flowers in the large entrance hall: tall, slender trumpet vases standing on cloth-covered tables on either side of the fireplace, filled with tall, spreading, fulsome arrangements. (These trumpet vases still stand in their traditional places, filled with flowers.) On a cabinet against the wall are five large oriental vases with long, branching stems of blossom. One of Sybil's watercolours shows an unusual wrought-iron stand in the form of a screen covered with pots of ferns in the hall. Another shows that most of the space in an alcove off the library is taken up by a banded wooden wine cooler, filled with tall red flowers, perhaps camellias, with a hanging basket of greenery dangling overhead. A third shows that even a bedroom is furnished with a large rectangular wire stand on legs, full of what seem to be giant pink orchids.

But it is in the saloon, where the family often gathered, that the flowers were most spectacular. A photograph shows a tall spreading arrangement of larkspur and asparagus fronds in a vase raised high on a tall stand. Two more stands with arrangements flank a mirror, in front of which is a third, enormous arrangement of plants. The writing desk and every other flat surface is covered with a mixture of photographs and vases of flowers. The magic of the scene in the saloon at Christmas in 1906 stayed with Phyllis Legh all her life, until she wrote about it nearly fifty years later:

The door of the saloon opened on a scene of almost unreal loveliness; ... not the unreality of a stage setting, much more like an exquisite dream – a scene of comfort, elegance, beauty, not quite of this world .... Dividing the actual room from the one in the looking glass rose a hedge of chrysanthemums, scarlet poinsettias and lilies. Every-where stood pots of fuchsias and gloxinias. There were long-branching, many coloured carnations and small, clustering bright pink begonias, and on one table two or three lilies of the arum family, shaped like scarlet parasols with long yellow spikes, standing up stiffly in a tall vase.

The butler, Truelove, attended to the Christmas tree, which was no ordinary tree. 'The shape was now perfect, thanks to the additional branches, which no one, without being told, could possibly have detected. There were rainbow-coloured iridescent glass balls hanging singly and in garlands, showers of sparkling tinsel, small toy crocodiles and golliwogs, a figure of Father Christmas on the top-most branch and, of course, innumer-able candles.' On Christmas Day the 'great shimmering blazing tree' dominated the Long Gallery – 'the only light in the room except the fire' with its very tallest branches touching the ceiling.

Another glimpse of Christmas decorations is given by the 'decorator', one of twenty

Three watercolours by Sybil Legh showing how plants were used to decorate Lyme Park in 1898. FAR LEFT: a stand of wrought iron with five pots of ferns, in the Entrance Hall; LEFT: the Grand Staircase with a vase of ferns balanced on the newel post; ABOVE: the Yellow Bedroom with a plant stand probably filled with pink orchids.

The Saloon at Lyme, photographed in 1900. In the foreground, on a perilously thin stand, is an arrangement of larkspur and asparagus fern, two more stands with flowers flank the mirror, and orchids adorn a table. In front of the mirror is a large stand full of plants. Six years later Phyllis Legh was to describe this as 'a hedge of chrysanthemums, scarlet poinsettias and lilies … dividing the actual room from the one in the looking glass'.

gardeners employed at Cliveden in Berkshire, home of the Astor family. He received his orders from Lady Astor, sometimes arranging flowers in the house three times a day, in the early morning, before lunch and before dinner. He also travelled to London with flowers for the Astors' house in St James's Square. For Christmas:

> it had always got to be Poinsettias, they had always got to be six feet [1.8 metres] tall … the festooning took a fortnight to prepare, and it was always the butler's worry when it got crisp and dry, if there was a fire it would go like tinder. And the big hall, that was festooned from corner to corner, and all round the other loops, all down the stairs, and all the pillars was done with little ones, a terrific job, an orange tree had to go in, you know. If you hadn't got any oranges on it, well, you made some, bought some!

At Dunham Massey Hall in Cheshire, only twenty miles from Lyme Park, the Earl and Dowager Countess of Stamford's preference was for flower arrangements that were quiet and homely. These are remembered by Arthur Shufflebotham who started working there in 1934, aged fourteen, as 'vegetable boy'. After two years he was put on to helping out with the flowers in the house, under the tutelage of Mr Gillies, the head gardener. The style had not varied since the beginning of the century: one variety in a vase. All the Edwardian vases are still at Dunham, and continue in use.

Lady Stamford preferred small flowers such as fritillaries, forget-me-nots and rosebuds which she picked herself and put in her study. But this was the exception, Arthur Shufflebotham recalls, 'soon after seven a couple of chaps went and did the flowers in the hall [house] and that would go on until about quarter to nine . . .'. Not only were they arranged in the dining room and the summer parlour, but also the bedrooms, and even the pantry and the kitchen.

As the beds on the lawn were filled almost entirely with bedding plants, flowers for the house were grown with the fruit in the heated greenhouses in a large walled garden, half a mile away. In the Intermediate House grew white and pink camellias, which flowered for most of the winter and spring. They were followed by sweet peas which kept going until winter set in again. Seeds were sent from Holland, and the tendrils removed as they grew, achieving stems over 14 inches (36 centimetres) long. Red, pink and white single geraniums 'as tall as trees' grew against the back wall of the Vinery, alongside spray chrysanthemums in bronze, white, pink and cream, pots of *regale* or Easter lilies, and carnations.

The Peach House accommodated pink and blue hydrangeas in pots, followed by lace-caps that flowered through the winter. Hundreds of pots of arum lilies were forced in heated frames, while thousands of bulbs were coerced in greenhouses. Daffodils, narcissi and tulips were expected to be ready for picking a fortnight before Christmas, and to keep going until the ones in the woodland and pleasure gardens were in flower.

Lady Stamford was not keen on orchids, so only about half a dozen were grown in a pit cucumber house. But she loved chincherinchees, which were sent throughout the year, ready cut, from a sister in South Africa. In turn Lady Stamford sent camellias to her daughter, June Turnbull, in Kent, each branch fastened down separately and wrapped in cotton wool.

In addition to the greenhouse flowers, spring shrubs in the pleasure ground, such as jasmine, kerria and forsythia, provided blossom for the house. In summer, a susbstantial double herbaceous border in the kitchen garden, known as the Green Walk, yielded 'everything you can think of', including helenium, rudbeckia, scabious and golden rod.

Flowers in pots that had been scrubbed until spotlessly clean, were taken to the house in a handcart. Cut flowers were arranged in the pantry, where there was a good fire. Flower arrangements held fast to the tradition of one kind, one colour, apart from sweet peas and spray chrysanthemums. The arrangements were sparse – sweet peas 'so that one could see through them', although it was fashionable to intermix maidenhair fern. About five cut arum lilies were put with a few of their leaves, while orchids were displayed alone in a vase.

In the dining room at Dunham, ten vases of sweet peas when possible, or camellias or daffodils, stood in a line down the centre of the table, with the silver, on a white tablecloth.

Three pots of growing flowers were placed on each side-table, and for the very occasional parties given by the Stamfords they were put in 'great big silver punch bowls or wine cisterns with a cloth inside to prevent scratching, and moss on top of each pot – they looked best when filled with hydrangeas'. Two or three pots of lilies stood in each corner of the room. The corners of the saloon too were decorated with a few pots of mixed plants such as cyclamen, azaleas, cinerarias, hydrangeas. These also ran round the bay window.

For the visit of the Emperor Haile Selassie of Ethiopia in 1938, Dunham really came to life. The Emperor was given the Victorian Rooms looking on to a half moon of leaded roof over a bay window. 'Twelve of us had to carry, oh, hundred weights of moss from out of the old cricket ground, and spread it all over this leaded roof, and then we put palms and lilies and hydrangeas and all sorts of pot plants all over there, so that he could look out through the windows and see this lovely garden which was built on the top of the saloon roof.'

Spectacular plant arrangements were more the order of the day at Stourhead House in Wiltshire, home of the Hoare banking family. In 1897 Sir Henry and his wife Alda moved into the house. Lady Hoare was a woman of individual taste and strong opinions, who entirely controlled the household, rearranging the Georgian furniture without regard to original place or use. Many of the torchères or candlestands designed by Thomas Chippendale the Younger, *c*.1820, formerly standing in the corners of the rooms, were moved into the middle to serve as stands for palms and other trees.

The central part of Stourhead was gutted by fire in 1902, but photographs taken the previous year clearly show the flower and pot arrangements. The Picture Gallery, for instance, was filled with furniture and used as a living room. Two enormous rose bushes, as broad as they are tall, are perched on high torchères to dominate the centre of the room, and nearly touch the lofty ceiling. They are joined by eight palms on stands and tables in large oriental pots. Three bowls of maidenhair fern sit on the high back of the writing desk.

In the Library two tall torchères in the centre support palms, with four similar round the edge. Other foliage plants are dotted around the room, while vases of cut flowers together with photographs cover every flat surface. The effect is almost as cluttered as a Victorian drawing room of the 1860s, an example of how the 'old' families often took little notice of prevailing fashions, although the one kind of flower in a vase rule seems to have been universally adopted. Consuelo, Duchess of Marlborough, wrote in 1902 of the fashion in English homes for 'flowers massed on every table together with an array of autographed photographs'.

In contrast to this, houses of the newly rich often had 'decorators' to give them instant effects. An example of a fashionable home of the period is 24 Bedford Square, Bloomsbury, home of George Prothero, president of the Royal History Society and editor of the influential *Quarterly Review*. Bedford Lemere, the celebrated firm that specialised in photographing the interiors of fashionable homes, took a photograph of his drawing room in 1902. There are plenty of flowers on display, but not crowded onto table-tops as at Stourhead. Three of the fashionable, extremely tall glass cylinder-shaped vases are to be seen: one on the mantelpiece with a few tiger lilies and greenery, another on a small table with greenery and a few blossoms, and another on the piano with greenery and a lily or two. Between the sofa and the door is a large flower arrangement which appears to spring

The Picture Gallery at Stourhead House, photographed in 1901. Two enormous rose bushes on stands reach almost to the ceiling, accompanied by no less than eight palms on stands and tables in oriental pots.

out of a trumpet vase, probably 3 or 4 feet (90 or 120 centimetres) high. There is also a palm in an oriental pot, which might have once been a goldfish bowl, on an oriental stand.

From this turn-of-the-century photograph it can be seen that the tall, spreading flower arrangements of the Aesthetic Movement, once the exclusive province of a small avant garde, had become absorbed into mainstream taste. Mrs Panton, addressing an audience of suburban ladies of slender means, describes how to appear artistic for only a few shillings, recommending:

> some charming square stools made for 7s 6d each to hold large blue and yellow pots purchased at Whiteleys [the department store in Paddington] for 2s 11d each, and filled with palms, and these standing about in odd corners or in the centre of a bow window add very much to the appearance of any room, for nothing gives so Oriental or artistic an appearance as plenty of plants, ferns, and palms, and these need not be out of the reach of anyone who cares for pretty things, because with care they last and flourish for years.

Aspidistra elatior 'Variegata', appropriately known as the 'cast-iron plant', was almost indestructible.

Mrs Loftie, writing for a similar audience in *Social Twitters*, gives advice on how to achieve flowers that look artistic:

> The principle to aim at in the arrangement of all flowers is to place them as much as possible in a natural position. They should be made to look comfortable and at their ease – the drooping ones allowed to droop, the climbing ones allowed to climb. How such a barbarous invention as wiring flowers can be for a moment tolerated it is difficult to imagine. Nothing can be more inartistic than a gardener's bouquet, round, hard, regular in arrangement, outrageous in combination of colour, finished off by a piece of paper lace. We often wonder some prima donna is not seriously maimed by having these monstrosities thrown at her head.

Followers of the Arts and Crafts Movement remained faithful to their original vision, decorating their houses with simple garden flowers in unpretentious pots and vases. At Hilles in Gloucestershire, built by the Arts and Crafts architect Detmar Blow as his family home, the rooms were filled with large blue-and-white bowls of 'Gloire de Dijon' roses that grew up the walls of the house, or kingcups (marsh marigolds) and cowslips gathered from the streams and fields nearby.

Ellen Terry, the great Shakespearean actress, adopted the cottage style at her sixteenth-century house at Smallhythe in Tenterden in Kent. She adored daffodils, instituting a 'daffodil day' for the blind. Copious letters were sent to her gardener asking him to decorate the house with 'Sweet peas, heaps of them', to plant sweet smelling stocks under the front window, and to have all the geraniums in flower ready for her arrival. Her favourite house flowers were Madonna lilies, roses, bright blue anchusa and honesty.

In complete contrast to the cottage atmosphere of the half-timbered Smallhythe comes Waddesdon Manor, a magnificent mansion built and furnished in the style of a Loire château by Baron Ferdinand de Rothschild between 1874 and 1889. Our knowledge of the flowers and plants used at Waddesdon is extraordinarily complete thanks to The Red Book of photographs taken of all the main rooms in 1897, the year before the Baron's death. Also preserved in the archives is the head gardener's notebook of 1906. In careful handwriting he noted the varieties of plants and cut flowers to be used in the house and exactly where they should be placed in each room. The measurements for each plant were laid down so

Ellen Terry's dining room at Smallhythe Place comes as a complete contrast to the richly decorated interiors. The great actress loved cottage flowers and her taste can be seen in this photograph taken *c*.1900 which shows a simple arrangement of flowers on the table and pots of pelargoniums on the windowsill.

that it could fit into its allotted space and not overlap or hide in any way, even by an inch, the furniture, picture frames or tapestry adjacent. Some of the eighteenth-century Sèvres vases, of which there are many at Waddesdon (see page 80), were used for cut flowers and plants, and were described by the gardener as 'old fashioned vases'.

By 1906 the chatelaine at Waddesdon was the Baron's sister, Miss Alice. She was meticulous in continuing the tradition founded by Baron Ferdinand de Rothschild, keeping up his high standards and endeavouring to improve on them, creating what became known as 'the Rothschild standard of excellence'. A force to be reckoned with, she was famous for having dared to reprimand Queen Victoria when she inadvertently stepped onto a flower-bed, disturbing the perfectly raked earth.

The Red Book combined with the gardener's notebook not only provide a unique picture of the use of flowers and plants at Waddesdon at the beginning of the twentieth century, but also have proved invaluable in Lord Rothschild's recent restoration and refurbishment of the house and garden. The parterre has been replanted in front of the house, while tall kentia palms flourish again in their original places, and it is hoped that other original plants may in due course adorn the numerous rooms.

In 1906, for instance, the head gardener had to produce kentia palms (*Howea belmoreana* and *H. fosteriana*) for the Picture Gallery, East Gallery, Morning Room, Tower Room and Grey Drawing Room. Each palm was planted in a large oriental fish bowl on an oriental stand, and was underplanted or furnished with either maidenhair fern or caladiums (usually the lovely hybrid *candidum* with its sparkling white green-veined leaves), or *Begonia rex*. Smaller *Cocos weddelliana* (now *Lytocaryum weddellianum*) palms were

A page from The Red Book at Waddesdon Manor, showing the dining room in 1897. Roses – all of the same variety, as fashion dictated – are shown on the table, the mantelpiece and on a stand at the end of the room. Tendrils of greenery spread out from the roses to the edge of the table, as advocated by Robert Felton in *British Floral Decoration* published in 1910.

needed for recesses in the vestibule, and these were mixed with *Caladium* 'Tricolor', *Abutilon parvifolium* and *Carex argentea*.

Over a hundred foliage plants were needed to fill the plant stands and vases. Bright colours and variegation were the required qualities, so caladiums, crotons, *Begonia rex*, *Fittonia argyroneura* (silver net leaf plant) and marantas (herringbone plant) were the favoured varieties. Strict rules were applied to their growing size: in the library, for instance, 'On 2nd Bookcase Begonia Rex small leaved to be kept down 12″ [30 centimetres] high and no account to hide the tapestry', and on brackets flanking the fireplace Pandanus Veitchii (Screw Pine) should be accompanied by 'Caladium argyrites and splendens, Carex argentea and Hedera glechoma hanging down to just below the projection of the bracket.'

Hardy plants that didn't need to be grown in a hothouse were referred to by the gardener as 'tough stuff'. A combination of blue and yellow 'tough stuff' flowers were grown for some of the vases – larkspur, lupins, campanula, antirrhinum, gladiolus. This mixture of colour went against the fashion of the time, but as blue and yellow were the racing colours of the Rothschilds, an exception was made. For roses, however, usually one kind was provided for each vase: favoured white varieties were 'Souvenir de la Malmaison', with 'President Carnot' and 'Frau Lila Rautenstrauch' as second choices; pink – 'La France', 'Mme Caroline Testout', 'Mrs W. I. Grant'; yellow – 'Perle d'Or' and 'William Allen Richardson'; and buff – 'Gloire de Dijon'.

It was fashionable in grand houses to fill the fireplace completely with plant arrangements on staging that was, of course, invisible. At Waddesdon Baron Rothschild had a hothouse specifically devoted to raising the variegated crotons of dazzling colours which formed the mainstay of the decoration of the Red Drawing Room fireplace, where they were set off by palms and ferns. The 1906 notebook explains how the decoration was to be carried out: the palms, three dozen crotons and two dozen ferns had to be arranged in semi-circular bands. The frieze of the mantelpiece was to be 'lightly covered with small palms, not too stiff and using small ferns to cover pots'. '*Great Care* was to be taken that the foliage of palms or plants does not touch the sides of the screen.'

'Both fireplaces were completely hidden by exquisite flowers' wrote Arthur Beavan when describing the Indian Room at Marlborough House on 10 March 1888, the silver wedding day of the Prince and Princess of Wales. Orchids, roses, lilies, Malmaison carnations and hydrangeas seem to have been the most popular flowers for fireplace decoration, with the usual addition of palms and fronds. A photograph taken in 1896 by Bedford Lemere of the Foreign Secretary's Room in Whitehall shows the fireplace decorated presumably for a reception. Filling the entire opening of the fireplace and spilling out into the room is a veritable herbaceous border of bands of lilies at the top, daisies in the middle and hydrangeas below. The pots are hidden by a bed of moss and small palms. Groups of flowers are piled high above the mantelpieces – the top of the pyramid is formed by orchids with lilies, below are roses flanked by carnations, with the unmistakable large blooms of Malmaisons swooping down either side.

For those with smaller fireplaces in more modest houses who nevertheless wanted to keep up with fashion, Mrs Panton provided the answer in *Nooks and Corners*. 'A series of rings to hold flower pots which hang down from a slight rod just under the grate itself has just been brought out by Hamilton of the Quentin Matsys Forge, York Street, Westminster and looks very neat. It holds twelve pots of flowers and can be lifted out in a moment altogether should a fire be required, and would always look well put down in a corner of the room.'

When Mrs Greville gave a dinner followed by dancing at her London house in Charles Street, pink begonias entirely filled the fireplace of the white and gold ballroom, complementing the curtains of 'parchment-coloured brocade with great motifs of deep red roses' and the 'gold chairs upholstered in the same brocade ... that provided seating accommodation all round the room'. The pink theme continued into the hall, which was decorated with more begonias and chrysanthemums. All these flowers had been sent up specially from her country house, Polesden Lacey in Surrey. We know all this from an article dated December 1930, still kept in the Newspaper Cuttings Album at Polesden.

RIGHT: Bedford Lemere's photograph of the Foreign Secretary's Room in the Foreign Office in London, taken in 1896. Lilies, daisies and hydrangeas in pots are arranged in the fireplace, while a huge arrangement of palms, orchids, lilies, roses and Malmaison carnations adorn the mantelpiece.

FAR RIGHT: The fireplace of the dining room at Polesden Lacey, filled to overflowing with plants in the Edwardian style. A large orchid (*Cymbidium* hybrid) is in the middle, surrounded by lilies (*Lilium longiflorum*), michaelmas daisies and hydrangeas, with greenery provided by bird's nest ferns (*Asplenium nidus*) and Boston ferns (*Nephrolepsis exaltata*). The plants stand on the grate within the fireplace, and on stepped staging surrounding it, made up of wine boxes at the back and shoe boxes at the front. Some of the flowers are cut, placed in tubes of water, and stuck in the earth of the plants.

Polesden Lacey was purchased in 1906 for Maggie and her husband, the Hon. Ronald Greville, by her father, William McEwan, the wealthy Scottish brewer. Mrs Greville soon became one of the leading society hostesses: her parties at Polesden and at Charles Street were legendary. Guests included the King and other members of the English and European royal families, as well as leading politicians and society lions.

Mr Smith, her last head gardener, gives a glimpse of the lavish Edwardian lifestyle that continued right up to the Second World War. Mrs Greville conducted his job interview

from her bed, telling him, 'Smith, I want you to speak to me as if I were a man'. Before the First World War, fifteen gardeners had been employed to keep the garden manicured and provide cut flowers, fruit and vegetables for the house. By 1938, when Mr Smith was taken on, this number had been reduced by only one. The greenhouses used 30 tons of coke a year, and flowers and vegetables were sent up to Charles Street daily by train:

> Under glass we grew about 1,000 carnations in 6 inch [15 centimetres] pots, 200 Begonia Gloire de Lorraine, 200 Poinsettias and assorted other plants. We had a complete house of stove plants and another of orchids. A complete row of frames was devoted to Violets (the single type Princess of Wales) which were Mrs Greville's favourite flower, and these we had flowering from early November onwards.

The busiest week of the year was Ascot, when about twenty guests were staying, and in addition to all the flowers for the house, 'ten sprays of flowers, to match the colours of the dresses, and a similar number of carnations for button holes, red or white, would be requested'.

Mrs Greville was very particular to have flowers matching or harmonising with the colours of the walls or furnishings. The *Sunday Times* for 9 August 1936 described the library at Polesden Lacey, 'with its bright buttercup yellow coverings for chairs and sofas and great bowls filled with yellow gladioli [it] is as cheerful a spot as anyone could wish'.

Seven years earlier, the *Daily Mirror* admired the colour scheme of the dining room at Charles Street, where the crimson walls were matched by the table decoration of dark red, single chrysanthemums 'with two rows of tall silver candlesticks, plain parchment shades and white crested china', which on a long table covered with a white tablecloth 'combined to make a charming effect'. It was noted that 'Mrs Greville has never succumbed to the new fashion for table mats on her dining-table, but adheres to the large damask linen cloth'. The *Sketch* added that 'as most of the guests wore black, the effect of the background of crimson walls hung with Dutch paintings was admirable'. Such was the attention to detail at this time that it was not unusual for ladies to ascertain the colour of the rooms in their host's house in order to wear both dresses and flowers that would complement them.

Mrs Greville was maintaining the style of dining that had been fashionable in the last years of the nineteenth century, with flowers running down the centre of the table. Sometimes this could prove quite a barrier. When Victoria Sackville-West, later to be mistress of Knole and mother of Vita, was acting as hostess to her father, Lionel, 2nd Lord Sackville, who was the British Minister in Washington in the mid-1880s, she found herself at a diplomatic dinner in the White House. Dividing her from the guests on the opposite side of the table was a 5-foot (1.5 metre) long canoe made of white and crimson roses. On another occasion, she noted 'the long table with its boat-shaped centrepiece, a triumph of the White House gardeners … made the room almost sickly with the smell of hundreds of carnations'.

For the visit of Queen Victoria to Waddesdon in 1890, orchids – especially *Miltoniopsis vexillaria* – adorned the dining-room tables. But more usually roses or Malmaison carnations were chosen. A photograph from The Red Book shows a low openwork stand running down the middle of the table, on which are ten vases, a line of four central ones and a group of three at each end. The vases are scarcely visible, but combined they give the appearance of a hedge of roses. Delicate fronds of smilax, ivy and box trail out from the roses onto the white tablecloth. Vases of similar roses are on the mantelpieces and on a stand, all in porcelain vases. The Rothschild family always had porcelain vases in preference to silver. And the gardener's notebook records that the 'China vases on the Mantelshelf were *Always* to be filled with the same varieties of flowers or plants that are used on the dinner table.'

Table 11 shows the flowers provided by the head gardener for luncheon and dinner tables at Waddesdon in July and August 1906. It provides a unique record. When two varieties of flowers were mixed together, they were either of the same colour, such as yellow allamandas and gloriosas, or yellow and blue – exotic yellow allamandas mixed rather

---

TABLE 11   *July 1906 Dining Room*

	LUNCHEON	DINNER

1st	Large Party
	Allamanda [yellow] with cornflower traced with
	  smilax and chrysanthemum 'Morning Star'
	  on 3 round tables
		Large Party
		Carnations 'Souvenir de la Malmaison'
		  16 baskets with centrepiece
		  300 flowers

[no date]	Roses 'Ulrich Brunner'	Roses 'General Jacqueminot'
[no date]	Roses 'La France'	Pink roses 'Dorothy Perkins'
[no date]	Yellow antirrhinum with cornflowers	
[no date]	Pink roses	

August 1906 Dining Room

	LUNCHEON	DINNER
1st	Roses 'General Jacqueminot' and 'Frau Karl Drushka'	
3rd	Gloxinias	
[no date]	small caladiums mixed	Bourganvillea
9th	–	Allamanda and Gloriosa
11th	Verbena 'Miss Willmott'	
18th	yellow antirrhinum with cornflowers	Carnation 'Raby Castle'
19th	Roses 'Ulrich Brunner'	Allamanda and Gloriosa
[no date]	blue ageratum with carnation 'Raby Castle'	
20th	'Victor Hugo' and 'Frau Karl Drushka'	
[no date]	Roses 'Ulrich Brunner'	
21st	–	Roses 'Mrs Grant'

Colour illustrations from Mrs Beeton's *Book of Household Management*, 1907 edition.

ABOVE: *Dinner Table à la russe* – the entire centre of the table is taken up with gigantic red and yellow chrysanthemums. They are mixed with maidenhair fern in bowls that form a loose hedge down the centre, and with smilax or jasmine foliage when decorating the arch that rises out of the central bowls. Each table corner is decorated with an attractive pendant consisting of one red and one yellow bloom, with trailing smilax and asparagus greenery pinned onto the cloth.

BELOW: *Supper Buffet for Ball Room or Evening Party* – a white and yellow colour scheme has been chosen. Perhaps it was Mrs Beeton who introduced the fashion for garlands dangling down between each place setting that appear in many photographs of this period. Here they are alternately studded with yellow and white single flowers. Miss Maling's stand (see page 166) would seem to have been used in the three tall arrangements, with single chrysanthemums in the trumpet and double blooms in the lower dish; both kinds mixed with jasmine and asparagus greenery. Three white double blooms in a pair of trumpet vases complete the decoration.

surprisingly with simple blue cornflowers, for instance. Such a combination was against the prevailing fashion, as noted earlier, but the blue and yellow represented the Rothschild racing colours.

A problem with having 'hedges' of flowers on the table marked the return of the difficulty, indeed impossibility, of seeing anyone sitting the other side, let alone talking to them. Lady Monkswell wrote in her diary on 4 June 1890, 'We dined with Shuttleworths and met Mr Gladstone.... As to the G.O.M. [Grand Old Man, a familiar name for Gladstone], he was hidden from my view by a huge bunch of red peonies; I occasionally heard his prophetic voice arising from out of the flowers, but I saw not even the top of his head .... So, on the whole my knowledge of old Gladstone has not been very much enlarged by this party.' The same problem was encountered in the United States, where Teddy Roosevelt used to be so irritated by the mass of tall flowers at a dinner party that he would go into the room and remove them just before the guests arrived, muttering 'If one goes for a picnic one doesn't sit round a bush.'

The florist Robert Felton, after a similar experience, decided to do something about it. At a dinner at the Guildhall in Cambridge the principal guests had speeches to make. 'The first was given by the Chairman, who, being a very tall man, was just able to peep over the top of the barricade of flowers which had been arranged in front of him; the second ... was unfortunately very short, and the audience called for the removal of the flowers since he was completely hidden. This was taken as a general signal to remove all the flowers, and so a very costly floral decoration finished its existence in various corners of the room.' As Mr Felton considered that low arrangements alone produced 'a very flat and inartistic effect', he invented what he called the Ellen Terry stand for use at diplomatic dinners or where speeches were to be given. It was very simple to make, the only accessories, apart from the flowers themselves, being a few bundles of moss, a stick 4 feet (120 centimetres) in length painted olive green and a saucer. This was one of several 'descendants' of the March stand introduced by Mr March in 1862 (see page 178).

For the Ellen Terry stand Mr Felton fixed a solid pad of moss into the saucer, then stuck the stick firmly into the moss, with another ball of moss fixed onto the top of the stick. Light sprays of asparagus fern could cover the moss and twine up the stick. Sprays of orchids, or roses of varying lengths, might then be pushed into the moss at the top and bottom of the stick in a 'perfectly natural way' and allowed to spread across the table. A similar arrangement by Mr Felton that won the championship prize at the Edinburgh Great International Show was filled entirely with yellow orchids: cattleyas, oncidiums and laelias, with a small amount of golden green foliage and a dozen or so long, thin, bronze croton leaves.

For dinners of a more private nature, Mr Felton advised that it was necessary only to make the stands of a height that would enable one to see through them when seated. The Ellen Terry stands did not interfere with any low flower decoration, but were able to decorate the room generally, carrying the eye upwards as well as downwards, creating a feeling of dining in a bower of flowers. As to the colours of those flowers, he explained how florists frequently had the patterns of the hostess' gowns sent to them 'to ensure the Floral Decoration being in harmony with them'.

Ellen Terry Stand

The Ellen Terry stand was invented in the early twentieth century by the florist Robert Felton for use at formal dinners where speeches were to be given. Its height and slim form enabled the speaker to be seen. It could be combined with low flower decorations, such as the 'hedge' used here.

The original Ellen Terry stand consisted of a tall stick with a ball of moss fixed at top and bottom. For this recreation, photographed in the dining room at Polesden Lacey, the stick has been replaced by a 4 feet (120 centimetres) high 'lily vase', and the moss by oasis.

The arrangement consists of dendrobian orchids 'James Storey', with caladium leaves (angel's wings).

A plastic saucer filled with oasis was placed on top of the lily vase, and the whole covered with 2 inches (5 centimetres) gauge wire netting secured around the neck of the vase with oasis tape. Sprigs of orchid were first pushed into the oasis, followed by the caladium leaves.

For the 'hedge' of flowers on the table, instead of troughs of sand or glass bowls of water, blocks of oasis were cut and set into oasis trays. The sprigs of orchid and leaves were then pushed in to create the hedge effect.

Photograph of a private dinner party, 31 December 1895, taken by Bedford Lemere at the Savoy Hotel in London. Palms rise from the table, reaching to the ceiling. At their bases are mounds of flowers and plants, linked along the table by ribbons. More palms and flowers are ranged around the room.

The fashion for putting palm trees through tables for special occasions continued, and on a grander scale. Bedford Lemere photographed a private dinner party on New Year's Eve 1895 at the Savoy Hotel in London. Gigantic palm trees, placed at intervals down the length of the table, rose to a great height, some touching the ceiling, spreading their fronds over the guests seated on either side. Mounds of plants and flowers clustered round the base of each tree and were placed at intervals down the centre of the table, joined together by a pattern of ribbons. Medallions of flowers hung from ribbons along the length of the wall and smaller palm trees stood on pedestals and on the floor round the edges of the room. One writer of the period recalled in his memoirs a dinner at the Savoy to celebrate a great *coup* on the Turf, where the winner's colours were festooned everywhere in ribbons and flowers, and palm trees rose as though planted in the tables. Perhaps this was the occasion.

To have tables beribboned had for some time been the fashion in America. It is recorded that President Grant's dinner tables were 'loaded with mountains of flowers and trailing ribbons'. And Ellen Mary Slaydon, the wife of a Texan Congressman, wrote in her journal in 1898 that fashionable tables were 'too much beribboned' for her taste as 'ribbons and gravy are not so compatible'. She was not impressed by 'broad satin stripes running diagonally across with big bows, like a little girl's sash, at each corner'.

In 1888 Mrs Panton published *From Kitchen to Garret* 'for the British matron who begins life with little money and less experience'. A ringing endorsement soon came from Lady Campbell, 'I give every bride I know a copy ... I cannot tell how many copies have passed through my hands.'

For the dining-room table Mrs Panton suggested that it would be cheaper to have a palm surrounded by ferns rather than fresh flowers:

> In the centre of the table there should always be an art pot with a plant in it. . . . I know some people will think that expensive but let me tell you that since this time last year it has cost me just five shillings. I had my pot for years and this is not included in the outlay. In this pot I had planted a cocos palm 3s 6d, a most graceful plant, and the other 1s 6d went for three tiny ferns all of which are flourishing mightily, and will soon have to be transplanted and make room for smaller ones again . . . . Naturally cheaper plants are to be had, but the fine graceful foliage of the cocos is so pretty, and the plant lasts so long, that I can heartily recommend it from long experience.

Halls had dwindled over the centuries from the heart of the house in medieval times, the place for eating, assembling and even sleeping, to an entrance room. Despite this diminution in importance, halls in Edwardian times could provide plenty of room for large displays of exotic plants. In December 1892 the entrance hall at White Lodge, Richmond Park, then the home of the Duke and Duchess of Teck, was photographed by Bedford Lemere and reproduced in *The Opulent Eye*, a book illustrating many of their photographs compiled by Nicholas Cooper in 1976. The picture shows the room profusely decorated. In the many window embrasures are large low, rectangular plant stands filled with a crowded array of very tall flowering and foliage plants of various kinds, creating the illusion of a well-stocked herbaceous border. In addition there are Christmas decorations of branches of holly and evergreens in large jars over the pictures and twined between the antlers high on the wall.

For a small hall Mrs Panton thought that 'the top and back of an oak chest are charming with heavy jugs on, made too heavy to be blown over by filling them with sand, in which, when flowers are plentiful blossoms can be put, and when they are scarce, leaves and berries and pampas grasses show to great advantage. If any small tables are about, have plants and books on them.'

Large halls in hotels gave great scope for flower decoration. Mr Felton used the possibilities to the full when commissioned to decorate the reception hall at Claridges in June 1909 for a great diplomatic reception to mark the visit of H. H. Prince Nashimoto of Japan. He was asked to carry out the scheme in roses, lilies (*Lilium auratum*, the golden-rayed lily of Japan) and wisteria (one of Japan's most loved flowers) to symbolise the friendliness of

Photograph from Robert Felton's *British Floral Decoration*, showing his decorations for a reception given in honour of their Royal Highnesses, Prince and Princess Nashimoto of Japan, held in June 1909 at Claridges. 'The advent [of wichuriana roses] has opened artistic possibilities which cannot be over-estimated' enthused Mr Felton. He has certainly made the most of the possibilities here, with roses outdoing the wisteria and scrambling wildly up the tall columns of the hall, over the frieze and onto the plasterwork of the ceiling. These roses could also be trained into 'fantastic forms' such as 'open umbrellas, windmills and elephants'.

the nations. Wisteria proving unobtainable, artificial flowers were resorted to, 'made in Yokohama, the flowers being of silk and each pip painted by hand. The length of the flower sprays varies from one to four and a half feet [30 to 135 centimetres], which to those who only know Wisteria in England, appears somewhat exaggerated, but in Japan four and a half feet is considered a very poor specimen .... Few would have noticed the deception.' The wisteria and climbing Wichuriana roses were made to clamber to the top of the very high pillars, while other roses and lilies in pots stood on tables, plant stands and on the floor.

The Edwardian taste for lavish, heavily scented hothouse flowers naturally found scope for expression in the decorations for parties and weddings. In August 1891 the wedding of Miss Bella Reid of Kilmardinny House near Glasgow was reported in the local newspaper:

> The entrance hall was lavishly decorated with banks of flowers as were also the wide staircase and tables. The array of pot plants was very magnificent, a perfect hedge of fuchsias lining the staircase, while on every side were to be seen large clusters of arum lilies. The air was heavy with the perfume of the flowers. In the centre of the hall stood the bride's cake, literally covered with white blossoms and Maidenhair ferns.
>
> The wedding ceremony took place in the drawing room ... which held a wealth of flowers. In one corner was an immense bank of Malmaison carnations, in another roses .... The bridesmaids carried bouquets of Malmaison carnations. Mrs Reid carried a bouquet of Gloire de Dijon roses. There was a handsome arch of evergreens at the principal entrance.

Constance Spry, 'floral expert and famous homemaker', photographed arranging flowers in her own home.

The First World War marked the culmination of the lavish lifestyle for many English country houses. As we have seen, some managed to continue in much the same way, albeit usually with reduced staff. It was the Second World War which finally put an end to the 'Edwardian' style.

A transformation in flower arranging had begun in the 1930s, due primarily to Constance Spry. In 1932 she opened a flower shop in Burlington Gardens in London, and two years later her first book, *Flower Decoration*, was published. As Sir William Lawrence wrote in the introduction, 'she caused flower arranging to become an "art form"', and this 'art' she taught to the pupils who enrolled at the flower school she opened in South Audley Street in 1935.

Constance Spry advocated the abandonment of the 'one kind of flower in a vase', encouraging instead the revival of 'mixed flowers'. Although some stuck determinedly to their single flower arrangements, mixed vases gradually became generally acceptable. Her

Louise Fisher at work in the West Hall of the Governor's Palace in Colonial Williamsburg, preparing an arrangement in a 'five-fingered posy holder' in early eighteenth-century style. 'It is not easy to arrange flowers in this holder' wrote Mrs Fisher, 'but the results can be most rewarding'.

other innovations met greater resistance: bare branches covered with lichen, branches of larch studded with cones, laburnum seed pods, cabbage leaves and artichokes. Her use of wooden bowls, baking tins, sauce boats and urns from the garden as containers for flowers was considered very strange.

Disliking a lot of vases dotted about, Constance Spry recommended concentrating on one handsome piece, and for this she introduced a tall, lightweight pedestal, which could be positioned anywhere in the room. Thus a bride and groom could welcome their guests at their wedding reception positioned next to a magnificent flower arrangement. The advent of 'oasis' in the 1960s enabled enormously high, triangular arrangements to be perched upon a pedestal.

In 1959 the National Association of Flower Arrangers was founded, attracting 100,000 members within 25 years and inspiring the formation of clubs in practically every town in Britain. Colleges arranged evening classes, City & Guilds offered examinations and qualifications. In 1981 the World Association of Flower Arrangers was set up.

Just as recent years have seen a revival of interest in music played on early instruments and recipes culled from historical cookery books, so the idea of having displays of period flowers and plants has developed. Louise Fisher was the first in the field. As we have seen, soon after arriving at Colonial Williamsburg in 1930 she introduced eighteenth-century flower arrangements into many of the restored buildings that are open to the public (see page 79). Her tradition has been followed ever since, and the flower arrangements that she pioneered are famous all over the world.

Forty or so years later, at the Palace of Het Loo in Holland, her example was followed in conjunction with the restoration of the magnificent gardens. Recently Hampton Court Palace has begun to display period flowers in the King's apartments, and has restored the privy garden.

For the National Trust, the way was paved at Osterley Park, where a remarkable collection of eighteenth-century flowers has been built up by a team of volunteers. These are displayed in eighteenth-century vases in every room of the house. Other National Trust houses are following, with flowers of the early nineteenth century at Ickworth in Suffolk, and of the second half of the century at Hughenden Manor in Buckinghamshire. The Edwardian style can be seen at Lyme Park and at Polesden Lacey. At Waddesdon Manor, palm trees are back in their original places, as stipulated over a century ago by Baron Ferdinand de Rothschild.

At other National Trust houses, the style of arrangements follows a person rather than a period. At Basildon Park in Berkshire, for instance, Lady Iliffe established a very distinctive style which the National Trust aims to follow. Indeed, as she still lives in a part of the house, she is on hand to put them right. At Uppark, flowers have been reintroduced in the style developed by Lady Meade-Fetherstonhaugh in the mid twentieth century.

One of the Trust's most modern houses is 2 Willow Road in Hampstead, designed and lived in by Ernö Goldfinger, the Hungarian-born architect of the Modern Movement. Photographs show the house soon after it was built in 1938, with occasional plain glass vases containing a few stems. Later the house was taken over by family life, with the balcony a riot of geraniums and marigolds in boxes, and the sitting room a jungle of large green plants. Today boxes of red geraniums are back on the balcony, while one or two vases are placed in the rooms. In this way, 2 Willow Road, like the old, great country houses belonging to the National Trust, can once more provide a living, comfortable setting, even though the family has departed.

An eighteenth-century fish bowl of *famille rose* on a nineteenth-century ebonised stand in the West Gallery at Waddesdon Manor. The bowl contains a kentia palm (*Howeia forsteriana*) underplanted with *Begonia × hiemalis* and ivy, *Hedera helix*.

Lists of Plants

PLANT INTRODUCTIONS

These lists give the botanical and common names of practically every plant mentioned in the text, with a few others that might be useful for period flower arrangements. I have listed the country of origin for each, as I think it gives an added attraction to a flower to know whence it originally came, and to be aware of how much we owe to the plant hunters.

With the help of Tony Lord, whose knowledge in this field is unsurpassed, and in particular D. J. Mabberley's *The Plant-Book* and Clive Stace's *New Flora of the British Isles*, I have had access to the most recent research on the subject. However, research continues, and there will always be some difference of opinion.

The alphabetical lists are divided into periods (which relate to the chapters of the text) so that you can see which plants were available at a specific period. It must be remembered that some took a long time to find their way into vases and plant stands indoors. 'N' indicates plants and flowers native to Britain.

1: *Before 1677*

Botanical Name	Common Name	Countries of Origin	Date of Introduction to Britain
Acanthus mollis	bear's breeches	W and C Med.	1548
Achillea millefolium	sneezewort		N
Aconitum napellus	monkshood		N
Adiantum capillus-veneris	maidenhair fern		N
Agave americana	century plant	Mexico	1554
Agrostemma githago	corn cockle	Med.	unknown
Alcea rosea	hollyhock (double, various colours)	W Asia	1275
Alchemilla xanthochlora	lady's mantle		N
Amaranthus caudatus	love-lies-bleeding, flower gentle, velvet flower	S America	1596
Amberboa moschata (syn. *Centaurea moschata*)	sweet sultan	E Med.	1629
Anemone coronaria	poppy anemone	S Europe	1596
Antirrhinum majus	snapdragon, calves' snouts	SW Europe	1500
Aquilegia vulgaris	columbine, granny's bonnet		N
Artemisia abrotanum	southernwood	S Europe	c.900
Asphodeline lutea	king's spear	S Europe	1596
Aster tradescantii	starwort	N America	1633
Astrantia major	greater masterwort	Switzerland and Asia Minor	1596
Borago officinalis	borage	S Europe	unknown

Botanical Name	Common Name	Countries of Origin	Date of Introduction to Britain
Buxus sempervirens	box tree, common box		N
Calendula officinalis	pot marigold	origin unknown	*c.*900
Campanula medium	Canterbury bells	Italy and SE France	1578
Campanula persicifolia	peach-leaved bellflower	Europe, N Africa, N and W Asia	1596
Campanula pyramidalis	chimney bellflower, steeple bells	Italy, Yugoslavia	1594
Capsicum annuum	sweet pepper, chilli pepper	N America	1548
Celosia argentea var. *cristata*	cockscomb	pantropical	1570
Centaurea cyanus	cornflower, corn bottle		N
Citrus aurantium	Seville orange	tropical Asia	1595
Citrus limon	lemon	Asia	1648
Citrus sinensis	sweet orange	S China	1595
Consolida ajacis	larkspur	Med.	1573
Convallaria majalis	lily of the valley		N
Convolvulus tricolor	dwarf convolvulus	S Europe	1629
Crocus sativus	saffron crocus (autumn)	Greece	*c.*1350
Crocus vernus	crocus (spring)	Italy, Austria, E Europe	1597
Cyclamen purpurascens (syn. *C. europaeum*)	cyclamen (autumn)	C and E Europe	1596
Cyclamen repandum	cyclamen (spring)	C and E Med.	1629
Cytisus scoparius	broom		N
Daphne mezereum	mezereon		N
Dianthus barbatus	sweet William	S Europe	*c.*1200
Dianthus caryophyllus	carnation	Med.	1475
Dianthus plumarius	pink, clove pink, gillyflower, July flower, sops-in-wine	C Europe	1560
Dictamnus albus	dittany, fraxinella, burning bush		1596
Digitalis lutea	small yellow foxglove	France	1596
Digitalis purpurea	foxglove, virgins' fingers		N
Digitalis purpurea f. *albiflora*	white-flowered foxglove		N
Echinops ritro	globe thistle	SE and S Europe	1570
Erysimum cheiri	wallflower	S Europe	*c.*1260
Filipendula ulmaria	meadowsweet		N
Fritillaria imperialis	crown imperial	Iran to N India	before 1590
Fritillaria meleagris	snake's head fritillary		N
Fritillaria persica	Persian fritillary	Cyprus to Iran	1596
Galanthus nivalis	snowdrop		possibly native
Galanthus nivalis 'Flore Pleno'	double snowdrop		possibly native
Gentiana asclepiadea	willow gentian	C Europe	1629
Geranium pratense	meadow cranesbill		N
Geum spp.	avens		N
Gladiolus communis	eastern gladiolus	S Europe, N Africa	1596

Botanical Name	Common Name	Countries of Origin	Date of Introduction to Britain
Gladiolus communis subsp. *byzantinus*	Byzantine gladiolus	E Med.	1629
Helianthus annuus	sunflower	N America	1596
Helichrysum stoechas	immortelle, everlasting flower	W Med.	1629
Helleborus niger	Christmas rose	Alps and Apennines	*c.*1300
Helleborus viridis	green hellebore		N
Hepatica nobilis	liverwort (white, blue, red)	Europe	1573
Hesperis matronalis	sweet rocket	C and S Europe	*c.*1300
Hyacinthus orientalis	common hyacinth (single and double)	C and S Turkey, NW Syria, Lebanon	1596
Hyacinthus orientalis var. *albulus*	Roman hyacinth	origin unknown	1596
Impatiens balsamina	balsam (double scarlet and double purple)	India	1596
Iris 'Florentina' *Iris germanica* *Iris pallida*	flower-de-luce	S Europe	*c.*900
Jasminum humile	yellow jasmine, Indian jasmine	Himalayas	1656
Jasminum officinale	common white jasmine, jessamine	China	*c.*1500
Laburnum anagyroides	laburnum	C and S Europe	1560
Lathyrus latifolius	everlasting pea	Europe	unknown
Laurus nobilis	bay tree, sweet bay	Med.	995
Lavandula angustifolia	lavender	W Med.	*c.*1200
Legousia speculum-veneris (syn. *Specularia speculum-veneris*)	Venus's looking glass	Europe	1596
Leucanthemum vulgare	ox-eye daisy, marguerite		N
Lilium bulbiferum	fire lily	C and E Europe	1596
Lilium candidum	Madonna lily	E Med	before *c.*900
Lilium martagon	Turk's-cap lily, martagon lily	Europe	1596
Lobelia cardinalis	cardinal flower, scarlet lobelia	N America	1629
Lonicera periclymenum	honeysuckle, woodbine		N
Lunaria annua	honesty, satin flower	S Europe	1595
Lupinus albus	white lupin	Aegean	*c.*1300
Lychnis chalcedonica	Maltese cross, cross of Jerusalem	N Russia	by 1576
Lychnis coronaria	campion, rose campion	SE Europe	1596
Lycopodium spp.	club moss		N
Lythrum salicaria	purple loosestrife, willow herb		N
Lytocaryum weddellianum (syn. *Cocos weddelliana*)	cocos palm	SE Brazil, W Europe to E Asia	1597
Matthiola incana	stock, stock-gillyflower	S Europe	*c.*1260
Mirabilis jalapa	marvel of Peru	Mexico	1596
Muscari botryoides	grape hyacinth (white and dark blue)	C and SE Europe	1596
Myrtus communis	common myrtle	Med.	1562

Botanical Name	Common Name	Countries of Origin	Date of Introduction to Britain
Narcissus 'Albus Multiplex'	double white daffodil	garden	before 1629
Narcissus jonquilla	jonquil	Spain, Portugal	1596
Narcissus poeticus	pheasant's eye, poet's narcissus	S Europe	before 1538
Narcissus pseudonarcissus	Lent lily, wild daffodil		N
Narcissus tazetta	polyanthus narcissus, bunch-flowered narcissus	Med.	1597
Nepeta cataria	catmint		N
Nerine sarniensis	Guernsey lily	S Africa	1659
Nerium oleander	oleander, rose bay	S Europe	1596
Nicotiana tabacum	tobacco plant	NE Argentina, Bolivia	1570
Nigella damascena	love-in-a-mist	Med.	1570
Olea europaea	olive	Med.	1570
Ornithogalum umbellatum	star of Bethlehem	Europe, N Africa	unknown
Osmunda regalis	royal fern		N
Paeonia officinalis	peony	S Europe	c.900
Paeonia tenuifolia		SE Europe to Caucasus	1594
Pancratium illyricum		W Med., S Europe	1615
Papaver somniferum	opium poppy	SW Asia	c.900
Passiflora incarnata	May apple, May pops		before 1629
Philadelphus coronarius	syringa, mock orange	Europe, SW Asia	c.1580
Phillyrea latifolia	phillyrea	S Europe, SW Asia	1597
Physalis alkekengi	Chinese lantern	W Asia to Japan, C and S Europe	1548
Polemonium caeruleum	Jacob's ladder		N
Polianthes tuberosa	tuberose	S America	1629
Polygonatum multiflorum	Solomon's seal		N
Primula auricula	auricula, bear's ears, dusty miller	Alps	1596
Prunus lusitanica	Portugal laurel	Spain and Portugal	1648
Punica granatum	pomegranate	SE Europe to Himalayas	before 1400
Ranunculus acris 'Flore Pleno'	double meadow buttercup, bachelor's buttons		N
Ranunculus asiaticus	Persian buttercup, turban buttercup	SE Europe and SW Asia	1596
Rosa × *alba*	white rose		ancient
Rosa × *alba* 'Alba Maxima'	Jacobite rose, white rose of York		ancient
Rosa × *alba* 'Alba Semiplena'			ancient
Rosa canina	dog rose		
Rosa × *centifolia*	cabbage rose, Provence rose	garden origin	1596
Rosa × *damascena*	Damask rose	Asia Minor	1573
Rosa × *damascena* var. *semperflorens*	Autumn Damask rose, monthly rose	Middle East	
Rosa gallica	French rose	S Europe to W Asia	probably 13th cent.

Botanical Name	Common Name	Countries of Origin	Date of Introduction to Britain
Rosa gallica var. *officinalis*	apothecary's rose, red rose of Lancaster		probably 13th cent.
Rosa gallica 'Versicolor'	Rosa Mundi		before 1500
Rosa moschata	musk rose	Iran to Himalayas	1540
Rosa rubiginosa (syn. *R. eglanteria*)	sweet briar, eglantine		N
Rosmarinus officinalis	rosemary	Europe	1338
Rudbeckia laciniata	cone flower	N America	1640
Salvia sclarea	clary, clear eye	S Europe to C Asia	1562
Scabiosa atropurpurea	sweet scabious	S Europe	1629
Scilla hyacinthoides		Med., Portugal	1585
Sedum telephium	orpine, live-forever		N
Solidago virgaurea	golden rod		N
Syringa vulgaris	lilac	SE Europe	c.1580
Tagetes erecta	African marigold	Mexico	1596
Tagetes patula	French marigold	Mexico	1573
Tanacetum parthenium	feverfew	SE Europe	unknown
Tradescantia virginiana	spiderwort	E and N America	1629
Tulipa Rembrandt Group		Turkey	1577
Tulipa sylvestris	wild tulip		N
Valeriana officinalis	common valerian		N
Veronica spicata	spiked speedwell		N
Viburnum opulus	guelder rose		N
Viburnum tinus	laurustinus	S Europe	1560
Viola odorata	sweet violet		N
Viola tricolor	heartsease, wild pansy		N
Yucca gloriosa	yucca	SE USA	c.1550

2: *1677–1740*

Botanical Name	Common Name	Countries of Origin	Date of Introduction to Britain
Agapanthus africanus	African lily	S Africa	1692
Aloe humilis	spider aloe	S Africa	1731
Amaranthus hypochondriacus	prince's feather	America	1684
Amaryllis belladonna	belladonna lily	S Africa	1712
Argyranthemum frutescens	Paris daisy	Canary Islands	1699
Aster novi-belgii	Michaelmas daisy, New York daisy	N America	1710
Callistephus chinensis	China aster (red, white, yellow, blue)	China	1731
Gomphrena globosa	globe amaranth	America, Australia	1714
Helenium autumnale	sneezeweed	N America	1729
Kalmia latifolia	calico bush, mountain laurel	E and N America	1736

Botanical Name	Common Name	Countries of Origin	Date of Introduction to Britain
Kniphofia uvaria	red hot poker	S Africa	1707
Lathyrus odoratus	sweet pea	Crete, Sicily, S Italy	1700
Lupinus angustifolius	blue lupin	Med.	1686
Lilium superbum	swamp lily	America	1727
Magnolia grandiflora	bull bay, loblolly	SE USA	c.1728
Opuntia ficus-indica	cactus: Indian fig, prickly pear	Mexico	1731
Papaver orientale	Oriental poppy	SW Asia	1714
Passiflora caerulea	blue passion flower	S Brazil, Argentina	1699
Phlox paniculata	phlox	N America	1732
Polygala myrtifolia		S Africa	1707
Populus balsamifera	balm of Gilead	N America	1692
Rosa × centifolia 'Muscosa'	common moss rose, old pink moss rose	garden origin	1696
Syringa × persica 'Alba'	white Persian lilac		1700
Tropaeolum majus	nasturtium, Indian cress	Peru	1686
Verbena bonariensis	verbena	S America	1732
Zantedeschia aethiopica	arum lily	S Africa	1731

3: 1740–1800

Botanical Name	Common Name	Countries of Origin	Date of Introduction to Britain
Acacia longifolia	mimosa, Sydney golden wattle	SE Australia	1792
Alstroemeria pelegrina	Peruvian lily	Chile	1753
Anemonella thalictroides	rue-leaved anemone	America	1768
Asparagus asparagoides (syn. *A. medeoloides*)	smilax	S Africa	1752
Aucuba japonica	Japanese laurel	E Asia	1783
Banksia spp.	Australian honeysuckle	Australia	1788
Bouvardia ternifolia		Mexico, Texas	1794
Buddleja globosa	orange ball tree	Chile and Peru	1774
Camellia japonica	common camellia	SE Asia	1739
Campanula americana	American bellflower	N America	1763
Chimonanthus praecox	wintersweet	China	1766
Chrysanthemum × morifolium (incurved)		China	1796
Clethra arborea	lily of the valley tree	Madeira	1784
Cobaea scandens	cup and saucer plant	Mexico	1787
Cordyline fruticosa (syn. *C. terminalis*)	dracaena palm, good luck plant (USA)	E Asia to Polynesia	1770
Crinum americanum		S USA	1752
Crinum bulbispermum	Cape lily	S Africa	1752

Botanical Name	Common Name	Countries of Origin	Date of Introduction to Britain
Cyrtanthus elatus (syn. *Vallota speciosa*)	vallota, Scarborough lily	S Africa	1774
Daphne odora		China	1770
Delphinium grandiflorum		Siberia, W and N America	1741
Dionaea muscipula	Venus's fly-trap, tippitiwitchet	SE USA	1768
Erica conspicua and other species	tree heath	The Cape	1774
Fuchsia coccinea		Brazil	1792
Fuchsia magellanica		S Chile, Argentina	1793
Gardenia augusta (syn. *G. jasminoides*)	Cape jasmine	China	1754
Gypsophila paniculata	baby's breath, chalk plant	C Europe to C Asia	1759
Heliotropium arborescens	heliotrope, cherry pie	Peru	before 1757
Hydrangea macrophylla	mop-headed hydrangea, Chinese guelder rose	Japan, Korea	1789
Illicium floridanum	purple anise	SE USA	1766
Ixia odorata	African corn lily	S Africa	1757
Lobelia erinus	common bedding lobelia	S Africa	1757
Lophospermum scandens (syn. *Maurandya scandens*)	maurandya	W and S America	1796
Lygodium microphyllum	climbing fern	E Indies	1793
Monarda didyma	scarlet bergamot, bee balm	E and N America	1744
Nephrolepis exaltata 'Bostoniensis'	Boston fern	tropics	1793
Ornithogalum thyrsoides	chincherinchee	S Africa	1757
Osmanthus fragrans		Asia	1770
Paeonia suffruticosa	moutan (tree peony)	China	1770
Pelargonium peltatum	ivy-leaved geranium		1701
Pelargonium zonale	zonal geranium		1710
Pelargonium inquinans			1714
Penstemon barbatus	beard tongue	N America	1794
Reseda odorata	mignonette	N Africa	1752
Rhododendron luteum	yellow azalea	Caucasus	1793
Rhododendron ponticum	common rhododendron	W and E Med.	1763
Rosa banksiae var. *normalis*	Banksian rose (single white)	China	1796
Rosa chinensis	China rose	China	1769
Rosa × odorata	hybrid China rose, old blush rose		1759
Solenostemon scutellarioides	coleus	New Guinea	1764
Sophora microphylla	kowhai	New Zealand	1771
Sparmannia africana	house lime, indoor linden	S Africa	1790
Strelitzia reginae	bird-of-paradise, crane flower	S Africa	1773
Zinnia elegans		Mexico	1796

4: *1800–1850*

Botanical Name	Common Name	Countries of Origin	Date of Introduction to Britain
Abutilon pictum		Brazil	1837
Allamanda cathartica 'Grandiflora'		Brazil	1844
Anchusa azurea		Med.	1810
Anemone hupehensis var. *japonica*	Japanese anemone	China	1844
Aspidistra elatior	cast-iron plant	China	1823
Begonia incarnata 'Gloire de Lorraine'	(winter)	Mexico	1822
Begonia semperflorens	(summer)	China	1829
Bougainvillea spectabilis		S America	1829
Calceolaria cana	slipper flower	Chile	1820s
Calomeria amaranthoides (syn. *Humea elegans*)	incense plant, plume plant	Australia	1800
Campanula lactiflora		Caucasus	1814
Chrysanthemum × *morifolium* × *indicum*	Chusan daisy, pompon chrysanthemum	China	1846
Clarkia unguiculata (syn. *C. elegans*)		California	1823
Codiaeum variegatum var. *pictum*	croton	Papuasia and W Pacific	1810
Cortaderia selloana	pampas grass	S America	1848
Dahlia coccinea		Mexico	1798 but died and reintroduced 1804
Dahlia pinnata		Mexico	1798 but died and reintroduced 1804
Deutzia gracilis		Japan	1843
Epacris spp.	Australian heath (sweet scented)	Australia	1803
Eryngium giganteum	silver thistle, Miss Willmott's ghost	Caucasus	1826
Eschscholzia californica	California poppy	California	1826
Euphorbia pulcherrima	poinsettia	S Africa	1834
Forsythia suspensa		China	1845
Freesia refracta		S Africa	1815
Fuchsia fulgens		Mexico	1830
Lapageria rosea	Chilean bellflower	Chile	1847
Lilium lancifolium (syn. *L. tigrinum*)	tiger lily	E China, Korea, Japan	1804
Nephrolepis cordifolia	ladder fern, sword fern	pantropical	1841
Nymphaea lotus	Egyptian water lily	Egypt to tropical and SE Africa	1802
(Orchid) *Cattleya skinneri*		Guatemala	1836
(Orchid) *Dendrobium nobile*		N India, Assam, China	1836
(Orchid) *Laelia anceps*		Mexico	1834

Botanical Name	Common Name	Countries of Origin	Date of Introduction to Britain
(Orchid) *Miltonia clowesii*		Brazil	1840
(Orchid) *Oncidium aureum*		Peru	1838
(Orchid) *Phalaenopsis amabilis*	moth orchid	Java	1847
Pericallis × hybrida	florist's cineraria	Canary Islands	1839
Petunia integrifolia		Brazil	1831
Plumbago auriculata (syn. *P. capensis*)	Cape leadwort	S Africa	1818
Rhodanthe manglesii		W Australia	1832
Rhododendron arboreum	(red, pink, white)	Himalayas	1817
Rhododendron calendulaceum	fiery azalea (scarlet, orange)	N America	1806
Rosa banksiae 'Lutea'	Banksian rose (double yellow)	China	1824
Rosa × borboniana	Bourbon rose	Île de Bourbon	1817
Rosa 'Rose du Roi'	(forerunner of the Hybrid Perpetuals)		1816
Rosa × odorata 'Odorata'	Hume's blush rose, tea rose (tea-scented)	China	1809
Rosa rugosa	hedgehog rose, Japanese rose	China, Korea, Japan	1845
Salvia patens	(blue)	Mexico	1838
Salvia splendens	(scarlet)	Brazil	1822
Sinningia speciosa	gloxinia	Brazil	1815
Stephanotis floribunda	Madagascar jasmine	Madagascar	1839
Weigela florida		China, Japan, Korea	c.1844
Wisteria sinensis		China	1816

5: *1850–1890*

Botanical Name	Common Name	Countries of Origin	Date of Introduction to Britain
Anthurium andreanum	flamingo flower	Columbia	1876
Begonia rex	elephant ear, king begonia	Assam	1858
Caladium humboldtii	angel wings	S America	1858
Crocosmia × crocosmiiflora	montbretia	raised in France	1880
Dianthus 'Souvenir de la Malmaison'	Malmaison carnation	France	1857
Eucharis × grandiflora	(often sold as *Eucharis amazonica*)	Columbia	1854
Exacum affine	Persian violet	Oman, Africa, Madagascar	1881
Fittonia albivenis Argyroneura Group	silver net leaf plant	Peru	1867
Howea forsteriana	kentia palm	Lord Howe's Island, Australia	1872
Ligustrum japonicum	Japanese privet	Korea, Japan, N China	1845
Lilium auratum	golden-rayed lily of Japan	Japan	1862
Maranta leuconeura	prayer plant	Brazil	1875

Botanical Name	Common Name	Countries of Origin	Date of Introduction to Britain
Pandanus veitchii	screw palm	Polynesia	1868
Rosa 'La France'	(first Hybrid Tea rose)		1867
Selaginella kraussiana	creeping club moss	S Africa	1878

6: *1890–1930*

Botanical Name	Common Name	Countries of Origin	Date of Introduction to Britain
Carex brunnea	brown sedge	Himalayas, Australia	1892
Delphinium elatum Belladonna Group			1924
Hydrangea macrophylla var. *normalis*	lace-cap hydrangea	China and Japan	1917
Lathyrus odoratus 'Countess Spencer'	Sweet pea (first waved variety)		1900
Lilium henryi		Central China	1890
Lilium regale	regal lily	W China	1903
Prunus sargentii	flowering cherry, Sargent cherry	E Russia, Korea, Japan	1893
Rosa wichuriana	memorial rose	E China, Korea, Formosa, Japan	1891

ALPHABETICAL LIST OF COMMON NAMES

The common names for plants are arranged alphabetically, with their botanical names and the periods within which they appear in the list of plant introductions. I have not included plants such as fuchsia or heliotrope, as the common and botanical genus names are more or less identical. The general index provides an indication of where the plants appear in the text.

Common Name	Botanical Name	Period	Common Name	Botanical Name	Period
African corn lily	*Ixia odorata*	3	Baby's breath	*Gypsophila paniculata*	3
African lily	*Agapanthus africanus*	2	Bachelor's buttons	*Ranunculus acris* 'Flore Pleno'	1
African marigold	*Tagetes erecta*	1	Balm of Gilead	*Populus balsamifera*	2
American bellflower	*Campanula americana*	3	Balsam	*Impatiens balsamina*	1
Angel wings	*Caladium humboldtii*	5	Banksian rose (double yellow)	*Rosa banksiae* 'Lutea'	4
Anise	*Illicium floridanum*	3	Banksian rose (single white)	*Rosa banksiae* var. *normalis*	3
Apothecary's rose	*Rosa gallica* var. *officinalis*	1	Bay tree	*Laurus nobilis*	1
Arum lily	*Zantedeschia aethiopica*	2	Beard tongue	*Penstemon barbatus*	3
Auricula	*Primula auricula*	1	Bear's breeches	*Acanthus mollis*	1
Australian heath	*Epacris* spp.	3	Bear's ears	*Primula auricula*	1
Australian honeysuckle	*Banksia* spp.	3			
Azalea	*Rhododendron luteum*	3			

Common Name	Botanical Name	Period
Bee balm	*Monarda didyma*	3
Belladonna lily	*Amaryllis belladonna*	2
Bergamot	*Monarda didyma*	3
Bird of paradise	*Strelitzia reginae*	3
Borage	*Borago officinalis*	1
Boston fern	*Nephrolepis exaltata* 'Bostoniensis'	3
Bourbon rose	*Rosa* × *borboniana*	4
Box	*Buxus sempervirens*	1
Broom	*Cytisus scoparius*	1
Brown sedge	*Carex brunnea*	6
Bull bay	*Magnolia grandiflora*	2
Bunch-flowered narcissus	*Narcissus tazetta*	1
Burning bush	*Dictamnus albus*	1
Byzantine gladiolus	*Gladiolus communis* subsp. *byzantinus*	1
Cabbage rose	*Rosa* × *centifolia*	1
Cactus	*Opuntia ficus-indica*	2
Calico bush	*Kalmia latifolia*	2
California poppy	*Eschscholzia californica*	4
Calves' snouts	*Antirrhinum majus*	1
Camellia	*Camellia japonica*	3
Campion	*Lychnis coronaria*	1
Canterbury bells	*Campanula medium*	1
Cape jasmine	*Gardenia augusta*	3
Cape lily	*Crinum bulbispermum*	3
Cardinal flower	*Lobelia cardinalis*	1
Carnation	*Dianthus caryophyllus*	1
Cast-iron plant	*Aspidistra elatior*	4
Catmint	*Nepeta cataria*	1
Century plant	*Agave americana*	1
Chalk plant	*Gypsophila paniculata*	3
Cherry pie	*Heliotropium arborescens*	3
Chilean bellflower	*Lapageria rosea*	4
Chimney bellflower	*Campanula pyramidalis*	1
China aster	*Callistephus chinensis*	2
China rose	*Rosa chinensis* R. × *odorata*	3
Chincherinchee	*Ornithogalum thyrsoides*	3
Chinese guelder rose	*Hydrangea macrophylla*	3
Chinese lantern	*Physalis alkekengi*	1
Christmas rose	*Helleborus niger*	1
Chusan daisy	*Chrysanthemum* × *morifolium* × *indicum*	4
Cineraria	*Pericallis* × *hybrida*	4
Clary, clear eye	*Salvia sclarea*	1
Climbing fern	*Lygodium scandens*	3
Clove pink	*Dianthus plumarius*	1
Cockscomb	*Celosia argentea* var. *cristata*	1
Cocos palm	*Lytocaryum weddellianum*	1
Coleus	*Solenostemon scutellarioides*	3
Columbine	*Aquilegia vulgaris*	1
Comfrey	*Symphytum officinale*	1

Common Name	Botanical Name	Period
Cone flower	*Rudbeckia laciniata*	1
Corn bottle, cornflower	*Centaurea cyanus*	1
Corn cockle	*Agrostemma githago*	1
Cotton lavender	*Santolina chamaecyparissus*	1
Crane flower	*Strelitzia reginae*	3
Cranesbill	*Geranium* spp.	1
Creeping club moss	*Selaginella kraussiana*	5
Cretan brake	*Pteris cretica*	4
Crocus	*Crocus vernus*	1
Cross of Jerusalem	*Lychnis chalcedonica*	1
Crown imperial	*Fritillaria imperialis*	1
Croton	*Codiaeum variegatum* var. *pictum*	4
Cup and saucer plant	*Cobaea scandens*	3
Cyclamen (autumn)	*Cyclamen purpurascens*	1
Cyclamen (spring)	*Cyclamen repandum*	1
Daffodil (wild)	*Narcissus pseudonarcissus*	1
Damask rose	*Rosa* × *damascena*	1
Dittany	*Dictamnus albus*	1
Dog rose	*Rosa canina*	1
Dracaena palm	*Cordyline fruticosa*	3
Dusty miller	*Primula auricula*	1
Dwarf convolvulus	*Convolvulus tricolor*	1
Eastern gladiolus	*Gladiolus communis*	1
Eglantine	*Rosa rubiginosa*	1
Elephant ear	*Begonia rex*	5
Everlasting flower	*Helichrysum stoechas*	1
Everlasting pea	*Lathyrus latifolius*	1
Feverfew	*Tanacetum parthenium*	1
Fiery azalea	*Rhododendron calendulaceum*	4
Fire lily	*Lilium bulbiferum*	1
Flamingo flower	*Anthurium andraeanum*	5
Fleur-de-lys, flower-de-luce	*Iris pallida, I. germanica, I.* 'Florentina'	1
Flower gentle	*Amaranthus caudatus*	1
Flowering cherry	*Prunus sargentii*	6
Foxglove	*Digitalis* spp.	1
Fraxinella	*Dictamnus albus*	1
French marigold	*Tagetes patula*	1
French rose	*Rosa gallica*	1
Gillyflower or July-flower	*Dianthus plumarius*	1
Globe amaranth	*Gomphrena globosa*	2
Globe thistle	*Echinops ritro*	1
Gloxinia	*Sinningia speciosa*	4
Golden-rayed lily of Japan	*Lilium auratum*	5
Golden rod	*Solidago virgaurea*	1
Good luck plant	*Cordyline fruticosa*	3
Granny's bonnet	*Aquilegia vulgaris*	1
Grape hyacinth	*Muscari botryoides*	1

Common Name	Botanical Name	Period
Greater masterwort	*Astrantia major*	1
Grass of Parnassus	*Parnassia palustris*	1
Guelder rose	*Viburnum opulus*	1
Guernsey lily	*Nerine sarniensis*	1
Heartsease	*Viola tricolor*	1
Hedgehog rose	*Rosa rugosa*	1
Hollyhock	*Alcea rosea*	1
Honesty	*Lunaria annua*	1
Honeysuckle	*Lonicera periclymenum*	1
House lime	*Sparrmannia africana*	3
Hyacinth	*Hyacinthus orientalis*	1
Immortelle	*Helichrysum stoechas*	1
Incense plant	*Calomeria amaranthoides*	4
Indian cress	*Tropaeolum majus*	2
Indian jasmine	*Jasminum humile*	1
Indoor linden	*Sparrmannia africana*	3
Ivy-leaved geranium	*Pelargonium peltatum*	3
Jacobite rose	*Rosa × alba* 'Alba Maxima'	1
Jacob's ladder	*Polemonium caeruleum*	1
Japanese anemone	*Anemone hupehensis* var. *japonica*	4
Japanese laurel	*Aucuba japonica*	3
Japanese privet	*Ligustrum japonicum*	5
Japanese rose	*Rosa rugosa*	1
Japanese royal fern	*Osmunda regalis*	1
Jasmine, jessamine	*Jasminum officinale*	1
Jonquil	*Narcissus jonquilla*	1
Kentia palm	*Howea forsteriana*	5
King begonia	*Begonia rex*	5
King's spear	*Asphodeline lutea*	1
Lace-cap hydrangea	*Hydrangea macrophylla* var. *normalis*	6
Ladder fern	*Nephrolepis cordifolia*	4
Lady gloves	*Digitalis* spp.	1
Lady's mantle	*Alchemilla xanthochlora*	1
Larkspur	*Consolida ajacis*	1
Laurustinus	*Viburnum tinus*	1
Lavender	*Lavandula angustifolia*	1
Lemon	*Citrus limon*	1
Lent lily	*Narcissus pseudonarcissus*	1
Lilac	*Syringa vulgaris*	1
Lily of the valley	*Convallaria majalis*	1
Little club moss	*Selaginella kraussiana*	5
Live-forever	*Sedum telephium*	1
Liverwort	*Hepatica nobilis*	1
Loblolly	*Magnolia grandiflora*	2
Loosestrife	*Lythrum salicaria*	1

Common Name	Botanical Name	Period
Love-in-a-mist	*Nigella damascena*	1
Love-lies-bleeding	*Amaranthus caudatus*	1
Madagascar jasmine	*Stephanotis floribunda*	4
Madonna lily	*Lilium candidum*	1
Maidenhair fern	*Adiantum capillus-veneris*	1
Malmaison carnation	*Dianthus* 'Souvenir de la Malmaison'	5
Maltese cross	*Lychnis chalcedonica*	1
Marigold	*Calendula officinalis*	1
Marguerite	*Leucanthemum vulgare*	1
Marvel of Peru	*Mirabilis jalapa*	1
Masterwort	*Astrantia* spp.	1
Maurandya	*Lophospermum scandens*	3
May apple, May pops	*Passiflora incarnata*	1
Meadowsweet	*Filipendula ulmaria*	1
Memorial rose	*Rosa wichuriana*	6
Mezereon	*Daphne mezereum*	1
Michaelmas daisy	*Aster novi-belgii*	2
Mignonette	*Reseda odorata*	3
Mimosa	*Acacia longifolia*	3
Miss Willmott's ghost	*Eryngium giganteum*	4
Mock orange	*Philadelphus coronarius*	1
Monkshood	*Aconitum napellus*	1
Montbretia	*Crocosmia × crocosmiiflora*	5
Monthly rose	*Rosa × damascena* var. *semperflorens*	1
Mop-headed hydrangea	*Hydrangea macrophylla*	3
Moss rose	*Rosa × centifolia* 'Muscosa'	2
Mountain laurel	*Kalmia latifolia*	2
Moutan	*Paeonia suffruticosa*	3
Musk rose	*Rosa moschata*	1
Myrtle	*Myrtus communis*	1
Nasturtium	*Tropaeolum majus*	2
New York daisy	*Aster novi-belgii*	2
Old blush rose	*Rosa × odorata* 'Pallida'	3
Old pink moss rose	*Rosa × centifolia* 'Muscosa'	2
Oleander	*Nerium oleander*	1
Olive	*Olea europaea*	1
Opium poppy	*Papvaer somniferum*	1
Orange ball tree	*Buddleja globosa*	3
Oriental poppy	*Papaver orientale*	2
Orpine	*Sedum telephium*	1
Ox-eye daisy	*Leucanthemum vulgare*	1
Pampas grass	*Cortaderia selloana*	4
Pansy	*Viola* spp.	1
Paris daisy	*Argyranthemum frutescens*	2
Passion flower	*Passiflora caerulea*	2
Peach-leaved bellflower	*Campanula persicifolia*	1

Common Name	Botanical Name	Period
Peony	*Paeonia officinalis*	1
Persian buttercup	*Ranunculus asiaticus*	1
Persian fritillary	*Fritillaria persica*	1
Persian lilac	*Syringa × persica* 'Alba'	2
Persian violet	*Exacum affine*	5
Peruvian lily	*Alstroemeria pelegrina*	3
Pheasant's eye	*Narcissus poeticus*	1
Pink	*Dianthus plumarius*	1
Plume plant	*Calomeria amaranthoides*	4
Poet's narcissus	*Narcissus poeticus*	1
Poinsettia	*Euphorbia pulcherrima*	4
Polyanthus narcissus	*Narcissus tazetta*	1
Pomegranate	*Punica granatum*	1
Pompon chrysanthemum	*Chrysanthemum × morifolium × indicum*	4
Poppy anemone	*Anemone coronaria*	1
Portugal laurel	*Prunus lusitanica*	1
Pot marigold	*Calendula officinalis*	1
Prayer plant	*Maranta leuconeura*	5
Prince's feather	*Amaranthus hypochondriacus*	2
Provence rose	*Rosa × centifolia*	1
Red hot poker	*Kniphofia uvaria*	2
Red rose of Lancaster	*Rosa gallica*	1
Regal lily	*Lilium regale*	6
Roman hyacinth	*Hyacinthus orientalis* var. *albulus*	1
Rosa Mundi	*Rosa gallica* 'Versicolor'	1
Rose bay	*Nerium oleander*	1
Rose campion	*Lychnis coronaria*	1
Rosemary	*Rosmarinus officinalis*	1
Royal fern	*Osmunda regalis*	1
Rue-leaved anemone	*Anemonella thalictroides*	3
Rush lily	*Sisyrinchium bermudiana*	4
Saffron crocus	*Crocus sativus*	1
Sargent cherry	*Prunus sargentii*	6
Satin flower	*Lunaria annua*	1
Scabious	*Scabiosa atropurpurea*	1
Scarborough lily	*Cyrtanthus elatus*	3
Screw palm	*Pandanus veitchii*	5
Sea thrift	*Armeria maritima*	1
Seville orange	*Citrus aurantium*	1
Silver net leaf plant	*Fittonia albivenis* Argyroneura Group	5
Silver thistle	*Eryngium giganteum*	4
Slipper flower	*Calceolaria cana*	4
Smilax	*Asparagus asparagoides*	3
Snake's head fritillary	*Fritillaria meleagris*	1
Snapdragon	*Antirrhinum majus*	1
Sneezewort	*Achillea millefolium*	1
Snowdrop	*Galanthus nivalis*	1

Common Name	Botanical Name	Period
Snowdrop (double)	*Galanthus nivalis* 'Flore Pleno'	1
Solomon's seal	*Polygonatum multiflorum*	1
Sops-in-wine	*Dianthus plumarius*	1
Southernwood	*Artemisia abrotanum*	1
Spider aloe	*Aloe humilis*	1
Spiderwort	*Tradescantia virginiana*	1
Spiked speedwell	*Veronica spicata*	1
Starwort	*Aster tradescantii*	1
Star of Bethlehem	*Ornithogalum umbellatum*	1
Steeple bells	*Campanula pyramidalis*	1
Stock-gillyflower	*Matthiola* spp.	1
Sunflower	*Helianthus annuus*	1
Sweet bay	*Laurus nobilis*	1
Sweet briar	*Rosa rubiginosa*	1
Swamp lily	*Lilium superbum*	2
Sweet orange	*Citrus sinensis*	1
Sweet pea	*Lathyrus odoratus*	2
Sweet rocket	*Hesperis matronalis*	1
Sweet sultan	*Amberboa moschata*	1
Sweet violet	*Viola odorata*	1
Sweet William	*Dianthus barbatus*	1
Sword fern	*Nephrolepis cordifolia*	4
Sydney golden wattle	*Acacia longifolia*	3
Syringa	*Philadelphus coronarius*	1
Tea rose	*Rosa × odorata* 'Odorata'	4
Tiger lily	*Lilium lancifolium*	4
Tippitiwitchet	*Dionaea muscipula*	3
Tobacco plant	*Nicotiana tabacum*	1
Tree heath	*Erica conspicua* and other species	3
Tree peony	*Paeonia suffruticosa*	3
Tuberose	*Polianthes tuberosa*	1
Tulip – Rembrandt	*Tulipa* Rembrandt Group	1
Tulip – wild	*Tulipa sylvestris*	1
Turban buttercup	*Ranunculus asiaticus*	1
Turk's cap lily	*Lilium martagon*	1
Valerian	*Valeriana officinalis*	1
Vallota	*Cyrtanthus elatus*	3
Velvet flower	*Amaranthus caudatus*	1
Venus's fly-trap	*Dionaea muscipula*	3
Venus's looking-glass	*Legousia speculum-veneris*	1
Virgins' fingers	*Digitalis* spp.	1
Wallflower	*Erysimum cheiri*	1
Water lily (Egyptian)	*Nymphaea lotus*	4
Willow gentian	*Gentiana asclepiadea*	1
Willow herb	*Lythrum salicaria*	1
Wintersweet	*Chimonanthus praecox*	3
White rose of York	*Rosa × alba* 'Alba Maxima'	1
Woodbine	*Lonicera periclymenum*	1

Select Bibliography

As I have used an enormous number of books and sources in my research, this is a selection of titles. The place of publishing is only given when it is not in England.

GENERAL

AMHERST, The Hon Alicia, *A History of Gardening in England*, 1885.
BALFOUR, A. P., *Annual and Biennial Flowers*, 1959.
COATS, Alice M., *Flowers and their Histories*, 1956.
– *Garden Shrubs and their Histories*, 1956.
DAVIS, B. and KNAPP, B., *Know Your Common Plant Names*, 1992.
FISHER, John, *The Origins of Garden Plants*, 1982.
GIROUARD, Mark, *Life in the English Country House*, 1978.
GRIEVE, M., *A Modern Herbal*, 1992 (first printed 1931).
HADFIELD, Miles, *A History of British Gardening*, 1960.
HARVEY, John H., *The Availability of Hardy Plants of the Late Eighteenth Century*, 1988.
HENIGER, J. and OLDENBURGER-EBBERS, C. S., *Ornamental Plants in the Sixteenth and Seventeenth Centuries*, 1975.
HILLIER NURSERIES, *Manual of Trees and Shrubs*, sixth edition, 1991.
JACKSON-STOPS, Gervase and PIPKIN, James, *The English Country House: A Grand Tour*, 1985.
JACKSON-STOPS, Gervase and PIPKIN, James, *The Country House Garden*, 1987.
JELLITO, L. and SCHACHT, W., *Hardy Herbaceous Perennials*, 1990.
MABBERLEY, D. J., *The Plant-Book*, 1997.
ROYAL HORTICULTURAL SOCIETY, *The New Royal Horticultural Society Dictionary of Gardening*, 1992.
– *RHS Plant Finder*, 1998.
SINCLAIR ROHDE, Eleanour, *The Story of the Garden*, 1932.
SMITH, Georgiana, *Table Decoration*, 1968.
STACE, Clive, *New Flora of the British Isles*, 1997.
STUART, D. C., *The Kitchen Garden*, 1984.
TAYLOR, M. and HILL, C., *Hardy Plants introduced to Britain by 1799*, 1982.

CHAPTER I

BOSTWICK, David, 'Plaster to Puzzle Over', *Country Life*, 12 July and 19 July, 1990.
COLEMAN, John, 'Mysterious Blooms', *Country Life*, 6 March 1997.
D'AUVERGNE, Anne de La Tour, 'Lapis Specularis: Scagliole of the Reich Kapelle', *FMR Magazine*, New York, No. 77, December 1995.
FERRARI, G. B., *De Florum Cultura*, Rome, 1633.
GERARD, John, *Herball or Generall Historie of Plantes*, 1597.
GLANVILLE, Philippa, *Silver in Tudor and Early Stuart England*, 1990.
HAMNER, Thomas, *The Garden Book of Sir Thomas Hanmer Bart*, printed from the MS of 1659, edited by Ivy Elstob, 1933.

LAWSON, William, *The Countrie Housewife's Garden*, 1617.
LEITH-ROSS, Prudence, *The John Tradescants*, 1984.
LEVEY, Santina M., *An Elizabethan Inheritance: The Hardwick Hall Textiles*, 1998.
LYTE Esq, Henry, *A Nieuwe Herball or Historie of Plantes*, 1578.
PARKINSON, John, *Paradisi in Sole Paradisus Terrestris*, 1629.
PAVORD, Anna, *The Tulip*, 1999.
PEPYS, Samuel, *Diary*, edited by R. Latham and W. Matthews, 1983.
PLATT, Sir Hugh, *Floraes Paradise*, 1608.
– *The Garden of Eden* (a revised edition of *Floraes Paradise* brought out after the author's death, with a second part in 1660), 1653.
ROUTH, E. M. G., *Sir Thomas More and his Friends 1477-1535*, 1934.
THORNTON, Peter, *Seventeenth Century Interior Decoration in England, France and Holland*, 1983.
TUSSER, Thomas, *A Hundred Pointes of Good Husbandrie*, 1557.
WOLLEY, Hannah, *The Queen-like Closet or Rich Cabinet*, third edition, 1675.
WOODS, May and WARREN, Arrete, *Glasshouses: A History of Greenhouses, Orangeries and Conservatories*, 1988.

CHAPTER 2

The Gentleman's Magazine, 17 August 1732.
ARCHER, Michael, *Delftware*, 1997.
BRADLEY, Richard, *Gentleman & Gardeners' Kalender*, 1718.
DEFOE, Daniel, *A Tour through the Whole Island of Great Britain*, edited by Pat Roger, 1971.
DE LA QUINTINIE, Monsieur, *The Compleat Gard'ner or Directions and Right Ordering of Fruit Gardens and Kitchen Gardens*, translated by John Evelyn, 1693.
DIXON HUNT, John and DE JONG, Erik, *The Anglo-Dutch Garden in the Age of William and Mary*, 1988.
ERKELENS, A. M. L. E., *Queen Mary's Delft Porcelain*, Zwolle, 1996.
EVELYN, John, *Directions for the Gardener at Sayes Court*, 1687.
– *The Diary of John Evelyn*, edited by E. S. de Beer, 1955.
FAIRCHILD, Thomas, *The City Gardener*, 1722.
FIENNES, Celia, *The Journeys of Celia Fiennes c.1682-c.1712*, edited by Christopher Morris, 1947.
FURBER, Robert, *The Flower Garden Display'd*, second edition, 1734 (first published in 1732).
HILL, John, *Eden, or Compleat Body of Gardening*, 1757.
JACQUES, David and VAN DER HORST, Arend Jan, *The Gardens of William and Mary*, 1988.
LANGLEY, Batty, *New Principles of Gardening*, 1728.
MASSIALOT, François, *Nouvelles Instructions pour les Confitures, les Liqueurs et les Fruits*, Paris, 1698.
SOMERS COCKS, Anna, 'The Nonfunctional Use of Ceramics in the English Country House during the Eighteenth Century', *The Fashioning and Functioning of the British Country House – Studies in the History of Art 25*. Washington, D.C., 1989.

SWITZER, Stephen, *Nobleman, Gentleman and Gardener's Recreation*, 1715.
– *Iconographia Rustica*, second edition, 1741.
VAN OOSTEN, Henry, *The Dutch Gardener*, 1711.

CHAPTER 3

ABERCROMBIE, John, *The Hot House Gardener*, 1789.
AUSTIN, John C., *Chelsea Porcelain at Williamsburg*, Williamsburg, 1977 (The appendix includes a facsimile of Mr Ford's catalogue of the Chelsea factory sale in March 1755).
COOKE, Samuel, *Complete English Gardening or Gardening Made Perfectly easy*, c.1793.
DELANY, Mrs, *Autobiography and Correspondence of Mary Granville, Mrs Delany*, edited by Lady Llanover, 1861-2.
DUTTON, Joan Parry, *The Flower World of Williamsburg*, Williamsburg, revised edition, 1973.
FERGUSON, Patricia F., 'The Eighteenth Century Mania for Hyacinths', *Antiques*, New York, June 1997.
FISHER, Louise B., *An Eighteenth-Century Garland: The Flower and Fruit Arrangements of Colonial Williamsburg*, Williamsburg, 1951.
FITZGERALD, Brian, *Emily, Duchess of Leinster 1731-1814*, Dublin, 1949.
GARRICK, David and COLMAN, G., *The Clandestine Marriage*, 1766.
HANBURY, Rev. William, *A Complete Body of Planting and Gardening*, 1770-1.
HEDLEY, Olwen, *Queen Charlotte*, 1975.
LANGE, Amanda, 'English Ceramic Wall Pockets', *Ars Ceramica*, New York, No. 15, 1998/1999.
LYBBE-POWYS, Mrs, *Passages from the Diary of Mrs Lybbe-Powys*, edited by E. J. Climenson, 1899.
MARSDEN, Christopher, *Palmyra of the North*, 1943.
MASSIALOT, François, *Nouvelles Instructions pour les Confitures, les Liqueurs et les Fruits*, Paris, 1776 and 1791.
MILLER, Philip, *Gardeners Dictionary*, 1731 and later editions.
POWELL, Anthony, *The Royal Gardener or Complete Calendar of Gardening*, 1769.
SAVILL, Rosalind, *The Wallace Collection: Catalogue of Sèvres Porcelain*, 1988.
STRONG, Roy, *Royal Gardens*, 1992.
TILLYARD, Sheila, *Aristocrats: Caroline, Emily, Louisa and Sarah Lennox*, 1994.
WALPOLE, Horace, Earl of Orford, *Letters*, edited by Peter Cunningham, 1857.
WHITWELL, Benjamin, *Universal Calendar*, 1726.
WOODFORDE, The Reverend James, *The Diary of a Country Parson 1758-1802*, edited by John Beresford 1949.
YETTER, George Humphrey, *Williamsburg Before and After: The Rebirth of Virginia's Colonial Capital*, Williamsburg, 1994.
Invoices for plants ordered by Sir Nathaniel Curzon, Bart from John Broadhurst between January and April 1760. Kedleston Hall Archives.
Letter from Sir John Dick, British Consul at Leghorn in Italy to Thomas Anson at Shugborough Hall in Staffordshire 1771. Staffordshire County Records Office D615/P(A)/2.
Mrs Kennedy's Diary 1793-1816. The Royal Archives, Windsor Castle.
Transcripts of Josiah Wedgwood's letters, Commonplace Book I, Shape Book No 1. Trustees of the Wedgwood Museum, Barlaston, Stoke-on-Trent, Staffordshire.

CHAPTER 4

The Morning Post, 30 July 1821.
ACKERMANN, Rudolph, *Repository of the Arts*, 1808-28.
ANON, *A Visit to the Bazaar*, 1818.
DISRAELI, Benjamin, *Letters*, six volumes, edited by John Matthews, Toronto, 1982-97.
EDGEWORTH, Maria, *Life and Letters*, edited by A. J. C. Hare, 1894.
– *Letters to America 1813-1844*, edited by C. Colvin, 1971.
GERE, Charlotte, *Nineteenth-Century Decoration*, 1989.
– *Nineteenth-Century Interiors: an Album of Watercolours*, 1992.
HEDLEY, Olwen, 'How the Christmas Tree came to the English Court', *The Times*, 22 December 1958.
HIBBERD, Shirley, *Rustic Adornments for Homes of Taste*, 1856.
HIBBERT, Christopher, *George IV: Regent and King 1811-1830*, 1973.
JACKSON-STOPS, Gervase, *An English Arcadia 1600-1990*, 1992.
KENT, Elizabeth, *Flora Domestica or the Portable Flower-Garden*, 1823.
LACHAUME, Jules, *Les Fleurs Naturelles: traité sur l'art de composer les couronnes, les parures, les bouquets etc. de tous genres pour bals et soirées*, Paris, 1847.
LE ROUGETEL, Hazel, *A Heritage of Roses*, 1988.
LONDONDERRY, Lady, *Russian Journal of Lady Londonderry 1836-37*, edited by W. A. L. Seaman and J. R. Sewell, 1973.
LONGSTAFFE-GOWAN, Todd, *The London Town Garden*, 2000.
LOUDON, John, *The Greenhouse Companion*, 1824.
LUMMIS, Trevor and MARSH, Jan, *The Woman's Domain*, 1990.
LUCY, Mary Elizabeth, *The Memoirs of Mary Elizabeth Lucy, Mistress of Charlecote*, edited by Alice Fairfax-Lucy, 1983.
MEADE-FETHERSTONHAUGH, Margaret and WARNER, Oliver, *Uppark and its People*, 1964.
MORLEY, John, *Regency Design 1790-1840*, 1993.
NICOL, Walter, *The Villa Garden Directory*, 1809.
PAUL, William, *The Rose Garden*, eighth edition, 1881 (first published 1848).
PÜCKLER-MUSKAU, Prince, *The English Tour of Prince Pückler-Muskau described in his letters 1826-1828*, edited by E. M. Butler, 1957.
PUGIN, Augustus C., *Engravings of Fashionable Furniture*, 1823.
PYNE, W. H., *History of the Royal Residences*, 1817-19.
RIVERS, Thomas, *The Rose Amateurs Guide*, 1837.
SOLMAN, David, *Loddiges of Hackney: The Largest Hothouse in the World*, 1995.
STEVENSON, Arthur L., *The Wild Irish Girl: The Life of Sydney Owenson, Lady Morgan 1776-1859*, 1936.
WEBBER, Ronald, *The Early Horticulturists*, 1968.
George IV Accounts, Invoice 25536, to His Royal Highness the Prince Regent from Curtis and Salisbury Nurserymen, The Botanic Garden Brompton, June 1811. The Royal Archives, Windsor Castle.
Invoice to Sir Harry Fetherstonhaugh from Mr Charles Pepper, 1826; Invoice to Sir Harry Fetherstonhaugh from William Summers, 1835. Uppark Archives.
Letter written by Lady Boringdon, 1810. Saltram Archives.

CHAPTER 5

'Decoration of the Dinner Table', *The Lady*, 2 July 1885.
'Festivities at Trentham to celebrate the Majority of the Marquis of Stafford', *The Illustrated London News*, 5 January 1850.

ABDY, Jane and GERE, Charlotte, *The Souls*, 1984.

ALLEN, David Elliston, *The Victorian Fern Craze*, 1969.

ANON, *The Private Life of the Queen: by One of Her Majesty's Servants*, 1979 (first published 1897).

BANHAM, Joanna, PORTER, Julia and MACDONALD, Sally, *Victorian Interior Style*, 1991.

BEETON, Mrs Isabella, *The Book of Household Management*, 1861 and later editions.

BURBIDGE, F. W. T., *Domestic Floriculture*, 1874.

CAVENDISH, Lady Frederick, *The Diary of Lady Frederick Cavendish*, edited by John Bailey, 1927.

CONDER, Josiah, *The Flowers of Japan and The Art of Floral Arrangement*, Tokyo, 1891.

ELLIOTT, Brent, 'The First Table Decoration Competition', *Journal of the Royal Horticultural Society*, 1987.

GIROUARD, Mark, *Sweetness and Light: The Queen Anne Movement 1860-1900*, 1977.

– The Victorian Country House, 1979.

GLADSTONE, Mary, *Diaries and Letters*, edited by Lucy Masterman, 1930.

HASSARD, Annie, *Floral Decorations for Dwelling Houses*, 1875.

HAYDEN, Peter, *Biddulph Grange: A Victorian Garden Rediscovered*, 1989.

HENDERSON, Peter, *Practical Floriculture*, New York, 1869.

HIBBERD, Shirley, *The Fern Garden*, 1869.

– *New and Rare Beautiful-Leaved Plants*, 1870.

JEKYLL, Gertrude, *Home and Garden*, 1900.

MALING, Miss, *Flowers for Ornament and Decoration and how to arrange them*, 1862.

MARCH, T. C., *Flower and Fruit Decoration*, 1862.

MONKSWELL, Mary, Lady, *A Victorian Diarist: Extracts from the journals of Mary, Lady Monkswell 1873-1895*, edited by Hon E. C. F. Collier, 1944.

MORGAN, Joan and RICHARDS, Alison, *A Paradise out of a Common Field*, 1990.

PERKINS, John, *Floral Decorations for the Table*, 1877.

ROBINSON, William, *The Wild Garden*, 1870.

SMITH, John, *Ferns: British and Foreign*, 1866.

STANLEY, The Hon Eleanor, *Twenty Years at Court: From the Correspondence of the Hon Eleanor Stanley, maid of honour to her late Majesty Queen Victoria, 1842-1862*, edited by Mrs Stewart Erskine, 1916.

TREVELYAN, Raleigh, *A Pre-Raphaelite Circle*, 1978.

WILLS, John, 'Plants for House Decoration', *Journal of the Royal Horticultural Society*, March 1892.

A Gardener's Day Book 1881-1886. Royal Archives, Windsor Castle RA/Vic/ADD C29.

Letters published in *The Journal of Horticulture*, *The Garden* and *The Gardener's Chronicle*.

CHAPTER 6

'Famous Gardeners at Home: At the Gardens, West Dean Park, Chichester', an interview with Mr W. H. Smith, head gardener at West Dean, *Garden Life*, August 1904.

Pall Mall Magazine I, 1893.

ALSOP, Susan Mary, *Lady Sackville: A Biography*, 1978.

BEATON, Cecil, *The Glass of Fashion*, 1954.

BEAVAN, Arthur, *Marlborough House and its Occupants*, 1896.

BROTHERSTON, R. P., *The Book of Cut Flowers*, 1906.

COOPER, Nicholas, *The Opulent Eye*, 1976.

COXHEAD, Elizabeth, *Constance Spry: A Biography*, 1975.

FELTON, Robert, *British Floral Decoration*, 1910.

JEKYLL, Gertrude, *Flower Decoration in the House*, 1907.

KEPPEL, Sonia, *Edwardian Daughter: Reminiscences*, 1958.

LAURIE, Kedrun, *Cricketer Preferred*, undated.

LOFTIE, Mrs M. J., *Social Twitters*, 1879.

PANTON, Mrs Ellen Jane, *From Kitchen to Garret*, 1888.

– *Nooks and Corners*, 1889.

– *Leaves from a Housekeeper's Book*, 1914.

ROTHSCHILD, Mrs James de, *The Rothschilds at Waddesdon Manor*, 1979.

SANDEMAN, Phyllis, *Treasure on Earth*, 1906.

SPRY, Constance, *Flower Decoration*, 1934.

VANDERBILT BALSAN, Consuelo (Duchess of Marlborough 1895-1921), *The Glitter and the Gold*, 1953.

WESTMINSTER, Loelia, Duchess of, Recollection of Loelia, Duchess of Westminster in *The Country House Remembered*, edited by Merlin Waterson, 1985.

Description of Miss Bella Reid's wedding at Kilmardinny House near Glasgow, *Stirling Journal and Advertiser*, 5 August 1891.

Discussion with Arthur Shufflebotham, gardener at Dunham Massey 1934-1984, Mary Rose Blacker and James Rothwell, 1999.

Memories of a gardener at Cliveden. Cliveden Archives.

Notebook of the head gardener at Waddesdon Manor, 1906. Waddesdon Archives.

Newspaper Cuttings Album. Polesden Lacey Archives.

Recollections of Mr Henry Smith, gardener at Polesden Lacey 1938-64 and last head gardener to Mrs Greville. Polesden Lacey Archives.

List of Plates

The author and publishers would like to acknowledge the many institutions and individuals who have granted permission to reproduce their material in these pages.

Please note that figures in bold refer to page numbers.

NTPL – National Trust Photographic Library
NT – National Trust Regional Libraries and Archives
NMR – National Monuments Record

Index